Music Theory

FOR

DUMMIES®

by Michael Pilhofer and Holly Day

Wiley Publishing, Inc.

Music Theory For Dummies®

Published by
Wiley Publishing, Inc.
111 River St.
Hoboken, NJ 07030-5774
www.wiley.com

Copyright © 2007 by Wiley Publishing, Inc., Indianapolis, Indiana

Published by Wiley Publishing, Inc., Indianapolis, Indiana

Published simultaneously in Canada

For general information on our other products and services, please contact our Customer Care Department within the U.S. at 877-762-2974, outside the U.S. at 317-572-3993, or fax 317-572-4002.

For technical support, please visit www.wiley.com/techsupport.

Wiley also publishes its books in a variety of electronic formats. Some content that appears in print may not be available in electronic books.

Library of Congress Control Number: 2007920019

ISBN: 978-0-7645-7838-0

Manufactured in the United States of America

12 11 10 9 8

WILEY

About the Authors

Michael Pilhofer: Michael Pilhofer teaches music theory and percussion at McNally Smith College of Music in St. Paul, Minnesota, where he serves as department head of the Ensembles Department. He has worked as a professional musician for more than 18 years and has played and performed with Joe Lovano, Marian McPartland, Kenny Wheeler, Dave Holland, Bill Holman, Wycliffe Gordon, Peter Erskine, and Gene Bertoncini.

Holly Day: Holly Day has written about music for numerous publications internationally, including *Computer Music Journal*, *ROCKRGRL*, *Music Alive!*, *Guitar One*, *Brutarian Magazine*, *Interface Technology*, and *Mixdown* magazine. Over the past couple of decades, her writing has received an Isaac Asimov Award, a National Magazine Award, and two Midwest Writer's Grants. Her previous books include *The Insider's Guide to the Twin Cities* (3rd, 4th, and 5th Editions), Shakira, and *Behind the Orange Curtain: A History of Orange County Punk Rock*.

Dedication

To Wolfegang and Astrid, with much love.

Authors' Acknowledgments

Special acknowledgement goes to all the musicians and composers who took the time out of their very busy schedules to share their thoughts on writing music with us.

Steve Reich, Philip Glass, Irmin Schmidt, Barry Adamson, Jonathan Segel, John Hughes III, Nick Currie, Andrew Bird, Fred Sokolow, Rachel Grimes, Christian Frederickson, Pan Sonic, Mark Mallman, Leslie Hermelin, Corbin Collins, and Matt Wagner: thank you.

Special thanks goes to Tom Day, whose patience both in and out of the production booth is always amazing.

R.I.P., Dr. Robert Moog.

Publisher's Acknowledgments

We're proud of this book; please send us your comments through our Dummies online registration form located at www.dummies.com/register/.

Some of the people who helped bring this book to market include the following:

Acquisitions, Editorial, and Media Development

Project Editor: Corbin Collins

Acquisitions Editor: Stacy Kennedy

Copy Editor: Corbin Collins

Technical Editor: Delbert Bowers

Media Project Supervisor: Laura Moss-Hollister

Media Development Specialist: Kit Malone

Editorial Manager: Michelle Hacker

Editorial Supervisor and Reprint Editor: Carmen Krikorian

Editorial Assistants: Erin Calligan Mooney, Joe Niesen, David Lutton, Leeann Harney

Cartoons: Rich Tennant (www.the5thwave.com)

Composition Services

Project Coordinator: Patrick Redmond

Layout and Graphics: Carl Byers, Joyce Haughey, Laura Pence, Heather Ryan, Rashell Smith

Special Art: W.R. Music Service/Woytek and Krystyna Rynczak

Anniversary Logo Design: Richard Pacifico

Proofreaders: Aptara, Jessica Kramer, Susan Moritz, Todd Lothery

Indexer: Aptara

Publishing and Editorial for Consumer Dummies

Diane Graves Steele, Vice President and Publisher, Consumer Dummies

Joyce Pepple, Acquisitions Director, Consumer Dummies

Kristin A. Cocks, Product Development Director, Consumer Dummies

Michael Spring, Vice President and Publisher, Travel

Kelly Regan, Editorial Director, Travel

Publishing for Technology Dummies

Andy Cummings, Vice President and Publisher, Dummies Technology/General User

Composition Services

Gerry Fahey, Vice President of Production Services

Debbie Stailey, Director of Composition Services

Contents at a Glance

Table of Contents

Introduction

● ●

*W*elcome to *Music Theory For Dummies*!

What do you think of when you hear the phrase *music theory*? Does the image of your elementary school music teacher scowling at you from behind the piano pop into your head? Or perhaps a later image of fellow college students in theory classes determinedly trying to notate theremin whistles? If either of these ideas is anything close your own perception of what music theory is, then hopefully, this book will be a pleasant surprise.

For a lot of self-taught musicians, the idea of theory seems daunting and even a little self-defeating. After all, if you can already read guitar tabs and play some scales, why would you want to cheese what you already know with theory?

Even the most basic music theory training will give you the keys to expand your range and abilities as a musician. A decent amount of note-reading ability will enable you to play classical piano music, whereas some basic knowledge about chord progressions will show you the way to writing your own music.

About This Book

Music Theory For Dummies is designed to teach you everything you need to know to become fluent at knocking out a solid beat, reading musical scores, and learning to anticipate where a song should go, whether you're reading someone else's music or writing your own.

Each chapter is as self-contained as possible, you don't *have* to read every single chapter to understand what the next one is talking about. It does help, though, as knowledge of music builds from simple concepts to complex ones.

To find the information you need, you can use the Table of Contents as a reference point, or you can just flip through the Index at the back of the book.

Whom This Book Is For

This book is written for all types of musicians, from the absolute beginner, to the classical student who never learned how to improvise, to the seasoned musician who knows how to put music together but never bothered to find out how to read music beyond guitar tabs and lead sheets.

The absolute beginner

We wrote this book with the intent that it will accompany the beginning musician from his very first steps into note-reading and tapping out rhythms all the way into the first real attempts at composing music by using the principles of music theory. Beginning musicians should start at the beginning of the book, with Part I, and just keep going. The book is organized to follow the lesson plan that college music theory classes would offer you, depending on how fast a learner you are.

The music student who quit

This book is also written for the musician who took instrument lessons as a child and still remembers how to read sheet music, but who was never exposed to the principals of building scales, basic improvisation, or how to jam with other musicians. There are a lot of those people out there, and this book is designed to gently ease you back into the joy of playing music. It shows you how to work outside the constraints of playing from a piece of music and truly begin to improvise and even write your own music.

The experienced performer

Music Theory For Dummies is also intended for the seasoned musician who already knows how to play music but never got around to working out how to read sheet music beyond the basic fakebook or lead sheet. You, too, may want to start with Part I, because it specifically discusses the note values used in sheet music. If you're already familiar with the concepts of eighth notes, quarter notes, and so on, then Part II may be where you want to start out. In this part of the book, we lay out the entire music staff and match it to both the piano keyboard and the guitar neck for easy reference.

How This Book Is Organized

Music Theory For Dummies is organized into five parts. The first four are each based around a particular aspect of music, and the fifth, the Part of Tens, contains information about fun aspects of music theory that have little or nothing to do with actually playing it. This system makes it easy for you to find what you need to know quickly — because, after all, this is a reference book, and nobody wants to spend all day thumbing through pages to find one simple technique.

Part I: Rhythm: Keeping the Beat

Without rhythm, music would be one long, unbroken, unwavering note, and that would be awfully tricky to dance to. Rhythm is the most basic component of any type of music, and being able to keep proper rhythm can make or break a performer. In this section, we discuss the various values of notes and rests used in written music, as well as more advanced concepts like time signatures and syncopation.

Part II: Melody: The Part You Hum

Melody is the lead line of the song that stays stuck in your head, long after the song is over. It's the essential musical theme that runs through a piece of music, or a part of a piece of music, that ties the whole thing together. In this section, we cover basic note reading and some silly mnemonics to help remember the order of the notes on the grand staff. Staffs for both piano and guitar notation are included.

Part III: Harmony: Fleshing It Out

Harmony is the part of a song that fills out the melody. Harmony can turn the simplicity of "Twinkle, Twinkle, Little Star" into a full orchestral number. In this part, we go over interval basics, major and minor scales, building chords, and how to use the all-important Circle of Fifths. We also talk about basic chord progressions and musical cadences. There are tons of musical examples in this section that you can hear on the book's CD, performed on both piano and guitar.

Part IV: Form: How It's Shaped

In this chapter, we show you how to put it all together to start writing your own real music. The structure of various types of classical music — including such forms as fugues and sonatas — are dissected and discussed, as are popular forms like the 12-bar blues, 32-bar blues ballads, and rock and pop forms.

Part V: The Part of Tens

In this section of the book, we introduce you to a few things to do with theory outside of playing music. We answer some of the most common questions people have about music theory. We profile some fascinating music theorists without whom this book, or any other book like it, would not be possible. And we point you to furthering your musical exploits by listing additional music theory and history books, as well as Internet resources.

Icons Used in This Book

Icons are handy little graphic images that are meant to point out particularly important information. You'll find the following icons in this book, conveniently located along the left margins.

This icon indicates good advice and information that will help you understand key concepts.

When we discuss something that might be problematic or confusing, we use this icon.

This icon flags information that's, well, technical, and you can go ahead and skip it if you want to.

When we make a point or offer some information that we feel you should keep with you forever, we toss in this icon.

This points out tracks on the CD that relate to the point currently being discussed in the book.

We hope you enjoy reading this book as much as we did writing it. Sit back, read, and then start your own musical adventure!

Where to Go from Here

If you're a beginning music student, or want to start again fresh, then go ahead and plow into Part I. If you're already familiar with the basics of rhythm and want to simply find out how to read notes, then head on into Part II. If you are a trained musician w ho wants to know how to improvise and begin to write music, Part III covers the basics of chord progressions, scales, and cadences. Part IV discusses a variety of musical forms you can start plugging your own musical ideas into.

So relax and have fun with this. Listening to, playing, and writing music are some of the most enjoyable experiences you'll ever have. *Music Theory For Dummies* may have been written by teachers, but we promise, no clock-watching tyrants will show up at your door to check how fast you're plowing through this book!

Part I
Rhythm: Keeping the Beat

The 5th Wave   By Rich Tennant

"It's a jazz metronome. It's like a regular metronome except it takes a 32-bar solo during each practice session."

In this part . . .

This part introduces you to the backbone of all music: rhythm. Here's where you'll see which notes and rests mean what, find out how to count out the beat, determine how to read time signatures, and get acquainted with tempo and dynamics. If you're new to music theory, this is where you should start.

Chapter 1

What Is Music Theory Anyway?

*O*ne of the most important things to remember about music theory is that music came first. Music existed for thousands of years before theory came along to explain what people were trying to accomplish by pounding on their drums. So, don't ever think that you can't be a good musician just because you've never taken a theory class. In fact, if you *are* a good musician, you already know a lot of theory. You just may not know the words or scientific formulas for what you're doing.

The concepts and rules that make up music theory are very much like the grammatical rules that govern written language — which also came along after people had successfully learned how to talk to one another. Just as being able to transcribe language made it possible for people far away to "hear" conversations and stories the way the author intended, being able to transcribe music makes it possible for other musicians to read and play compositions exactly as the composer intended. Learning to read music is almost exactly like learning a new language, to the point where a fluent person can "hear" a musical "conversation" when reading a piece of sheet music.

There are plenty of people in the world who can't read or write but can communicate their thoughts and feelings verbally just fine. In the same way, there are plenty of intuitive, self-taught musicians out there who have never learned to read or write music and find the whole idea of learning music theory tedious and unnecessary. However, just like the educational leaps that can come with learning to read and write, music theory can help musicians learn new techniques, perform unfamiliar styles of music, and develop the confidence they may need to try new things.

How Will Theory Help My Music?

If you didn't know better, you might think that music was something that could start on any note, go wherever it wanted to, and just stop whenever the performer felt like getting up for a glass of iced tea. Although it's true that many of us have been to musical performances that actually do follow that style of "composition," for the most part those performances are confusing, annoyingly self-indulgent, and feel a little pointless.

The only people who can pull off a spontaneous jam *well* are people who know music thoroughly enough to stack chords and notes next to one another so that they *make sense* to listeners. And, because music is inherently a form of communication, connecting with your listeners is the important thing.

Learning about music theory is also incredibly inspiring. There's just no describing the light bulb that goes off in your head when you suddenly know how to put a 12-bar blues progression together and build a really good song out of it. Or when you can look at a piece of classical music and find yourself looking forward to playing through it for the first time. Or the first time you sit down to jam with your friends and find you have the confidence to take the lead.

It's our intention that the readers of this book will end up putting it down on a regular basis because the urge try out a new musical technique is just too hard to resist.

The Old Lady and the Yardstick

Yep, this is the image that a lot of us get when we think about music lessons: angry, elderly piano teachers who tap out the beat with yardsticks, sometimes inches from your knuckles. We promise, right here and now, that no angry old ladies with yardsticks will show up at your house upon purchase of this book. You can go through the chapters and principles as quickly, or as slowly, as you'd like without worrying about your knuckles.

However, the inescapable fact is this: what you get out of music is what you put into it. If you want to be able to play classical music, you must memorize sight-reading and know how to keep a steady beat. If you plan on becoming a rock guitarist, then knowing what notes you need to play in a given key is especially important. Learning to play music takes a lot of personal discipline, but in the end, it's worth all the hard work.

Plus, of course, playing music is *fun*, and knowing how to play music well is *incredibly* fun. Everybody loves a rock star/jazz man/Mozart.

And now for a little history.

The Birth of Music and Theory

From what we can tell, by the time the ancient world was beginning to estab-lish itself — approximately 7000 B.C. — musical instruments had already achieved a complexity in design that would be carried all the way into the pre-sent. Bone flutes with five to eight drilled holes were being produced in the Henan Province in China that could play notes in both the five-note Xia Zhi scale and the seven-note Qing Shang scales of the ancient Chinese musical system. Some of the flutes found from this time period are still playable, and short performances have been recorded on them for modern listeners to hear.

All over the world, people were playing music — and not just on bone whis-tles and empty turtle shells. Pictographs and funerary ornaments have shown that by 3500 B.C., Egyptians had invented the harp — or at least were using it a lot — as well as double-reed clarinets, lyres, and their own version of the flute. By 2500 B.C., their neighbors across the Mediterranean, the Cycladians, eventually responsible for forming Greek culture, had adopted the lyre as well, while in faraway Denmark, the Danes had invented the first known trumpet.

By 1500 B.C., the Hittites of northern Syria had modified the traditional lute/harp design of the Egyptians and invented the first two-stringed guitar, with a long, fretted neck, tuning pegs at the top of the neck, and a hollow soundboard to amplify the sound of the strings being plucked. Guitars may look a lot sexier now and have a few more strings, but they follow the same basic design laid out more than 3,000 years ago.

There are a lot of unanswered questions about ancient music, not the least being why so many different cultures came up with so many of the same tonal qualities in their music completely independent of one another. Many theorists have concluded that certain patterns of notes *just sound right* to lis-teners, and certain patterns *don't*. Music theory, then, very simply, could be said to be a search for how and why music sounds right or wrong.

It's only common sense to assume that if a Neanderthal, say, built a really awesome flute or laid out a catchy rhythm on the ol' hollow log, there had to be someone nearby who asked, "How the heck did you do that?" Voila! The birth of music theory. The purpose of music theory is to both explain *why* something sounded the way it did, and *how* that sound can be made again.

The Greeks: First Theorists

Many people consider ancient Greece to be the actual birthplace of music theory. This is because, in that great, ancient Greek way of theirs, the ancient Greeks started entire schools of philosophy and science built around dissecting every single aspect of music then known. Even Pythagorus (the triangle guy) got into the act by creating the 12-pitch octave scale that we still use today. He did this via the very first Circle of Fifths (see the Cheat Sheet in the front of this book for an example), a device still religiously used by musicians from all walks of life.

Another famous Greek scientist and philosopher, Aristotle, is responsible for many books about music theory. He began a rudimentary form of music notation that stayed in use in Greece and subsequent cultures for nearly a thousand years after his death.

In fact, so much music theory groundwork was laid out in ancient Greece that there didn't seem to be a need to make any substantial changes to it until the European Renaissance nearly 2,000 years later. Neighbors and conquerors of Greece were all more than happy to incorporate Greek math, science, philosophy, art, literature, and music into their own cultures.

Yet without the benefit of the unique social perspective and structure of Greek culture — that is, the belief that smart people should be allowed to just think about things for the benefit of society — the newcomers were pretty hard-pressed to expound on these ideals. Besides, ancient Mediterranean peoples had more than enough other things to keep them busy, such as wars, slave revolts, threats from barbarian hordes, the destruction of Rome, and the overall oppressive atmosphere that permeated the Dark Ages.

The Keyboard and Music Notation

Prior to the Renaissance period, there were few truly innovative changes in music technology. Stringed instruments, woodwind, horns, and percussion instruments had been around for thousands of years, and although they had undergone many, many improvements in design and playing technique, they were essentially the same instruments used by the people of ancient Mesopotamia. It wasn't until the 1300s that a brand new musical interface appeared: the keyboard.

The first primitive keyboards had actually been in use since 300 B.C., when Ktesibios of Greece invented the one-note pipe organ. Romans adopted the design later for use in their arenas. It was absolutely the loudest instrument around and was perfectly suited to herald the beginning and end of spectacles such as the Roman Games. Still, considering that if you were in the ring when you heard it, you were probably about to wrestle a lion, this early organ was probably not a very popular instrument among anybody but Roman aristocracy.

Pipe organs were also a fixture in the Catholic Church since the late 700s, but were only played at the whimsy of whichever Pope was presiding. St. Augustine was apparently uncomfortable with music and did not allow it to be played during services. Pope Gregory forbade priests from playing musical instruments, which meant that only the human voice was allowed in service. Outside of the Church, there were no keyboards for folk musicians to experiment on. Pipe organs are way too big to steal, so if a church was attacked and razed, the organ went down right along with it.

Because of the Church affiliation, too, organs (therefore keyboards) were considered much too sacred an instrument for ordinary people to learn how to play. So, when the harpsichord became available for public consumption, it was almost immediately considered a far superior instrument than the "peasant" instruments that had been around for millennia. When royalty wanted a music performance written and performed for an occasion, more than likely they wanted that performance to be on a harpsichord. This perception of the keyboard instrument belonging to a superior class carried on into the Baroque and Classical periods of music and has hold over public perception even today.

With the invention of the keyboard came the beginning of modern musical *notation* — written music. The keyboard-notation link has to do with the ease of composing for full orchestras on the keyboard, as well as the fact that most newly commissioned work was for keyboard instruments because of the previously mentioned superior public perception of the instrument.

Fifteenth-century French composers began adding as many lines as they needed to their musical *staffs (or staves* — see Chapter 7 to find out all about the musical staff). They also wrote music with multiple staffs to be played simultaneously by different instruments. Because there were so many notes available on a keyboard, a separate staff for left- and right-handed playing began to be used: the bass clef and the treble clef.

Keyboards also had the advantage of being incredibly easy to build chords on (Chapter 13 has a lot of discussion about this), and the principles of intervals (Chapter 10) and chord building were heavily explored by famous Baroque composers such as Heinrich Schütz (1585–1672), Jean-Baptiste Lully (1632–1687), Henry Purcell (1659–1695), Johann Sebastian Bach (1685–1750), George Frideric Handel (1685–1759), George Philipp Telemann (1681–1767), and Antonio Vivaldi (1678–1741).

By the 17th century, the five-lined staff was considered standard for most musical instrumentation — probably because it was easier and cheaper to print just one kind of sheet music for musicians to compose on. The system hasn't changed much over the past four centuries, and probably won't change again until a new, sexier, more appealing instrument interface enters the scene.

But now that you know about how music theory started, let's get on to the real reason you picked up this book: to learn how music theory works.

Chapter 2

Counting Out Notes

- -

In This Chapter

▶ Understanding rhythm, beat, tempo, and note values

▶ Counting (and clapping) out notes

▶ Getting to know ties and dotted notes

▶ Mixing up note types and counting them out

- -

*J*ust about everyone has taken some sort of music lessons, either formal paid lessons from some crinkly old piano teacher or just the state-mandated rudimentary music classes offered in public school. Either way, we've all been asked at some point to knock out a beat, if only by clapping our hands.

Maybe the music lesson seemed pretty pointless at the time, or just a great excuse to bop your grade-school neighbor on the head. However, counting out a beat is exactly where we have to start with music. Without a discernible rhythm, there is no order to music and nothing to dance to or nod our heads to. Although all the other parts of music (pitch, melody, harmony, and so on) are pretty darned important, without rhythm, you don't really have a song. So rhythm is where we start in this book.

Don't worry. You don't have to be a perfect metronome of a percussionist to keep a beat. Everything around you has a rhythm to it, from birds to automobiles to babies, and that includes you.

In music, the rhythm is the pattern of regular or irregular pulses. The most basic thing you're striving for in music is to find the rhythm in songs. Luckily, written music makes it easy to interpret other composers' works and produce the kind of rhythm they had in mind for their songs.

Meet the Beat

A *beat* is a pulse of time. A ticking clock is a good example. Every minute, the second hand ticks 60 times, and each one of those ticks is a beat. If you speed up or slow down the second hand, you're changing the *tempo* of the beat. *Notes* in music tell you what to play during each of those clicks.

Let's sum up:

✔ **Rhythm:** A pattern of regular or irregular pulses in music

✔ **Beat:** A series of repeating, consistent pulsations of time that divide time into equal lengths. Each pulsation is also called a beat

✔ **Tempo:** The rate or speed of the beat

✔ **Note:** A notation that tells the performer how long and how often to play a certain musical pitch within the beat

When you think of the word *note* as associated with music, you may think of a sound. However, in music the official reason for notes is to explain exactly how long a specific pitch should be held by the voice or instrument. The *time value* of notes determines what kind of rhythm the resulting piece of music will have, whether it will run along very quickly and cheerfully, or slowly and somberly, or in some other way.

Notes and Note Values

If you think of music as a language, then notes are like letters of the alphabet — they're that basic to the construction of a piece of music. Studying how note values fit against each other in a piece of sheet music is even more important than their musical pitches because if you change the notes values in a piece of music, you end up with completely different music. In fact, when musicians talk about performing a piece of music "in the style of" Bach, or Beethoven, or Philip Glass, they're more than likely talking about using the rhythm structure and pace characteristics of that particular composer's music than any particular love of chord progressions or melodic choices.

The big picture

As you may remember from school or music lessons, notes come in different flavors, each with its own note *value*. Before we go into detail on each kind of note, have a look at Figure 2-1, which shows most of the kinds of notes you'll encounter in music arranged so that their values add up the same in each row. The value of a half note is half that of a whole note, the value of a quarter note is a quarter that of a whole note, and so on. Each level of the "tree of notes" is equal to the others.

Figure 2-1:
Each level
of this tree
of notes
lasts as
many beats
as every
other level.
At the top is
the whole
note, below
that half
notes, then
quarter
notes,
eighth
notes, and
finally
sixteenth
notes on the
bottom.

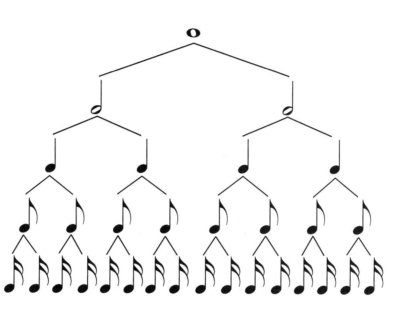

Another way to think of notes that you may find helpful is to imagine a whole note as a pie, which is easy because it is round. To divvy up the pie into quarter notes, cut it in quarters. Cutting the pie into eight pieces gives you eighth notes, and so on.

Depending on the time signature of the piece of music (see Chapter 4), the number of beats per note varies. In the most common time signature, 4/4 time, also called *common time*, a whole note is held for four beats, a half note is held for two, and a quarter note lasts one beat. An eighth note lasts half a beat and a sixteenth note just a quarter of a beat in 4/4 time.

Often, the quarter note equals one beat. If you sing, "MA-RY HAD A LIT-TLE LAMB," each syllable is one beat (you can clap along with it) and each beat gets one quarter note. You'll find out much more about this in Chapter 4.

The way notes look

Notes are made up of up to three specific components: *note head, stem,* and *flag* (see Figure 2-2). Every note has a head. It's the round part of a note. A note stem is the vertical line attached to the note head. A note flag is the little line that comes off the top or bottom of the note stem.

By the way, stems can point either up or down, depending where on the *staff* they appear (pointing up or down makes no difference in the value of the note — and you'll find out all about staffs in Chapter 7). Only eighth notes and smaller notes have flags. Quarter notes and half notes have stems but no flags. Whole notes have neither stems nor flags.

Instead of each note getting a flag, though, notes with flags can also be connected to each other with a *beam*, which is really just another, more organized-looking incarnation of the flag. For example, Figure 2-3 shows how two eighth notes can be written as each having a flag, or as connected by a beam.

Figure 2-4 shows four sixteenth notes with flags, grouped into two pairs connected by a double beam, and all connected by one double beam. It doesn't matter which way they are written. They would sound the same when played.

Figure 2-4:
These three groups of sixteenth notes, written in three different ways, would all sound alike when played.

Likewise, eight thirty-second notes could be written in either of the ways shown in Figure 2-5. Note that thirty-second notes get *three* flags (or three beams).

Figure 2-5:
Like eighth notes and sixteenth notes, thirty-second notes can be written separately or "beamed" together.

Using beams instead of individual flags on notes is simply a case of trying to clean up an otherwise messy-looking piece of musical notation.

Finding and following the beat

When figuring out how to follow the beat, rhythm sticks (fat cylindrical hard wood instruments) come in real handy. So do drum sticks. If you've got a pair, grab 'em — if not, clapping or smacking your hand against bongos or your desktop works just as well.

It is absolutely fundamental that you eventually "feel" a beat in your body while you play music, whether you're reading a piece of sheet music or jamming with other musicians. The only way you're going to be able to do this is *practice, practice, practice*. Following along with the beat in music is something you're going to have to pick up if you want progress in music.

Perhaps the easiest way to practice working with a steady beat is to cheat: Buy yourself a metronome. They're pretty cheap, and even a crummy one should last you for years. The beauty of a metronome is that you can set it to a wide range of tempos, from very, very slow to hummingbird fast. If you're using a metronome to practice with — especially if you're reading from a piece of sheet music — you can set the beat to whatever speed you're comfortable with and gradually speed it up to the composer's intended speed when you've figured out the pacing of the song.

Whole Notes

The whole note is the big daddy note of them all, as implied by its name. It lasts the longest of all the notes. Figure 2-6 shows what it looks like.

Figure 2-6:
A whole note is a hollow oval.

There's something comforting about the idea of a whole note, isn't there? Like a whole donut, or a whole sandwich, or possibly something that has nothing at all to do with food. Coming across a whole note in a piece of music can also be very comforting, especially to a beginning music student, because a whole note is held for an entire four beats (in 4/4 time — see Chapter 4 for more on time signatures). For four whole beats, you don't have to do anything with that one note except play and hold it. That's it.

When counting out beats, you only count as high as the highest-valued note in a selection. This means that (again, in 4/4 time) you only count as high as the number four, no matter how many whole notes are thrown at you.

So if you were to see a line of whole notes like the ones shown in Figure 2-7, you would count them out like this:

CLAP two three four CLAP two three four CLAP two three four.

Figure 2-7: Three whole notes in a row mean each one gets its own "four-count."

"CLAP" means you clap your hands, and "two three four" is what you say out loud as the note is held for four beats.

Even better for the worn-out musician is coming across a *double* whole note. You don't see them a whole heck of a lot, but when you do, they look like Figure 2-8.

Figure 2-8: A double whole note is held for twice as long as a normal whole note.

When you see a double whole note, you have to hold the note for an entire eight counts, like so:

CLAP two three four five six seven eight

Another common way to show a note that lasts for eight counts is when two whole notes are tied together. *Ties* are discussed later in this chapter.

Half Notes

It's simple logic what comes next. A half note is held for half as long as a whole note. Half notes look like Figure 2-9.

Figure 2-9:
A half note is held for half as long as a whole note.

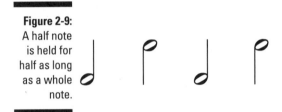

When you count out the half notes in Figure 2-9, it sounds like this:

CLAP two CLAP four CLAP two CLAP four

You could have a whole note followed by two half notes, as shown in Figure 2-10.

Figure 2-10:
A whole note followed by two half notes.

In that case, you would count out the three notes as follows:

CLAP two three four CLAP two CLAP four

Quarter Notes

Divide a whole note (worth four beats) by four, and you get a quarter note with a note value of one beat. Quarter notes look like half notes except that the note head is completely filled in, as shown in Figure 2-11.

Figure 2-11:
These four quarter notes get one beat apiece, meaning together they last as long as one whole note.

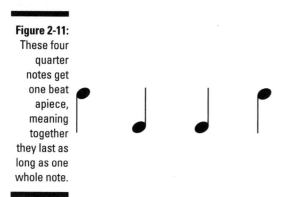

Four quarter notes are counted out like this:

CLAP CLAP CLAP CLAP

Because the highest valued note is a quarter note, you would only count up to one.

Suppose we replace one of the quarter notes with a whole note, and one with a half note, as shown in Figure 2-12.

Figure 2-12:
A mixture of whole, half, and quarter notes is getting closer to what you find in music.

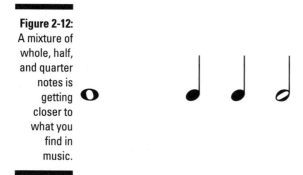

In that case, you would count out:

CLAP two three four CLAP CLAP CLAP four

Eighth Notes and Beyond

This is the point where sheet music starts to look a little scary. Usually, just one or two clusters of eighth notes in a piece of musical notation isn't enough to frighten the average beginning student, but when you open to a page that is littered with eighth notes, sixteenth notes, or thirty-second notes, you just know you've got a lot of work ahead of you. Why? Because these notes are *fast*.

An eighth note looks like Figure 2-13.

Figure 2-13:
An eighth note is held for one eighth as long as a whole note.

As you may expect, an eighth note has a value of half of a quarter note. Eight eighth notes would last as long as one whole note, which means an eighth note last half a beat (in 4/4, or common, time).

How could you have half a beat? Easy. Tap your toe for the beat and clap your hands twice for every toe tap.

CLAP-CLAP CLAP-CLAP CLAP-CLAP CLAP-CLAP

Or you can count it out as follows:

ONE-and TWO-and THREE-and FOUR-and

The numbers represent four beats, and the "ands" are the half beats.

Yet another way to think of eighth notes is to use the metronome. Just think of each tick as an eighth note instead of a quarter note. That means a quarter note is now two ticks, a half note is four ticks, and a whole note lasts eight ticks. That's perfectly legitimate.

If you have a piece of sheet music with sixteenth notes in it, then each sixteenth note can equal one metronome tick, an eighth note two ticks, a quarter note four ticks, a half note eight, and a whole note can equal sixteen ticks.

A sixteenth note has a note value of one quarter of a quarter note, which means it lasts one sixteenth as long as a whole note. A sixteenth note looks like Figure 2-14.

Figure 2-14:
A sixteenth note is held for half as long as an eighth note.

While we're at it, take a look at the thirty-second note in Figure 2-15.

Figure 2-15:
A thirty-second note is held for half as long as a sixteenth note.

If you have a piece of sheet music with thirty-second notes in it, then with your metronome a thirty-second note equals one metronome tick, a sixteenth note equals two, an eighth note equals four, a quarter note equals eight, a half note equals sixteen, and a whole note equals thirty-two ticks.

You'll be glad to hear that you won't run into thirty-second notes very often.

Dotted and Tied Notes

Sometimes you want to add, even if slightly, to the value of a note. There are two main ways to extend a note's value in written music: *dotted notes* and *tied notes*.

Dotted notes

Occasionally, you'll come across a note followed by a small dot, called an *augmentation dot*. This means the note's value is increased by one half of its original value. The most common use of the dotted note is when a half note is made to last three beats instead of two, as shown in Figure 2-16.

Figure 2-16:
A dotted
half note is
held for half
again as
long as a
regular half
note.

 = 3 beats

Less common, but still applicable here, is the dotted whole note. This means the whole note's value is increased from four beats to six beats.

TECHNICAL STUFF

If there are two dots behind the note, then the time value of the note is increased by another quarter of the original note, on top of the half increase indicated by the first dot. A half note with two dots behind it would be worth two beats plus one beat plus one half beat, or three and a half beats. This is so very rarely seen in most modern music that you'll probably never come across it, but just in case you do, you know what it means. The composer Richard Wagner was very fond of the triple-dotted note.

Tied notes

Another way to increase the value of a note is by *tying* it to another note, like Figure 2-17 shows.

Figure 2-17:
Two quarter notes tied together are exactly equivalent to a half note. When you see a tie, simply add the notes together.

Ties connect notes *that are the same pitch* together to created one sustained note instead of two separate ones. Therefore, a quarter note tied to another quarter note equals one note held for two beats: CLAP-two!

Don't confuse ties with *slurs*. A slur looks kind of like a tie, except it connects two notes of *different pitches* (you find out more about slurs in Chapter 6).

Mixing It All Up

You're not going to work with many pieces of music that are composed entirely of one kind of note, so you're going to need to work with a variety of note values.

The four exercises shown in Figures 2-18 through 2-21 are exactly what you need to practice making a beat stick in your head and making each kind of note automatically register its value in your brain. Each exercise contains five groups (or *measures*) of four beats each.

In these exercises, you clap on the CLAPs and say the numbers aloud. Where you see a hyphenated CLAP-CLAP, it means two claps per beat (in other words, two claps in the space of one normal clap), and where you see CLAP-CLAPCLAPCLAP it means *four* claps per beat (four claps in the space of one normal clap).

Start out counting and then dive in after you count four.

Figure 2-18:
CLAP CLAP
CLAP CLAP |
CLAP two
three CLAP |
CLAP two
three four |
CLAP two
three four |
CLAP CLAP
CLAP four.

Figure 2-19:
CLAP two
three four |
CLAP two
three four |
CLAP CLAP
three CLAP |
CLAP two
CLAP four |
CLAP two
three four.

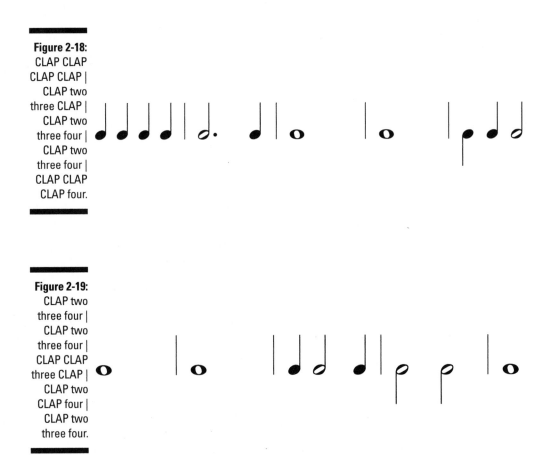

Figure 2-20:
CLAP CLAP-
CLAP CLAP
four | CLAP
two three
four | CLAP
two three
CLAP |
CLAP-CLAP
CLAP three
four | CLAP
two CLAP
four.

Figure 2-21:
CLAP two
CLAP four |
CLAP two
three CLAP |
CLAP two
three four |
one CLAP
three four |
CLAP two
three four.

Chapter 3

Giving It a Rest

. . . .

In This Chapter

▶ Talking about when not to sing or play

▶ Counting out the values of rests

▶ Mixing up notes and rests and counting them out

. . . .

Sometimes the most important aspects of a conversation are the things that aren't said. Likewise, many times it's the notes you *don't* play that can make all the difference in a piece of music.

These silent "notes" are called, quite fittingly, *rests*. When you see a rest in a piece of music, you don't have to do anything during it but keep on counting off the beats. Rests are especially important when it comes to writing down your music for other people to read — and in reading other composer's music — because rests make the rhythm of that piece of music even more precise than musical notes alone would.

Rests work particularly well with music for multiple instruments. Rests make it easy for a performer to count off the beats and keep time with the rest of the ensemble, even if the performer's instrument doesn't even come into play until later in the performance. Likewise, in piano music, rests tell the left or right hand — or both — to stop playing in a piece.

But don't let the name fool you. A rest in a piece of music is anything but nap time. If you don't continue to steadily count through the rests, just as you do when you are playing notes, your timing is going to be off, and eventually the piece will fall apart.

Continuing with Chapter 2's alphabet analogy, think of rests as the spaces between words and sentences in a written sentence. If those spaces weren't there, you'd just be stringing one long word together into gobbledygook.

Figure 3-1 shows the relative values of rests, ranging from a whole rest at the top to sixteenth rests at the bottom.

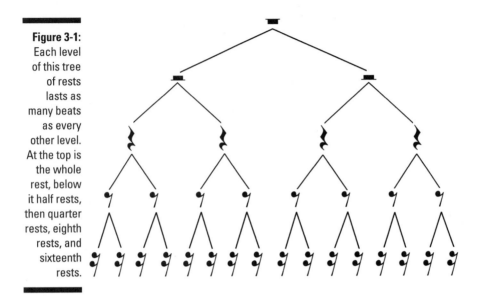

Figure 3-1:
Each level
of this tree
of rests
lasts as
many beats
as every
other level.
At the top is
the whole
rest, below
it half rests,
then quarter
rests, eighth
rests, and
sixteenth
rests.

Whole Rests

Just like a whole note, a whole rest is worth four beats (in the most common time signature, 4/4 — see Chapter 4 for all you need to know about time signatures). Look at Figure 3-2 for an example of a whole rest.

The whole rest looks like an upside down hat. You can remember this is the whole rest by imagining it is a hat that has been taken off and set down on a table, because this rest is the longest.

Figure 3-2:
A whole rest
looks like an
upside
down hat.

Even better than a double whole note for the worn-out musician is the rare double whole rest, which looks like Figure 3-3. When you see one of these in 4/2 music, you don't have to play anything for eight beats.

Figure 3-3:
You'll rarely
encounter
the double
whole rest,
but if you
ever do, this
is what it
looks like.

Half Rests

You're probably way ahead of us when it comes to the next kind of rest. If (in 4/4 time) a whole rest is held for four beats, then a half rest is held for two beats. Half rests look like Figure 3-4.

Half rests look like a hat. It's right side up because there's no time to lay it down on a table.

Figure 3-4:
The half rest
lasts half as
long as the
whole rest.

Take a look at the notes and rest in Figure 3-5.

Figure 3-5:
A whole
note, half
note, and
half rest.

If you were to count out the music written in Figure 3-5, it would sound like this:

CLAP two three four CLAP two three four

Again, rests don't get claps (or notes from instruments or voices). You just count them out in your head. Just remember to stop playing your instrument while you're counting.

Quarter Rests

See where this is going? Divide a whole rest by four, or a half rest by two, and you get a quarter rest. A quarter rest lasts one quarter as long as a whole rest. A quarter rest looks like Figure 3-6.

Figure 3-6:
A quarter rest, written like a kind of squiggle, is like a silent quarter note.

Figure 3-7 shows a whole note and a half note separated by two quarter rests.

Figure 3-7:
Two quarter rests tucked between notes.

You would clap out the music in Figure 3-7 as follows:

CLAP two three four one two CLAP four

Eighth Rests and Beyond

Eighth rests, sixteenth rests, and thirty-second rests are easy to recognize because they all have little curlicue flags, a little bit like their note counterparts. An eighth note (see Chapter 2) has one flag on its stem, and an eighth rest has a flag on its stem as well. A sixteenth note has two flags, and a sixteenth rest has two flags. (More rarely, a thirty-second note has three flags, and you can probably guess how many flags a thirty-second rest has.)

An eighth rest looks like Figure 3-8.

Figure 3-8:
An eighth
rest has a
stem and
one little
curling flag.

As you might imagine, thinking back to eighth notes in Chapter 2 (if you read it already), eighth rests can be as tricky to count out as their note equivalents. An eighth rest lasts half as long as a quarter rest, and this usually means less than a whole beat (Chapter 4 is about time signatures, which affects just how many beats are in a note or rest). There are eight eighth rests in a whole rest.

Getting a metronome to help count out notes and rests may be the best way to figure out a piece of music. You can assign the ticks of the metronome to be any portion of the beat that you like. Having a quarter note equal one beat may seem natural much of the time, but instead of trying to think about half beats, you can also assign an eighth note to equal one tick. Then a quarter note would equal two ticks, a half note four, and a whole note eight ticks. The relation among the different notes and rests always stays the same no matter how many metronome ticks in a whole note.

A sixteenth rest looks like Figure 3-9. It has a note value of $\frac{1}{16}$ of a whole rest. In other words, there are sixteen sixteenth rests in a whole rest.

Figure 3-9:
A sixteenth
rest is rarely
encoun-
tered and
has two
little curly
flags.

You will probably never encounter one, but a thirty-second rest looks like Figure 3-10.

Figure 3-10:
A thirty-
second rest
is very rare
and has
three little
curly flags.

A thirty-second rest has a value of one thirty-second of a whole rest. That is, there are thirty-two thirty-second rests in a whole rest.

Dotted Rests

Unlike notes, rests are never tied together to make them longer, so don't bother looking for tied rests in music. Rests are, however, sometimes dotted when the value of the rest needs to be extended. Just like with notes, when you see a rest followed by an *augmentation dot*, the rest's value is increased by one half of its original value.

Figure 3-11 shows a dotted half rest.

Figure 3-11:
A dotted half rest is held for a half rest and then one half of a half rest.

A dotted quarter rest is extended by another half of a quarter rest.

If there are two dots behind the rest, as shown in Figure 3-12, then the time value of the dotted rest is increased by another quarter of the original rest. Luckily, it is almost certain that you will never, ever encounter a double-dotted rest.

Figure 3-12:
Double-dotted rests are as rare as hen's teeth.

Mixing It All Up

The best way to really hear the way rests affect a piece of music is to mix them up with notes. To avoid adding to the confusion, we use only quarter notes in the following exercises.

The five exercises shown in Figures 3-13 through 3-18 are exactly what you need to practice making a beat stick in your head and making each kind of note and rest automatically register its value in your brain. Each exercise contains three groups of four beats each.

In these exercises, you clap on the CLAPs and say the numbers aloud. Start out counting and then dive in after you count four.

Figure 3-13:
CLAP CLAP
CLAP CLAP |
one two
three four |
CLAP two
three CLAP.

Figure 3-14:
One two
three four |
CLAP two
CLAP four |
CLAP two
three CLAP.

Figure 3-15:
One CLAP
three CLAP |
one two
three four |
CLAP two
three CLAP.

Figure 3-16:
One two
CLAP CLAP |
one two
three four |
CLAP CLAP
CLAP four.

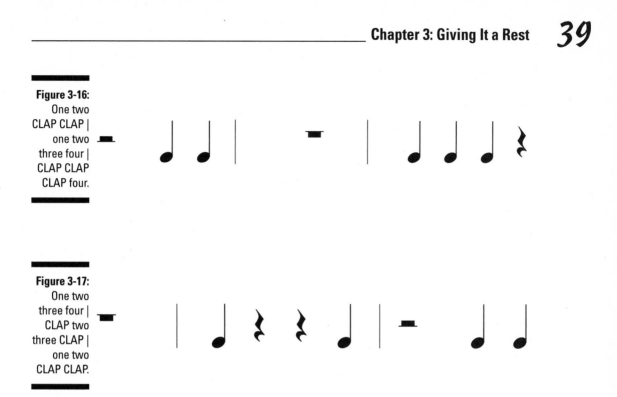

Figure 3-17:
One two
three four |
CLAP two
three CLAP |
one two
CLAP CLAP.

Chapter 4

Time Signatures

*I*n case you were wondering how you're supposed to keep track of where you are in a long piece of music, never fear. The geniuses who came up with music notation figured out a way to make order out of the onslaught of notes and rests. Once you're familiar with time signatures and the structure of the musical staff, including the concept of measures (or bars), all you really have to be able to do is keep counting out the beat.

Meet the Staff

Notes and rests in music are written on what we call a *musical staff* (called a *stave* when talking about more than one— you'll find out a good deal more about staves, in Chapter 7). A staff is made of five parallel, horizontal lines, containing four spaces between them, as shown in Figure 4-1.

Figure 4-1:
The two primary staves: On the left you see the treble clef staff, and on the right, the bass clef staff.

Treble and bass clefs

Notes and rests are written on the lines and spaces of the staff. Which particular musical notes are meant by each line and space depends on which *clef* is written at the beginning of the staff.

Look again at Figure 4-1. That cursive "G"-like marking at the beginning of the left-hand staff is called a *treble clef*. In the right-hand staff in Figure 4-1, the spiral "9"-like marking is called the *bass clef*. Basically, the treble clef is for higher notes, and the bass clef is for lower notes. In music for some instruments, such as piano, when both staffs are used, the treble clef is placed on top of the bass clef, and the result is called the *grand staff*. (Chapter 7 is all about the grand staff.)

Time signatures

In printed music, right after the clef at the beginning of the staff, you'll see a pair of numbers, one written over the other, three variations of which are shown in Figure 4-2.

Figure 4-2:
Three typical time signatures, read as "three-four time," "four-four time," and "six-eight time."

$$\begin{matrix} 3 \\ 4 \end{matrix} \qquad \begin{matrix} 4 \\ 4 \end{matrix} \qquad \begin{matrix} 6 \\ 8 \end{matrix}$$

The pair of numbers is called the *time signature*, which, incidentally, is the main character of this chapter. The time signature is there to tell you two things:

  ✔ **Number of beats in each measure:** The top number in the time signature tells you the number of beats to be counted off in each measure. If the top number is three, then each measure contains three beats.

  ✔ **Which note gets one beat:** The bottom number in the time signature tells you which type of note value equals one beat — most often, eighth notes and quarter notes. If the bottom number is four, then a quarter note is one beat. If it's an eight, then an eighth note gets one beat.

Measures

A *measure* (sometimes called a *bar*) is any segment of written music contained within two vertical bars that span the staff from top to bottom. Measures follow one another throughout a piece of written music, and each one contains as many beats as is indicated by the top number in the time signature.

A strong accent is put on the first beat of each measure, the "1" beat. The top number of the time signature lets you know how many beats are to be in a measure, as shown in Figure 4-3.

Figure 4-3:
The vertical lines here represent measures. Notice that given the 3/4 time signature, each measure contains three beats, and the quarter note equals one beat.

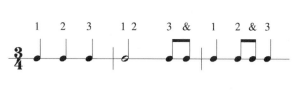

As we made clear in Chapters 2 and 3, continuously counting beats in your head while you're playing is incredibly important to the resulting sound. Timing is everything in music. You must become so comfortable with the inherent beat of whatever you're playing that you don't even know you're counting beats anymore. Practicing counting through measures is a great way to make sure you are playing the piece of music in front of you according to the beat chosen by the composer. (See Chapter 2 for all about beats.)

Counting beats according to the time signature is a lot like Driver's Ed in high school. The teacher repeatedly tells you to keep your eyes on the road ahead of you, because the rest of your body (and car) will be drawn to the space your eyes are focused on. After you become a relatively experienced driver, you don't even realize that your body and mind are constantly focused on that space on the road in front of you. Even when you're fiddling with the radio or talking to the person in the seat next to you, you're focused enough on the act of driving straight that you don't wobble all over the road when you answer difficult questions or pop a CD into the stereo. It's all about training your mind to follow the beat automatically, and once you have that down, you don't have to worry about consciously counting musical beats in your head — you just do it.

There are two types of time signatures:

- ✔ Simple
- ✔ Compound

Simple Time Signatures

Simple time signatures are the easiest to count, as a one-two pulse in a piece of music feels the most natural to a listener and a performer. Four requirements are necessary to make a time signature a simple time signature:

1. **Each beat is divided into two equal components.**

   This is most obvious when it is applied to eighth and smaller notes. In simple time, two eighth notes are always connected together with a bar called a *beam*, as are four sixteenth notes, or eight thirty-second notes. (If you have two sixteenth notes and one eighth note, those three notes, which equal one beat, are also beamed together.)

   Put another way, if there is more than one note in one single beat, they are always grouped together to equal one beat. Figure 4-4 shows the progression of how notes are beamed together in simple time.

2. **The note that gets one beat has to be an undotted note.**

   When you're counting a song out in your head, you're only going to be counting undotted, divisible-by-two notes. Usually this means quarter notes, but it can also mean half notes, whole notes, or, sometimes, eighth notes. In 4/4 time, for example, when you're counting out the measure, in your head you'll be counting, "One-two-three-four" over and over again. In 3/4 time, it'll be "one-two-three" over and over again. In 2/4 time, "one-two."

Figure 4-4:
Each level
of this tree
equals
every other
layer. In
simple time,
multiple
notes within
a beat are
always
grouped
together to
equal one
beat.

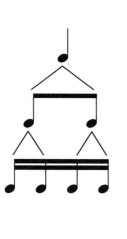

3. **The top number is not divisible by 3 except when it *is* 3.**

   For example, 3/4 and 3/8 are considered simple time signatures, whereas 6/4, 6/8, and 9/16 are not.

4. **The number of beats is the same in every measure.**

   Every measure, or bar, of music in a simple time signature has the same number of beats per measure throughout the song. Once you get into the groove of counting out the time, you don't have to worry about doing anything but making sure the notes in the song follow that beat, all the way through.

Measures and counting in simple time

Measures (or bars) were implemented specifically to help performers keep track of where they are in a piece of music and to help them play the appropriate beat. In simple time, the measure is where the true rhythm of a piece of music can be really felt, even if you're just reading a piece of sheet music without playing it.

In simple time, a slightly stronger accent is placed on the first beat of each measure. This means that when you see a line of music that looks like Figure 4-5, then the beat is counted off like this:

ONE two three four ONE two three four ONE two three four

Figure 4-5:
4/4 time
satisfies the
require-
ments of
simple time.

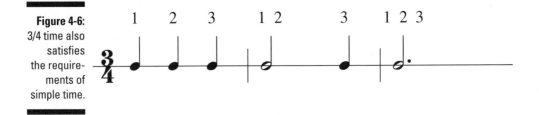

Figure 4-5: 4/4 time satisfies the requirements of simple time.

Again, the bottom number 4 tells you that the quarter note gets the beat, while the top number 4 tells you that there are four beats per measure, or four quarter notes (and only four) in each measure.

Here are three common examples of simple time signatures:

- ✔ **4/4:** Widely used in popular classical music, rock, jazz, country, bluegrass, hip-hop, and house music

- ✔ **3/4:** Used for waltzes and country and western ballads

- ✔ **2/4:** Used in polkas and marches

4/4 time is so often used in popular types of music (classical, rock, jazz, country, bluegrass, and most modern dance music) that it's referred to as *common time*. In fact, instead of writing "4/4" down for the time signature, some composers just write a large "C" instead. So if you see a "C" instead of a time signature, the piece is in 4/4 time.

If the time signature is 3/4, as in Figure 4-6, then the beat is counted like this:

ONE two three ONE two three ONE two three

Figure 4-6: 3/4 time also satisfies the requirements of simple time.

Here's a tricky one. If the time signature is 3/8, then the eighth note gets the beat, as shown in Figure 4-7.

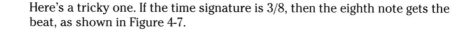
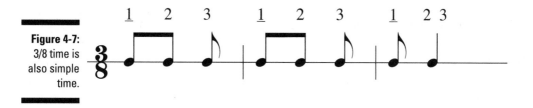

Figure 4-7:
3/8 time is
also simple
time.

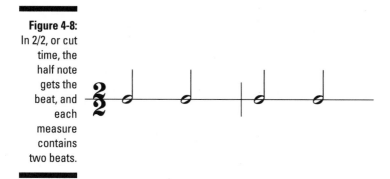

You would count out the beat of the music shown in Figure 4-7 like this:

ONE two three ONE two three ONE two three

3/8 and 3/4 have almost exactly the same rhythm structure in the way the beat is counted off — however, because 3/8 uses eighth notes instead of quarter notes, the eighth note gets the beat.

If the time signature is 2/2, also called *cut time*, then the half note gets the beat. And because the top number determines that there are two beats in the measure, there are two half notes in each measure, as seen in Figure 4-8.

Figure 4-8:
In 2/2, or cut
time, the
half note
gets the
beat, and
each
measure
contains
two beats.

You would count the music in Figure 4-8 like this:

ONE TWO ONE TWO

Time signatures with a 2 as the lower number were widely used in Renaissance music. Music from this period used a note value, called a minim, or a note played for half as long as a whole note.

Practicing counting beats in simple time

Using the information from this section, practice counting out the *beats* (not the notes) in Figures 4-9 through 4-13. When counting these beats out aloud, remember to give the first beat a slight stress.

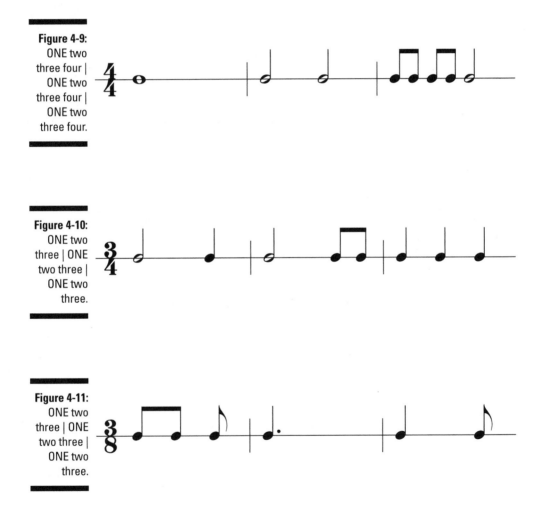

Figure 4-9:
ONE two three four | ONE two three four | ONE two three four.

Figure 4-10:
ONE two three | ONE two three | ONE two three.

Figure 4-11:
ONE two three | ONE two three | ONE two three.

Figure 4-12:
ONE two
three | ONE
two three |
ONE two
three.

Figure 4-13:
ONE two |
ONE two |
ONE two.

Compound Time Signatures

Just a wee bit trickier than simple time signatures are *compound* time signatures.

Here is a short list of rules that help you immediately tell when you're dealing with a compound time signature:

1. **The top number is evenly divisible by 3, with the exception of time signatures where the top number actually *is* 3.**

   Any time signature with a 6, 9, 12, 15, and so on is a compound time signature. 3/4 and 3/8 are not compound time signatures because the top number is 3. The most common compound time signatures are 6/8, 9/8, and 12/8. See Figure 4-14 for an example.

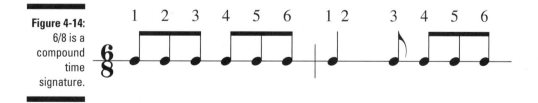

Figure 4-14:
6/8 is a
compound
time
signature.

2. **The beat is a dotted quarter note or three eighth notes.**

3. **Each beat is subdivided into three components.**

Again, this is most obvious when it is applied to eighth notes and beyond. In simple time, two eighth notes are always beamed together, as are even numbers of sixteenth notes. In compound time, *three* eighth notes are beamed together, as are *six* sixteenth notes.

Figure 4-15 shows the "three-based" grouping of beamed notes used in compound time.

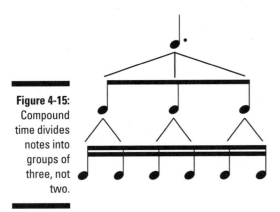

Figure 4-15: Compound time divides notes into groups of three, not two.

Measures and counting in compound time

One big difference between music in a simple time signature and music in compound time signature is that they *feel* different, both to listen to and to play.

In compound time, an accent is not only placed on the first beat of each measure, as in simple time, but a slightly softer accent is also placed on each successive beat. Therefore, there are two distinctly accented beats in each measure of music with a 6/8 time, three accents in a piece of 9/8 music, and four accents in a piece of music with a 12/8 time signature.

Two examples of compound time signature are:

- ✔ **6/8:** Used in mariachi music
- ✔ **12/8:** Found in 12-bar blues and doo-wop music

To determine the number of accents per measure under a compound time signature, divide the top number by three. This helps you find the pulse in the music you're playing and, therefore, where you put the accents in. In a piece of 6/8 music, for example, you would put the accent at the beginning of each measure, but you also would put a slight accent at the beginning of the second group of eighth notes in a measure, as shown in Figure 4-16.

Figure 4-16: In 6/8 time, a compound time signature, you add an accent on the second group of three eighth notes (on the *four* beat).

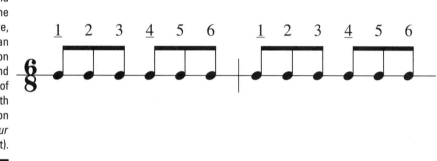

Therefore, the *beat accents* in Figure 4-16 would go like this:

ONE two three FOUR five six ONE two three FOUR five six

If the time signature is something scary, like 9/4, an example of which is shown in Figure 4-17, you would count off the beat (not the notes) like so:

ONE two three FOUR five six SEVEN eight nine

Figure 4-17: You'd better believe 9/4 is a compound time signature.

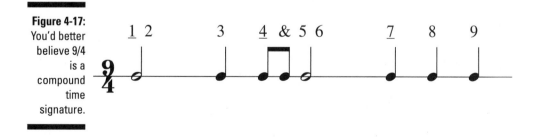

With simple time signatures, the beat of a piece of music can be broken down into two-part segments. In compound time signatures, the beat is broken down into three-part segments.

Practicing counting in compound time

Using the information from this section, practice counting out the beats in Figures 4-18 through 4-20. When counting these beats out aloud, remember to give the first beat a slight stress and put an additional stress at the "pulse points" of the measure, generally located after every third beat. (The *and*s in the captions are meant to capture the lilt of the some of the notes within the beat. We admit this is not a very scientific method, but it should give you a general idea of how to count out beats in different time signatures.)

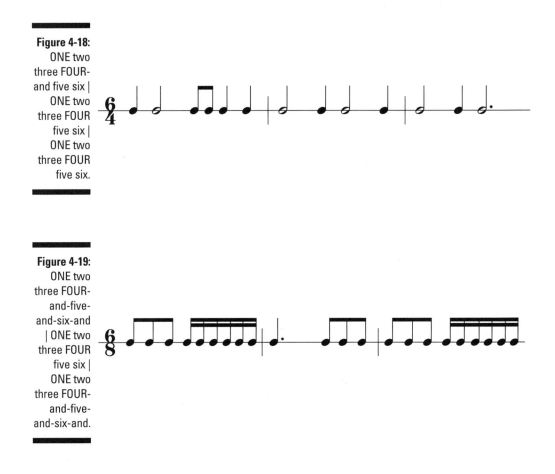

Figure 4-18:
ONE two three FOUR-and five six | ONE two three FOUR five six | ONE two three FOUR five six.

Figure 4-19:
ONE two three FOUR-and-five-and-six-and | ONE two three FOUR five six | ONE two three FOUR-and-five-and-six-and.

Figure 4-20:
ONE two three FOUR five six SEVEN eight nine | ONE two three FOUR-and-five-and six-and | SEVEN eight nine.

Asymmetrical Time Signatures

Asymmetrical time signatures (also sometimes called *complex* or *irregular* time signatures) generally contain five or seven beats, compared to the traditional two-, three-, and four-beat measure groupings we have looked at so far. Asymmetrical time signatures are very common in traditional music from around the world, both in European folk music and in Eastern (particularly Indian) popular and folk music.

When a piece of music with an asymmetrical time signature is played, the pulse, or beat, of the song feels and sounds quite a bit different than music written under simple or compound time signatures. For example, in Figure 4-21, the pulse is defined by the placements of the half notes in each grouping making the stresses fall on the third beat in the first measure and on the fourth beat in the second measure. In Figure 4-22, the beaming of the eighth notes shows where the stresses are to occur — on the first eighth note of each set of beamed notes.

Music with 5/4, 5/8, and 5/16 time signatures is usually divided up into two pulses, either two beats + three beats or vice versa. The stress pattern does not have to repeat itself from measure to measure — the only thing constant is that there are still five beats in each measure.

Figure 4-21:
ONE two
THREE four
five | ONE
two three
FOUR five.

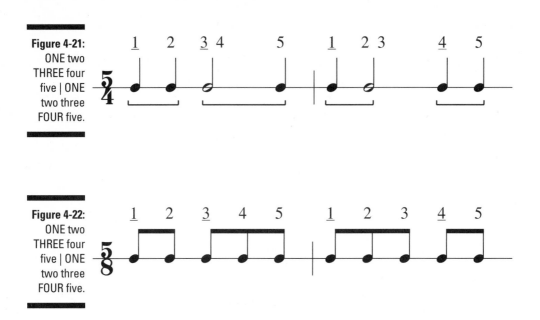

Music with 7/4, 7/8, and 7/16 time signatures looks like Figures 4-23 and 4-24. Again, the stress patterns don't have to stay the same from one measure to the next.

Figure 4-22:
ONE two
THREE four
five | ONE
two three
FOUR five.

Figure 4-23:
ONE two
three FOUR
five six
seven | ONE
two three
four FIVE six
seven.

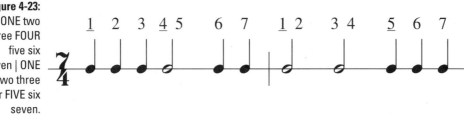

Figure 4-24:
ONE two
three FOUR
five SIX
seven | ONE
two THREE
four FIVE six
seven.

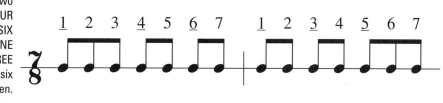

It should again be noted that asymmetrical time signatures are only considered "complex" from a Western point of view. Irregular time signatures have been used regularly throughout history and around the world, including ancient Greece and Persia, and can still be heard in Bulgarian folk music, for example. Modern Western composers and ensembles as diverse as Steve Albini, Beck, Dave Brubeck, June of 44, Andrew Lloyd Webber, Frank Zappa, Pink Floyd, Yo-Yo Ma, Bobby McFerrin, and Stereolab have all used asymmetrical time signatures in their music. A whole genre of rock, called *math rock*, is based around using complex time signatures like 7/8, 11/8, 13/8, and so on, in order to break away from the 4/4 time that is the rock standard.

Chapter 5

Naturalizing the Rhythm

As strict as the rules of notes and rests seem to be, it's probably obvious to even the most casual listener that music is not a force controlled by robotic percussionists and gigantic clicking metronomes. If the world itself was a perfectly ordered organism, with every living thing on it moving along in perfect time, music might be similar. However, even the healthiest human heart skips a beat now and then, and so does music.

The trick for composers and music theorists alike has been to translate these skipped beats into written notation, making such deviations fit naturally into the score. And that's what this chapter is all about.

Stress Patterns and Syncopation

The underlying rhythmic pulse of music is called the *beat*. In some ways, the beat is everything. It's what determines how people dance to music or even how they feel when they hear it. The beat helps determine whether people feel excited, agitated, mellow, or relaxed by music. When you're writing a piece of music down on paper, the way you group your notes together in a *measure* (the music contained within two *bar lines*) reflects the kind of pulse the music will have. As a musician, you can feel this natural pulse when you play music and count off the beats.

The general rule of placing stress

Generally, the first beat of a measure receives the strongest stress. If there are more than three beats in a measure, then there's usually a secondary strong beat halfway through the measure. There are lots of theories about why the brain seems to demand that music be broken up into units of two and three beats, not the least being that the beat of music tends to be similar to the beat of the human heart. But there's no real consensus on why music can be broken up into units of two or three beats.

In a piece of music with four beats in each measure, such as a piece in 4/4 time, there's a strong accent on the first beat in the measure and a slightly less strong beat on the third beat, counted as follows:

ONE two THREE four

A piece of music written in 6/8 time, which has six beats in each measure, is counted as follows:

ONE two three FOUR five six

And so on. (See Chapter 4 for more on time signatures.)

Syncopation: skipping the beat

Syncopation is, very simply, a deliberate disruption of the two- or three-beat stress pattern, most often by stressing an *off-beat*, or a note that is not on the beat.

Again, in 4/4 time, the general stress pattern is that the first and the third beats are strong, and the second and fourth are weak. Another way to say this is that *downbeats*, or accented beats, such as those at the beginning or halfway through a measure, are strong, and *upbeats*, or unaccented beats, are generally weak.

So if you had a piece of music that looked like Figure 5-1, the quarter rest where the natural downbeat is considered the point of syncopation in the music. The accent has been moved to the fourth beat of the measure, making for a different-sounding rhythm than you would normally have in 4/4 time music.

Figure 5-1:
This
measure
would be
counted off
as ONE-
two-(three)-
FOUR

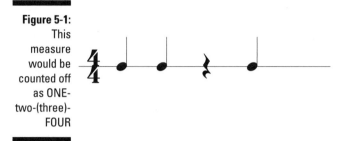

The natural stress of the meter has been disrupted — ONE-two-(three)-FOUR, which is weird, because we want to keep hearing that nonexistent quarter note that would carry the downbeat in the middle of the measure.

If you do anything that disrupts the natural beat with either an accent, or an upbeat with no subsequent downbeat being played, you have created a point of syncopation.

Syncopation is really tricky. It's often misunderstood by as being comprised of cool, complex rhythms with lots of sixteenth notes and eighth notes, as often seen in jazz music, but that isn't necessarily true.

For example, Figure 5-2 shows a bunch of eighth notes and then a bunch of sixteenth and thirty-second notes.

Figure 5-2:
These
measures
may look
complicated,
but they
don't show
syncopation.

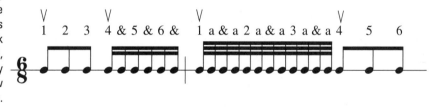

Just because Figure 5-2 is a very dense rhythm doesn't necessarily mean those rhythms are syncopated — as you can see from the accent marks, the downbeat is still on the "one" and "four" count in both measures, which is the normal downbeat.

Even if you have an entire measure of eighth notes, there's no syncopation there, because every eighth note has a subsequent *rhythmic resolution*: the downbeats still occur in the measure where they're supposed to be, on the accented notes shown in the figure. It's the same reason why a bunch of sixteenth notes in a row aren't syncopated because, again, even though you have some interesting notes that aren't on the downbeat, everything ends up always resolving to the beat of ONE two THREE four, or ONE two three FOUR five six.

However, look at the notes in Figure 5-3.

Figure 5-3:
This music shows three places where the note placement creates syncopation.

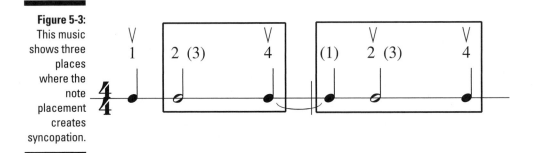

You have two points of syncopation in the measures, giving you a rhythm of ONE two three FOUR one TWO three FOUR. The natural stresses have been shifted over in both measures, resulting in a purposefully disjointed-sounding beat.

Try counting out the beats while listening to the Rolling Stones' "Satisfaction," and you'll hear some great examples of syncopation.

So, does syncopation involve a carefully placed rest or an accented note? The answer is both. Any point of a piece of music that moves your perspective of where the downbeat is is a point of syncopation because it's shifting where the strong and the weak accents are built.

Pick-Up Notes

Readers who have taken a poetry class have probably heard of anacrusis. In poetry, an *anacrusis* is one or more unstressed syllables at the very beginning of a verse that occurs before whatever metrical pattern being employed takes over.

Dr. Seuss was a great lover of anacrusis and used it in many of his classic books, such as *What Was I Scared Of?* That long poem begins like this:

Well . . .

I was walking in the night

And I saw nothing scary.

For I have never been afraid

Of anything. Not very.

In this example, the "Well . . ." is the poem's anacrusis, because it doesn't fit in with the rest of the meter of the poem at all, but serves as an idiosyncratic introduction. Anacrusis works the same way in music, too, although most people outside the world of classical music refer to it as *pick-up notes* or *a pick-up measure*.

A pick-up measure occurs when you have what looks like an odd or illegal measure at the beginning of a piece of music, as shown in Figure 5-4.

Figure 5-4:
The quarter note standing alone in the first measure is a pick-up note.

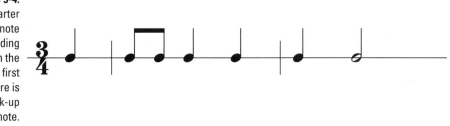

Looks pretty weird, right? Up until now, we have had to follow the rule that says 4/4 meter has four beats per measure. Every measure is like a jug of water; you've got to fill it right to the top, and you can't end up short and you can't spill any over. That's the rule.

But a pick-up measure allows us to break that rule. The measure shown in Figure 5-4 has only one beat in it where there should be three. From that point on, the song follows the rules set forth by the 3/4 time signature all the way to the very end, where you suddenly come across a measure that looks Figure 5-5.

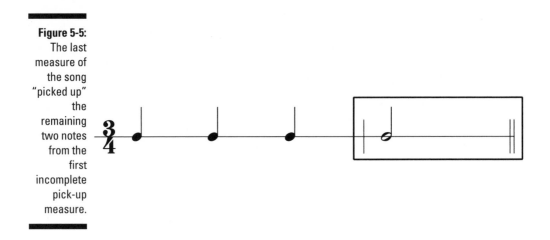

The final measure is the second part of the pick-up measure: the final two beats are considered the remainder part of that very first measure. The last measure "fixes" what looked wrong with that first measure, and therefore you have a piece of music written in perfect accordance with all the rules of music theory. Because you only filled the jug up a little bit in the beginning, the last measure finishes up whatever was incomplete in the first measure.

Now, in contemporary music, especially rock music, you can still have the first pick-up measure, but musicians don't necessarily have to adhere to this perfect rule of finishing it up in the final measure. Often a song starts with a pick-up measure, but the last measure is a complete, full measure. This is because a lot of the rules that governed music notation and composition prior to the 20th century have relaxed a whole bunch, and more people are happier about this than not.

Irregular Rhythms: Triplets and Duplets

Irregular rhythms are one example of the challenges that composers face when trying to get their already-composed music written down for others to play.

Triplets

Say you want to put a cool little musical *trill* (a quick sequence of two or three notes) where you'd normally play one quarter note. In 4/4 time, if you want to play an even number of notes in your trill, you can use a couple of eighth notes, or four sixteenth notes, or eight thirty-second notes. But what if you want to play an odd number of notes, and you absolutely want that odd number of notes to equal one beat?

The answer is to play a *triplet*, which is what you get when you have a note usually divisible by two equal parts divided into three equal parts. A quarter note divided into triplets looks like Figure 5-6.

Figure 5-6:
When a quarter note in 4/4 time is divided into three equal notes, the result is a triplet.

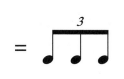

 A good way to count out the beats while playing triplets is to say the number of the beat followed by the word *triplet* (in two syllables), making sure to divide the triplet played into three equal parts.

For example, the measures in Figure 5-7 would be counted off like this:

ONE two THREE-trip-let four ONE-trip-let two THREE-trip-let four

Figure 5-7:
Irregular note divisions such as triplets allows for more complex rhythms than "regular" notation time normally allows.

The triplet notation can be shown in two ways: with the number *3* written over the group of three notes, or with a bracket as well as the number. We read triplet notation as meaning "three notes in the time of two."

Duplets

Duplets work like triplets, except in reverse. Duplets are used when a composer wants to put two notes in a space where there should be three.

An example would be dividing a dotted quarter note into two eighth notes instead of three eighth notes, as you would in a measure of music under a compound time signature. A good way to count duplets is to count the second note in each pair as *and* instead of assigning it a number value as you would any other beat in compound meter.

For example, the measures shown in Figure 5-8 would be counted out like this:

ONE two THREE FOUR-and ONE-and FOUR FIVE SIX

Figure 5-8:
Make sure that each duplet is given the same time value as the dotted note it replaced.

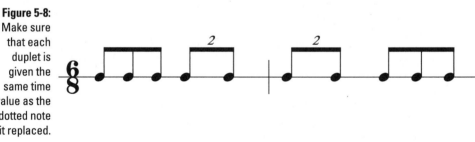

Chapter 6

Tempo and Dynamics

In This Chapter

▶ Figuring out sheet music notation for tempo and dynamics

▶ Keeping time with tempo

▶ Controlling loudness with dynamics

*E*verybody knows there's more to making good music than stringing a collection of notes together. Music is just as much about communication as it is about making sounds, and in order to really communicate to your audience, you need to grab their attention, inspire them, and wring some sort of emotional response out of them.

Tempo (speed) and *dynamics* (volume) are two tools you use to turn those carefully metered notes on sheet music into the elegant promenade of Liszt's Hungarian Rhapsody No. 2, the sweeping exuberance of Chopin's études, or, in a more modern context, the slow creepiness of Nick Cave's "Red Right Hand."

Tempo and dynamics are like musical punctuation — they're the markings in a musical sentence that tell you whether you're supposed to feel angry or happy or sad when you play a piece of music. As a performer, these are the markings that help you tell the composer's story to the audience.

Taking the Tempo of Music

Tempo means, quite basically, "time," and when you hear people talk about the tempo of a musical piece, they are referring to the speed at which the music progresses. The point of tempo is not necessarily how fast or slowly you can play a musical piece, however. What tempo really does is set the basic mood of a piece of music. Music that is played very, very slowly, or *grave*, can impart a feeling of extreme somberness, whereas music played very, very quickly, or *prestissimo*, can seem maniacally happy and bright.

The importance of tempo can truly be appreciated when you consider that the original purpose of much popular music was to accompany people dancing. Often the movement of the dancers' feet and body positions worked to set the tempo of the music, and the musicians followed the dancers.

Prior to the 17th century, though, composers had no real control over how their transcribed music would be performed by others, especially by those who had never heard the pieces performed by their creator. It was only in the 1600s that the concept of using tempo and dynamic markings in sheet music began to be employed.

The metronome: not just for hypnotists anymore

Despite what you may have gathered from horror movies such as Dario Argento's *Two Evil Eyes* and a number of Alfred Hitchcock's films, that pyramid-shaped ticking box does have a purpose besides turning human beings into mindless zombies.

Practicing with a metronome is the best possible way to learn to keep a steady pace throughout a song, and it's one of the easiest ways to match the tempo of the piece you're playing to the tempo conceived by the person who wrote the piece.

A brief history of time

The first person to write a serious book about tempo and timing in music was the French philosopher and mathematician Marin Mersenne. From an early age, Mersenne was obsessed with the mathematics and rhythms that governed our daily life — such as the heartbeats of mammals, the hoofbeats of horses, the wing flaps of various species of birds. This obsession led to his interest in the still-new field of music theory. In 1636, Mersenne introduced the concept of a universal music tempo, called the *minim*, which was equal to the beat of the human heart.

Mersenne's minim was greeted with open arms by the musical community. Since the introduction of written music hundreds of years before, composers had been trying to find some way to accurately reproduce the timing needed to properly perform their written works. Musicians loved the concept because having a common beat unit to practice with made it easier for individual musicians to play the growing canon of musical standards with complete strangers. Of course, not all hearts beat at the same rate, but most adult hearts beat at around 70 to 75 beats per minute (bpm) which was close enough to make the minim concept useful.

The metronome was first invented in 1696 by the French inventor Étienne Loulié. Loulié's first prototype consisted of a very simple weighted pendulum. The problem with his invention, though, was that in order to work with beats as slow as 40 to 60 beats per minute (bpm), the device had to be at least six feet tall.

It wasn't until more than 100 years later that two German tinkerers, Dietrich Nikolaus Winkel and Johann Nepomuk Maelzel, worked independently to produce the spring-loaded design that is the basis for analog (non-electronic) metronomes today. Maelzel was the first to slap a patent on the finished product, and as a result, his initial is attached to the standard 4:4 beat tempo sign, *MM=120*. *MM* is short for *Maelzel's metronome*, and the *120* means there will be 120 bpm, or 120 quarter notes, in the piece played.

Like the concept of the minim, the metronome was warmly received by musicians and composers alike. From then on, when composers wrote a piece of music, they could give musicians an exact number of beats per minute to be played. The metronomic markings were written over the staff so that musicians would know what to calibrate their metronomes to. For example, *quarter note=96*, or *MM=96*, means that 96 quarter notes are to be played per minute in a given song. These markings are still used today for setting mostly electronic metronomes, particularly for classical and avant-garde compositions that require precise timing.

Tempo notation

Although the metronome was the perfect invention for control freaks such as Beethoven and Mozart, most composers were happy instead to use the growing vocabulary of tempo notation to *generally* describe the pace of a song. Even today, the same words used to describe tempo and pace in music are used. They are Italian words, simply because when these phrases came into use (1600–1750), the bulk of European music came from Italian composers.

Table 6-1 lists some of the most standard tempo notations in Western music, usually found written above the time signature at the beginning of a piece of music.

Table 6-1	Common Tempo Notation
Notation	*Description*
Grave	The slowest pace. Very formal and very, very slow.
Largo	Funeral march slow. Very serious and somber.

(continued)

Table 6-1 *(continued)*

Larghetto	Slow, but not as slow as *largo*.
Lento	Slow.
Adagio	Leisurely. Think graduation and wedding marches.
Andante	Walking pace. Close to the original minim.
Andantino	Slightly faster than *andante*. Think Patsy Cline's "Walking After Midnight," or any other lonely cowboy ballad you can think of.
Moderato	Right smack in the middle. Not fast or slow, just moderate.
Allegretto	Moderately fast.
Allegro	Quick, brisk, galloping along.
Vivace	Lively, fast.
Presto	Very fast.
Prestissimo	Think "Flight of the Bumblebee."

Figure 6-1 shows an example of how tempo notation appears written above the time signature in a piece of music.

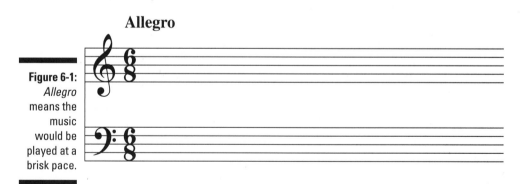

Figure 6-1:
Allegro means the music would be played at a brisk pace.

If you have a metronome, to properly appreciate the differences from one tempo setting to the next, you may want to try setting it to different speeds to get a feel of how different pieces of music might be played to each different setting.

Play Track 1 on the CD to hear examples of 80 (slow), 100 (moderate), and 120 (fast) beats per minute.

Just to make things a little more precise, modifying adverbs such as *molto* (very), *meno* (less), *poco* (a little), and *non troppo* (not too much) are sometimes used in conjunction with the tempo notation terms listed in Table 6-1. For example, if a piece of music says that the tempo is *poco allegro*, it means that the piece is to be played "a little fast," whereas *poco largo* would mean "a little slow."

Speeding up and slowing down: changing the tempo

Sometimes a different tempo is attached to a specific musical phrase within a song to set it apart from the rest. The following are a few tempo changes you're likely to encounter in written music:

- *Accelerando (accel.)*: Gradually play faster and faster.
- *Stringendo*: Quickly play faster.
- *Doppio movimento*: Play phrase twice as fast.
- *Ritardando (rit., ritard., rallentando,* or *rall.)*: Gradually play slower and slower.
- *Calando*: Play slower as well as softer.
- *A tempo*: Written at the end of musical phrases in which the tempo has been changed, this means return to the original tempo of the piece.

Dynamics: Loud and Soft

Dynamic markings have to do with how loudly or softly a piece of music is played. Like tempo, dynamic markings are used by composers to communicate how they want a piece of music to "feel" to an audience, whether it is quiet, loud, aggressive, or sad.

The most common dynamic markings, from softest to loudest, are as follows:

- ✔ *Pianissimo (pp)*: Play very softly.
- ✔ *Piano (p)*: Play softly.
- ✔ *Mezzo piano (mp)*: Play moderately softly.
- ✔ *Mezzo forte (mf)*: Play moderately loudly.
- ✔ *Forte (f)*: Play loudly.
- ✔ *Fortissimo (ff)*: Play very loudly.

Dynamic marking can be placed at the beginning or anywhere else within a piece of music. For example, in the music shown in Figure 6-2, *pianissimo (pp)* means that the piece is to be played very softly until you reach the next dynamic marking. The *fortissimo (ff)* means that the rest of the selection is to be played very loudly.

Figure 6-2:
The dynamic markings here mean you would play the first bar very softly and the second very loudly.

Modifying phrases

Sometimes when reading a piece of music, you may find one of the following markings attached to a musical phrase, or a section of music generally four to eight measures long:

- ✔ *Crescendo (cresc.<)*: Play gradually louder.
- ✔ *Diminuendo (dim.>)* or *decrescendo (decr.>)*: Play gradually softer.

In Figure 6-3, the long <, called a *hairpin*, means to play the selection gradually louder and louder until you reach the end of the *crescendo*.

Figure 6-3:
The crescendo here means play gradually louder and louder until the end of the hairpin.

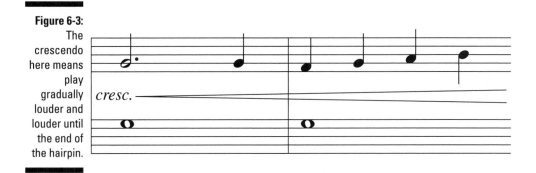

In Figure 6-4, the > hairpin beneath the phrase means to play the selection gradually softer and softer until you reach the end of the *diminuendo*.

Figure 6-4:
The *diminuendo*, or *decrescendo*, here means play gradually softer and softer until the end of the hairpin.

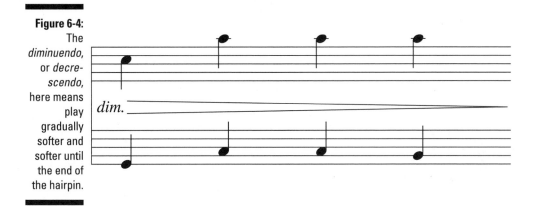

One more common marking you will probably come across is a *slur*. Just like when your speech is slurred and the words stick together, a musical slur is to be played with all the notes "slurring" into another. Slurs look like curves that tie the notes together.

Other tempo and dynamic markings

You probably won't see any of the following in a beginning-to-intermediate piece of music, but for more advanced pieces, you might find one or two of the following markings (listed alphabetically):

- ✔ *Agitato*: Excitedly, agitated
- ✔ *Animato*: With spirit
- ✔ *Appassionato*: Impassioned
- ✔ *Con forza*: Forcefully, with strength
- ✔ *Dolce*: Sweetly
- ✔ *Dolente*: Sadly, with great sorrow
- ✔ *Grandioso*: Grandly
- ✔ *Legato*: Smoothly, with the notes flowing from one to the next
- ✔ *Sotto voce*: Barely audible

Piano pedal dynamics

Additional dynamic markings have to do with using the three foot pedals located at the base of the piano (some pianos have only two pedals). The standard modern piano setup is, from left to right:

- ✔ **Soft pedal (or *una corda* pedal):** On most modern pianos, the soft pedal moves the resting hammers inside the piano closer to their corresponding strings. Because the hammers have less distance to travel to reach the string, the speed at which they hit the strings is reduced, and the volume of the resulting notes is therefore much quieter and has less sustain.

- ✔ **Middle pedal:** If it's present — and many modern pianos have only the two outer pedals to work with — the middle pedal has a variety of roles, depending on the piano. On some American pianos, this pedal gives the notes a tinny, "honky-tonk" piano sound when depressed. Some pianos have a bass sustain pedal as their middle pedal that works like a sustain pedal but for only the bass half of the piano keyboard. Still other pianos — specifically many concert pianos — have a *sostenuto* pedal for their middle pedal, which works to sustain one or more notes indefinitely, while allowing successive notes to be played without sustain.

- ✔ **Damper pedal (or sustaining or loud pedal):** The damper pedal does exactly the opposite of what the name would imply — when this pedal is pressed, the damper inside the piano *lifts off* the strings and allows the notes being played to "die out" naturally. This creates a ringing, echoey effect for single notes and chords (for example, the very end of The Beatles' "A Day in the Life"). The damper pedal can also make for a really muddled sound if too long of a musical phrase is played with the pedal held down.

Why all the Italian?

Since its inception, the piano has been the universal tool of choice for composing music, because almost every note you would ever want to work with is present on the keyboard, right there in front of you. Most pianos have at least 7 octaves to work with, and a few concert pianos can have 8.

You want to compose music for an oboe? The lower registers of the piano work quite nicely. Pieces written for strings can be easily hammered out in the middle and upper registers. And unlike most other instruments, you can hit chords and multiple notes simultaneously on a piano, which works well for trying to figure out how that multi-instrument orchestral piece you're writing will eventually sound.

You can blame the fact that the piano was invented by an Italian, Bartolomeo Cristofori, for the bulk of tempo and dynamic markings being Italian words. From day one of the piano's release to the initially Italian market, composers were finding new ways to write music on this spectacularly flexible instrument.

In sheet music notation, the entire musical phrase to be altered by use of pedals is horizontally bracketed, with the name of the pedal to be used listed beside or beneath it. If no pedal number is given, then the damper pedal is to be automatically used for the selection.

For example, in Figure 6-5, the "Ped." signifies that the damper pedal is to be depressed during the selection. The breaks in the brackets (^) mean that in these places, you briefly lift your foot off the pedal.

Figure 6-5:
Pedal dynamics show you which pedal to use and how long to hold it down.

Dynamic markings for other instruments

Although most dynamic markings are considered universal instructions — that is, applicable to all instruments — there are some that are aimed specifically at certain musical instruments. Table 6-2 lists some of these.

From clavichord to piano

The concept of using dynamic markings in sheet music came about around the same time as the piano — for good reason. Before the invention of the piano by Bartolomeo Cristofori in 1709, most composers were confined to writing most of their pieces for either the harpsichord or the clavichord; neither instrument had the capability to play both soft and loud sounds easily.

The reason for this is that the basic internal design of both the harpsichord and the clavichord follows the design of a stringed instrument. However, instead of having one's fingers in direct contact with the string, as with a guitar or a fiddle, harpsichord and clavichords are fitted with a plucking mechanism inside the instrument itself. When a certain key is pressed, the corresponding internal string is plucked by the mechanism. No matter how hard or soft you press the keys of either instrument, the result-ing volume is pretty much the same. Therefore, clavichords were used for quiet pieces of music that required lots of vibrato (quavering quality to notes that usually comes from a stringed instrument), whereas harpsichords were used for louder, brighter-sounding pieces.

Although the piano looks a lot like these two other instruments, it's really very different. The piano incorporates a hammer-and-lever mechanism that strikes each string with the same force as the human finger on the piano key did; this is why the piano is considered a *percussive* instrument. The piano made both quiet and loud sounds possible on the same instrument, and, therefore, in the same musical piece. This is why the piano was originally named the *gravicembalo col pian e forte*, or "harpsichord with soft and loud." The name was later shortened to *pianoforte* and, finally, to *piano*.

Table 6-2	Dynamic Markings for Specific Instruments
Notation	*What It Means*
Stringed instruments	
Martellato	A short, hammered stroke played with very short bow strokes
Pizzicato	To pluck the string or strings with your fingers
Spiccato	With a light, bouncing motion of the bow
Tremolo	Quickly playing the same sequence of notes on a stringed instrument
Vibrato	Slight change of pitch on the same note, producing a vibrating, trembling sound

Notation	What It Means
Horns	
Chiuso	With the horn bell stopped up (to produce a flatter, muted effect)
Vocals	
A capella	Without any musical accompaniment
Choro	The chorus of the song
Parlando or *parlante*	Singing in a speaking, oratory style
Tessitura	The average range used in a piece of vocal music

Part II
Melody: The Part You Hum

In this part . . .

In this part you begin to read music. You are presented with the grand staff, with the treble and bass clefs and all the note names. You find out more about how and why different instruments sound like they do. And you take the plunge into half steps and whole steps, the first steps of musical intervals.

Chapter 7

The Musical Staff

*J*ohannes Gutenberg's invention of the European printing press in 1450 is considered by many to be the official end of the Dark Ages for Europe. Eventually, his invention would make it possible for ordinary people to own books, and along the way, sheet music also began being printed for ordinary musicians to own. Soon, people with a little musical know-how could teach themselves all the principles of music theory previously unavailable to those outside the institutions of religion or higher learning.

As the proficiency of the "common" musician increased, the need for more new sheet music increased as well. Once composers learned they could now turn a decent profit by selling multiple, machine-printed copies of their music — instead of one laboriously hand-drawn copy at a time — they began flooding the market with new compositions.

All this eventually led to the standardization of sheet music. For years, composers were free to use as many staff lines as they wanted to express notation, but by the 1500s, the 5-line pair of clefs that we use today was gradually becoming universally accepted, at least in Europe.

The Clefs

Each clef can be thought of as a graph of *pitches*, or *tones*, shown as notes plotted over time on five lines and four spaces. Each pitch or tone is named after one of the first 7 letters of the alphabet: A, B, C, D, E, F, G, A, B, C . . . and it keeps on going that way indefinitely, repeating the note names as the pitches repeat in *octaves*, cycles where the note raises so high that it becomes a higher version of itself. The pitches go up as you go from A to G, with every eighth note — where you return to your starting letter — signifying the beginning of a new octave.

The treble clef

The *treble clef* is for higher-pitched notes. It contains the notes above middle C on the piano, which means all the notes you play with your right hand. On the guitar, the treble clef is usually the only clef you ever read. Most woodwind instruments stick solely to the treble clef, as well as high brass instruments and violins. Anything that makes *upper-register*, or high, sounds is going to have its music written for it in the treble clef.

The treble clef is also sometimes called the *G clef.* Note that the shape of the treble clef itself resembles a stylized G. The loop on the treble clef also circles the second line on the staff, which is the note G, as shown in Figure 7-1.

Figure 7-1:
The treble clef always tells you where the G is.

The notes are located on the treble clef on lines and spaces, in order of ascending pitch, as shown in Figure 7-2.

Figure 7-2:
The notes of the treble clef must be memorized in order for you to read music. There is no way around this. Sorry!

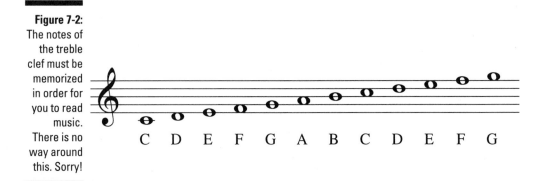

The bass clef

On the piano, the *bass clef* contains lower-pitched notes, the ones below middle C, including all the notes you play with your left hand. Music written in the bass clef is generally aimed at the lower wind instruments like the bassoon, the lower brass instruments like the tuba, and lower stringed instruments like the bass guitar.

Another name for the bass clef is the *F clef*. It looks a bit like a stylized F, if you use your imagination. The curly top of the clef also partly encircles where the F note is on the staff, and it has two dots that surround the F note, as shown in Figure 7-3.

Figure 7-3:
The bass clef looks a little bit like a cursive F.

F

The notes on the bass clef are also arranged in ascending order, as shown in Figure 7-4.

Figure 7-4:
The notes of the bass clef must also, alas, be memorized.

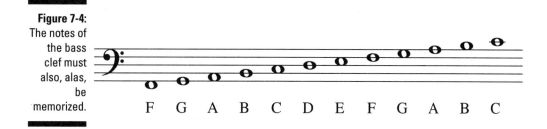

F G A B C D E F G A B C

The grand staff and middle C

Put the treble and bass clefs together, connected with by something called a *bracket*, and you get — can we get a drum roll? — the *grand staff*, as shown in Figure 7-5.

Figure 7-5:
The grand
staff
contains
both the
treble and
bass clefs,
connected
by ledger
lines and
middle C.

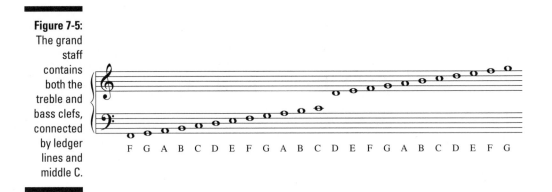

F G A B C D E F G A B C D E F G A B C D E F G

Take a good look at the grand staff in Figure 7-5. Note that piano's middle C is, indeed, right in the middle between the treble and bass clefs. But it's not *on* either clef. Instead it's on a *ledger* line. Ledger lines are lines written above the bass clef and below the treble clef that are necessary in order to connect the two clefs. Middle C is located one line below the treble clef and one line above the bass clef. Put it all together, and the notes flow smoothly from one clef to the other with no interruptions.

Alto and tenor clefs

Occasionally, you may come across an animal known as the C clef. The C clef is a moveable clef and can be placed on any line of the staff. The line that runs through the center of the C clef, no matter which line that is, is considered middle C, as seen in Figure 7-6.

C clefs were more commonly used before sheet music was standardized and able to easily accommodate a wide range of tones. Today, the only C clefs in common use are the alto clef, which puts the C on the third staff line, and the tenor clef, which puts middle C on the next-to-the-top line of the staff. The alto clef is most commonly used in writing music for the viola, whereas the tenor clef is used for writing cello music.

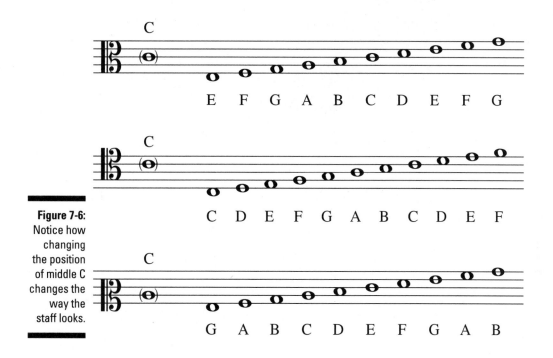

Intervals, Half Steps, Whole Steps, and Accidentals

When we're talking about the notes A, B, C, D, E, F, and G, we're referring to the *natural* notes — specifically, the notes that correspond to the white keys on the keyboard. Obviously, lots of other instruments don't have white or black keys, but because standardized musical notation evolved inside the Catholic church, and the sole instrument allowed in there was the keyboard-based pipe organ, all Western musical notation developed around the design of piano-like instruments.

The white keys of the keyboard were assigned the natural letter notes, which turn out to be the notes of the C major scale, beginning with C. However, since we're dealing with a musical vocabulary made up of 12 semitones we also have five black keys, repeated over and over, on the keyboard. The black keys were added much later than the original white keys in order to help build more perfect musical scales on the piano.

The modern piano keyboard is designed with each key, white or black, on the piano separated from the next by one *half step* (or *semitone*). For example,

Dr. Robert Moog, inventor, on keyboard alternatives

I think sound generation is a mature technology. Between analog and digital technology, you can make just about any sound you can imagine cheaply and easily. What we don't have cheap and easily yet are really good, new player interfaces — we're still working with the same old electronic organ principle. The same keyboards that were put into electronic organs 60 years ago, 50 years ago, are being used today, and there is very little difference. They feel the same, and, in fact, the organ keyboards that were developed in 1935 feel better than most keyboards that are designed today. A keyboard is just the starting point, especially if you think of all the ways that people like to move and push and touch when they're playing music. I think the field is wide open for developing really sophisticated, really human-oriented control devices.

But the problem for instrument designers is that people don't want to give up their keyboards.

Millions of people know how to play the piano. It's what there is when you're learning how to play music. If somebody were to start off at the age of 30 or 40 or 50 and learn a new control device, they'd have to practice as much as they did when they were learning how to play the piano when they were kids. You know what it's similar to — it's similar to the Dvorak keyboard, where you can type 20 or 30 percent faster than on a regular Qwerty keyboard. Anybody can do it, but very few people do it because it takes a certain amount of learning when you're an adult. Your mother's not going to teach you how to type on a Dvorak keyboard. Most adults already have plenty to do, and they're not going to relearn how to type. So new alternate controllers are like that, too. Designing them is going to be half the job — the other half is going to be musicians developing technique on those new interfaces. It's going to take decades.

The modern piano keyboard is designed with each key, white or black, on the piano separated from the next by one *half step* (or *semitone*). For example, the difference between the white C key on the keyboard and the black C sharp key is one half step. The difference between the white B key and the white C key is also one half step, because there is no black key between those two notes. This design also corresponds with the layout of frets on a modern guitar, with each fret being separated from the next by one half step.

Moving a whole step on the piano or guitar means you move *two* half steps from your starting position — for example, from the white C key to the white D key, or the black B flat key to the white C key. Half steps and whole steps are *intervals* (Chapter 10). Knowing the difference between whole steps and half steps is very important when working with the patterns used to build scales (as you see in Chapter 11) and chords (covered in Chapter 13).

Accidentals are notations used to raise or lower a natural note pitch on the staff by a half step. Accidentals come in three flavors:

✔ Sharp

✔ Flat

✔ Natural

A *sharp* is shown in Figure 7-7.

Figure 7-7:
Just remember that a sharp looks like a pound, or number, sign.

A sharp is placed before a note to indicate that the note is raised a half step higher, as shown in Figure 7-8.

Figure 7-8:
Notice how sharping the A means you play the black key to the *right* of the A, not the normal A. This black key, A sharp, is a half step up from A.

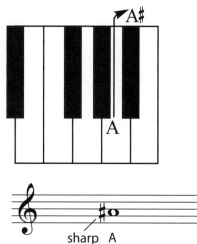

sharp A

A *flat* looks like Figure 7-9.

Figure 7-9:
Just
remember
that a flat
looks a bit
like a
lowercase
b.

A flat does just the opposite of a sharp. It lowers the note by a half step, as shown in Figure 7-10.

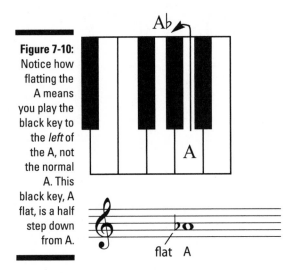

Figure 7-10:
Notice how
flatting the
A means
you play the
black key to
the *left* of
the A, not
the normal
A. This
black key, A
flat, is a half
step down
from A.

Every once in a while, you'll run into a *double* sharp or a *double* flat, which are shown in Figure 7-11.

Figure 7-11:
A double
sharp looks
kind of like
an X,
whereas a
double flat
is just two
flats in a
row.

The notation on the left in Figure 7-11 is a double sharp, and the one on the right is a double flat. The double sharp raises the natural note two half steps — or one whole step — whereas the double flat lowers the note two half steps, or one whole step.

Last but not least is the *natural*, shown in Figure 7-12.

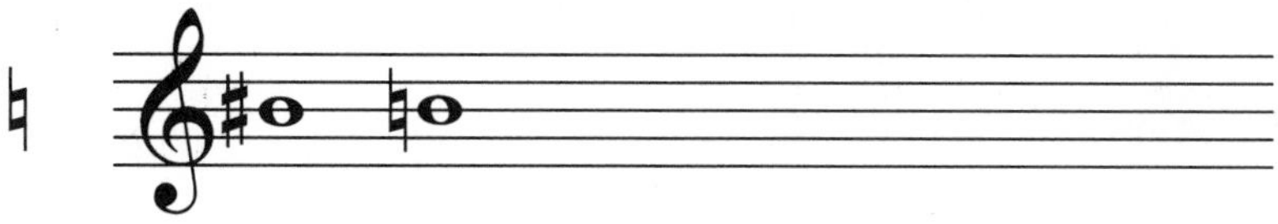

Figure 7-12:
A natural
cancels out
an already
established
sharp or flat.

When you see a natural sign next to a note, it means that any sharp or flat that is already in effect for the whole piece (given in the key signature — see Chapter 11 for more on key signatures) is cancelled. In other words, you're supposed to play the "natural" version of the note instead of whatever sharp or flat was in effect.

Finding the Notes on the Piano and Guitar

The figures in this section can be used as a handy reference when you can't quite remember which note is what on the piano or guitar.

Notes on the piano

Figure 7-13 shows it in all its glory: the piano keyboard — or at least a little over three octaves' worth of it. The corresponding natural notes on the grand staff have been labeled on the keyboard.

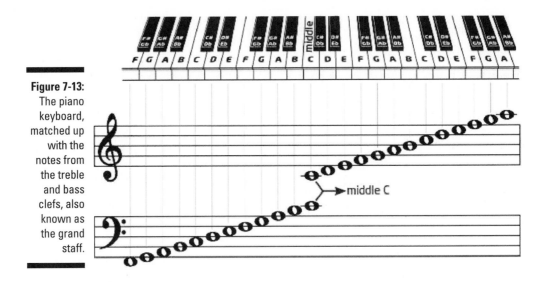

Figure 7-13: The piano keyboard, matched up with the notes from the treble and bass clefs, also known as the grand staff.

middle C

Notes on the Guitar

The trouble with laying out the neck of a guitar against musical notation is that notes repeat themselves all along the neck, and it can get confusing with so many options for playing notes in different ways. So what we've done is break the guitar neck up into three non-repeating sections to correspond along the natural notes on the staff, stopping at the 12th fret (which usually has two dots on it), also known as the octave mark.

Figures 7-14 through 7-16 show the notes of the first three frets of the guitar, then the next five, and then the next four.

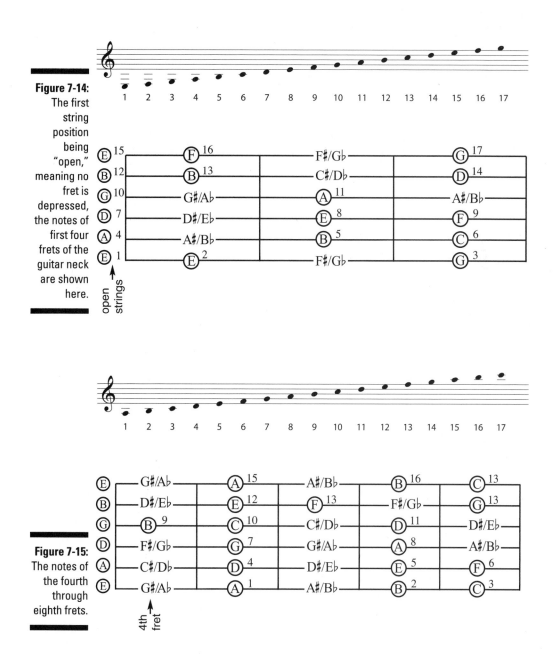

Figure 7-14:
The first string position being "open," meaning no fret is depressed, the notes of first four frets of the guitar neck are shown here.

Figure 7-15:
The notes of the fourth through eighth frets.

Figure 7-16:
The notes of the ninth through the twelfth frets. On many guitars, two dots on the twelfth fret signify the octave, meaning that it is the same note as the string played open, except one octave higher.

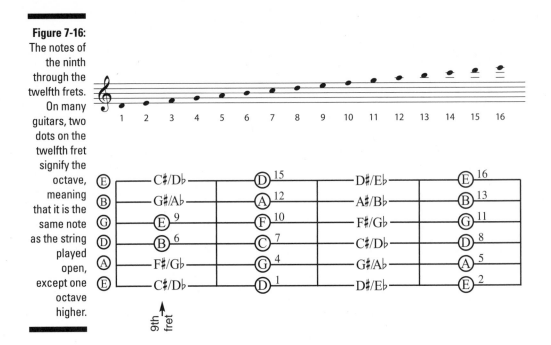

Tips on Remembering Notes

There are a zillion, silly ways to remember the order of the notes along the musical staff, probably enough to build an entire book around all on their own. Here are just a few to get you going — feel free to come up with your own *mnemonics* (memory helpers) to help keep things straight.

The treble clef

Here are some easy ways to remember the order of the notes of the treble clef staff lines, starting at the bottom, on E, and heading up through G, B, D, and F on the top line of the staff:

- ✔ Every Good Boy Deserves Favor
- ✔ Every Good Boy Deserves Fudge
- ✔ Every Good Boy Does Fine
- ✔ Every Good Bird Does Fly

The notes in the spaces are easy. They spell the word FACE, starting at the first space note, F, and heading up to the E in the top space on the staff. Everybody uses this one, and there's really no reason to try to come up with a complicated phrase when FACE is right there, staring you in the . . . .

The bass clef

Here are some easy ways to remember the order of the notes on the bass clef staff lines, starting at the bottom note, G, and heading up to the A at the top:

✔ Go Buy Donuts For Al

✔ Good Boys Do Fine Always

✔ Great Big Dreams For America

For the space notes, just remember:

✔ All Cows Eat Grass

✔ All Cars Eat Gas

✔ Alley Cats Eat Garbage

Chapter 8

Instrument Tone and Color

- -

In This Chapter

▶ Mixing up tone color

▶ Figuring out attack, timbre, and decay

▶ Getting acquainted with acoustics

▶ Understanding harmonics

- -

*H*ave you ever wondered why there aren't more songs that use a tuba or a bassoon for the lead instrument, or why so many great parts for instruments have been taken by pianos and guitars? Okay, maybe you haven't thought that much about it, but if you're thinking of writing music, you probably should.

The simple explanation for why some instruments are used for lead lines in music and others aren't is that the human ear reacts more favorably to higher-pitched sounds than to lower-pitched sounds. Notice that it is the higher-pitched range that babies and small children babble in, that birds sing in, and that pretty much all the happy little things make noise in. We can't get away from enjoying these sounds — it's part of our wiring.

There's also a greater sense of immediacy that's conveyed by high-pitched notes. You can work your fingers to the bone bowing on a cello, but it's not going to sound as urgent and lively as it would if the same passage were played at the same speed on a violin. It's just like in conversation: when you're trying to get an idea across, especially an important idea, your voice *tone* tends to drift up toward the higher registers, not down into the lower ones. This is why lead instruments are also sometimes called *talking* instruments.

Tone Color

The *tone color*, or character, of an instrument is made up of three basic components:

- Attack
- Timbre (or harmonic content)
- Decay

These three factors are what make every instrument sound different, so much so that even if you're just hearing the instrument through your car radio speakers, you can immediately tell, just by listening, what instrument is being played.

Attack

The *attack* is the very first sound you hear when you hear a note and is possibly the most distinguishing aspect of a note. For example, when you hear the first microsecond of a violin being played, you instantly know it's a violin because of that quick, raw sound of a bow being drawn across the familiar-sounding string. It's beautiful, immediate, and unmistakable. You don't even know you're hearing the first tiny point of contact, but it's there. If you were to slow down a recording of any virtuoso's violin solo, you would find that gorgeous, familiar rasp at the beginning of every bow stroke.

The attack of a piano is completely different. Each time you hit the key of a piano, a tiny hammer strikes three metal strings simultaneously, producing a beautiful, ringing sound. It's even more amazing to open up a piano and listen to how each note sounds when the frontpiece isn't muffling the sound.

The guitar also has its own distinctive attack, a sharp little twang when the metal strings are first plucked — a sound definitely less pronounced if the guitar has nylon strings. The different types of strings are partly responsible for the variety of guitar-playing styles by musicians. Electric rock guitars, pop acoustic, and country-and-western songs are usually played with metal-strung guitars because of that nice, crisp, aggressive-sounding twang. Classical, flamenco, and much of folk music use nylon-strung guitars because the attack is much softer-sounding, making for mellower music.

Timbre

The *harmonic* content, or *timbre*, of an instrument is what determines the middle part, or body, of each played note. When you remove the attack and the decay of some instruments' sounds with digital equipment, you find a lot of surprising similarities between instruments in this area, such as in flutes and violins. The timbre and pitch range of a flute and violin are almost identical, but because one is blown and one is bowed, that initial attack of each separate note is completely different and identifies these instrument by that very first split-second sound.

However, the harmonics between some instruments is pretty radically different, simply because of their construction. For example, the harmonic content between a note on a guitar and the same note on a piano are completely dissimilar, because one note on a guitar is one string being plucked, but one note on a piano is actually three strings tuned to three slightly different pitches being hit with a hammer (this has to do with harmonics, covered later in this chapter).

When the first synthesizers were developed, the designers were attempting to reproduce "natural" instruments instead of just synthetic sounds (the flat, artificial sound of a 1970s synthesizer, for example). The developers of the synthesizer discovered that the biggest challenge in making it sound natural was not in reproducing another instrument's timbre — which is what the engineers had primarily focused on from the onset — but in reproducing the attack and decay of each instrument. Eventually, they had to record samples of the instruments themselves into the synthesizers in order to make flute and violin sounds, for example, distinguishable from one another. Not to mention oboes and tubas.

Decay

Decay is the final part of an instrument's played note. There are two types of instrument decay:

- ✔ Impulsive
- ✔ Sustained

An *impulsive* decay belongs to instruments that need to be played continuously, or in pulses, in order to continue sounding. Tones are produced and immediately begin to decay until the next note played starts the process again. Common examples of instruments with an impulsive decay are those produced by plucking or striking, such as the guitar, most percussion instruments, and the piano.

A *sustained* decay is one for which the vibrating column of an instrument, such as the body of a flute, clarinet, or other column-shaped instrument, is excited continuously, so that the sound continues in a more or less steady state as long as the note is being played. Instruments producing sustained tones are those that are bowed or blown, such as violins and other bowed stringed instruments, woodwinds, free-reed instruments such as the accordion, and brass instruments.

Building the Band: a Little Bit About Acoustics

Next time you go out to see an orchestra or a big band play, or even when you watch one of those late-night show bands perform on TV, take a look at where the performers are sitting in relation to each other. Especially pay attention to which instrument is the "lead" instrument.

You should notice two things. First of all, especially in an orchestral setting, all the performers playing the same instruments are sitting together. This isn't because they all have to share the same piece of sheet music — it's because when you stick two violins or flutes or clarinets together they sound louder and fuller. Stick *ten* of them together, and you've got a wall of sound coming at you from that area of the orchestra.

This, incidentally, is one reason why instruments are so challenging to play — it's not just that they're particularly tricky to play well in themselves, but that you often have to play them in exact synchronicity with other performers.

Secondly, notice that the lead instruments are in front of all the other instruments, especially in acoustic performances. This is because of volume and perception: the sound waves from the instruments in the front of the orchestra pit will be heard a microsecond before the rest of the orchestra, and will therefore be perceived as being louder because you hear them a split second before the other instruments.

This principle applies to a regular four-piece band setting, too. If you want your singer to be heard above the guitars, make sure the amplifier carrying his or her voice is placed closer to the audience than the guitar and bass amp.

Incidentally, the best place to sit at an orchestral performance is as close to the conductor as possible. Conductors build each orchestra for each performance around where they stand so that they can hear exactly what is being played. This situation makes it pretty easy for a seasoned audio engineer to record an orchestral performance. Put the microphones right where the conductor's standing, and you'll record the piece of music exactly as the conductor intended for it to be heard.

Harmonics

Any sound, not matter what the source, is caused by something vibrating. Without vibration, there can be no sound. These vibrations cause the air particles next to the source to vibrate as well, and those air particles, in turn, cause the particles next to them to vibrate, and so on and so on, creating what we call a *sound wave*. Just like a wave in water, the further out the sound wave moves, the weaker it gets, until it completely dissipates. If the original vibration creates a strong enough wave, though, it eventually reaches your ears and registers as a sound.

When we hear a sound, it's because air vibrates against our eardrums, causing them to vibrate also. These vibrations are analyzed by our brains and registered as music, traffic, birds singing — whatever. Because sound waves are picked up by each unique eardrum and dissected by each unique brain, there's a good chance that nobody hears the same sound exactly the same as anybody else.

Each complete vibration of a sound wave is called a *cycle*. The number of cycles completed in one second is called the *frequency* of the vibration. One of the most noticeable differences between two sounds is the difference in pitch; it's is the frequency of a sound that mostly determines its pitch. Frequency is measured in *hertz*, with one hertz (Hz) being one cycle per second. One thousand hertz is called a kilohertz and is written as 1 kHz. A high-frequency vibration produces a high-pitched note; a low-frequency vibration gives a low-pitched note.

The human hearing range (audible range) is about 16Hz to 16kHz. The frequencies of notes that can be played on a piano range from 27.5 Hz to just over 4kHz.

The musical note produced by a tuning fork is called a *pure tone* because it consists of one tone sounding at just one frequency. Instruments get their specific sounds because their sound comes from many different tones all sounding together at different frequencies. A single note played on a piano, for example, actually consists of several tones all sounding together at multiples of the base frequency.

Chapter 9

Half Steps, Whole Steps, Sharps, and Flats

· ·

In This Chapter

▶ Understanding half steps

▶ Checking out whole steps

· ·

*A*s we have been mentioning, an octave is broken up, in Western music, into 12 equal segments called *half steps*, or *semitones*. But a musical *scale* contains eight notes, meaning that some of the distance between notes in a scale spans one semitone, and some spans at least two semitones. (See Chapter 12 for much more on scales.)

In other words, some half steps are skipped when building scales. On a piano, the white keys show you the C scale, over and over again. The black keys represent the semitones that are skipped in the C scale.

This chapter talks about the difference between half steps and whole steps in music.

Half Steps

In Western musical notation, the smallest difference between two pitches is the half step, or semitone. Notice we use the word *notation* here. Strictly speaking, musical pitch is a continuous spectrum, because it is determined by the frequency of vibration (see Chapter 8). Therefore, many other *microtonal* sounds actually exist between consecutive half steps.

Western musical notation only recognizes the division of pitch down to half steps.

In contrast, many Eastern instruments, particularly sitars and fretless stringed instruments, utilize *quarter tones*. Quarter tones are pitches located halfway between each half step.

Using the piano keyboard as a reference, if you pick a key, play it, and then play the key that is right next to it, on the left or right, whether that key is black or white, you've moved one half step in pitch. See Figure 9-1 for an illustration of this principle.

Figure 9-1:
Half steps are identified here to the left and right of the E key on the piano.

As you can see in Figure 9-1, if you start out playing an E on the piano, a half step to the left brings you to E flat/D sharp. A half step to the right, and you're on E sharp/F natural.

Note that every black key on a piano has two names. It can be referred to as the flat of the white key on its right, or the sharp of the white key on its left. It doesn't matter which way it's named. E flat and D sharp are the same note.

Incidentally, rarely will you hear F natural referred to as E sharp. The only reason "E sharp" is mentioned here at all is to help bring home the idea that when someone is referring to a note being *flatted*, that means you move one half step to the left of that natural note; if it's being *sharped*, you move one half step to the right.

Figures 9-2 and 9-3 show how flatting and sharping look in printed musical notation.

Figure 9-2:
E flat means
you move
one half
step down
in pitch from
the E.

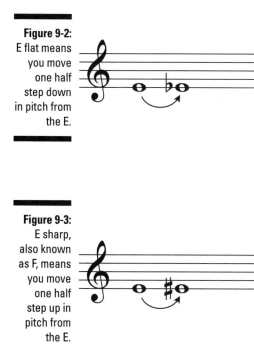

Figure 9-3:
E sharp,
also known
as F, means
you move
one half
step up in
pitch from
the E.

Here's another example. Start with the G key on the keyboard, as shown in Figure 9-4.

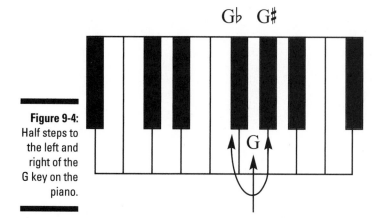

Figure 9-4:
Half steps to
the left and
right of the
G key on the
piano.

If you move one half step to the left of G (going down in pitch), you end up on the black key G flat/F sharp. If you move one half step to the right (moving up in pitch), you end up on the black key on the other side of G called G sharp/A flat.

A half step to the left flats the G (Figure 9-5), and a half step to the right sharps it (Figure 9-6).

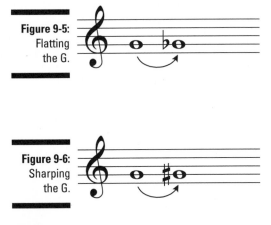

Figure 9-5:
Flatting the G.

Figure 9-6:
Sharping the G.

Half steps are even easier and more straightforward on the guitar. Each fret is a half step. You just move one fret up or one fret down from your starting point, and that move of one fret equals one half step.

Moving down the neck (toward the headstock of the guitar) flats the note (Figure 9-7), while up the neck (towards the body) sharps it (Figure 9-8).

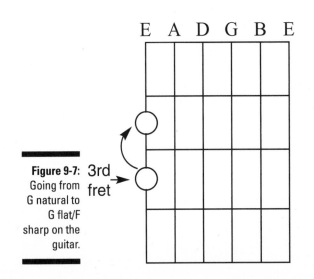

Figure 9-7:
Going from G natural to G flat/F sharp on the guitar.

3rd fret

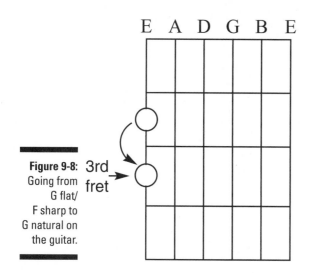

Figure 9-8:
Going from
G flat/
F sharp to
G natural on
the guitar.

3rd
fret

Whole Steps

Following the logic that a half step on the piano or guitar is one key or fret away from the starting point, it only makes sense that a *whole* step would be *two* keys or frets away from the starting point.

Let's say we start on E on the keyboard. One whole step to the left of E would be D, as shown in Figure 9-9.

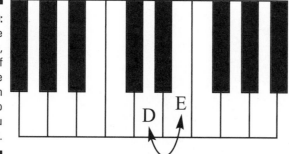

Figure 9-9:
Moving one
whole step,
or two half
steps, to the
left of E on
the piano
brings you
to D.

Meanwhile, one whole step to the *right* of E natural would be F sharp, as shown in Figure 9-10.

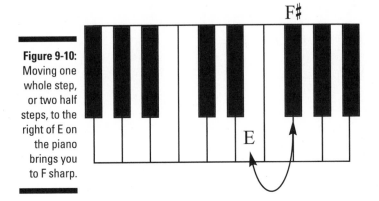

Figure 9-10: Moving one whole step, or two half steps, to the right of E on the piano brings you to F sharp.

On the guitar, a whole step is represented by a move of two frets up or down the neck.

Notice that the distance between the consecutive white piano keys E and F, and B and C, equal a half step, whereas the distance between the remaining white keys (G-A, A-B, C-D, D-E, F-G) is a whole step. That's because the piano is designed around the *C scale*.

Half steps and whole steps are *intervals*. There are lots of other kinds of intervals, and knowing them is where you begin to understand chords and harmony. The next chapter, Chapter 10, is all about these intervals.

Part III
Harmony: Fleshing It Out

The 5th Wave   By Rich Tennant

"First you play a G7 diminished, followed by an augmented 9th, then a perverted 32nd chord ending with a mangled 11th with a recovering 3rd."

In this part . . .

This is where you start dealing with many notes at a time: scales and chords. Beginning with intervals beyond half and whole steps, you find out the building blocks of chords and move on to start putting them together to make music. You also tackle key signatures and the Circle of Fifths, which shows the relation among the different keys and chords in music. The part finishes off with cadences, which work to resolve tension in music.

Chapter 10

Intervals

In This Chapter

▶ Understanding the different kinds of intervals

▶ Checking out fourths, fifths, and octaves

▶ Getting to know major, minor, augmented, and diminished

▶ Figuring out seconds, thirds, sixths, and sevenths

*T*his chapter goes over the types of intervals most commonly used in music and discusses how intervals are used in building scales and chords.

The distance between two musical pitches is called an *interval*. It's as simple as that.

Even if you have never heard the word *interval* used in relation to music before, if you've listened to music, you've heard how intervals work with one another. If you've ever played music, or even just accidentally set a coffee cup down on a piano keyboard hard enough to make a couple of jangly notes sound out, you've worked with intervals. Scales are built from intervals, and chords are built from intervals. Music gets its richness from intervals.

Harmonic and Melodic Intervals

There are two types of intervals:

✔ A *harmonic* interval is what you get when you play two notes at the same time, as shown in Figure 10-1.

✔ A *melodic* interval is what you get when you play two notes separately in time, one after the other, as shown in Figure 10-2.

Figure 10-1:
A harmonic interval is two notes played simultaneously.

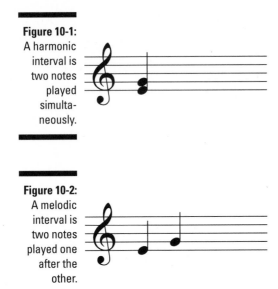

Figure 10-2:
A melodic interval is two notes played one after the other.

The *identity* of an interval, and this goes for both harmonic and melodic intervals, is determined by two things:

- ✔ Quantity
- ✔ Quality

Quantity: counting lines and spaces

The *quantity*, or *number size*, of the interval is based on the number of lines and spaces contained by the interval on the music staff. We use different names to indicate the quantity of intervals:

- ✔ Unison (or prime)
- ✔ Second
- ✔ Third
- ✔ Fourth
- ✔ Fifth
- ✔ Sixth
- ✔ Seventh
- ✔ Octave

All those names may sound tricky, but they really aren't. An interval's quantity is determined by simply adding up the lines and spaces included in the interval. Be sure to include the lines or spaces that contain the notes themselves.

Take a look at Figure 10-3 for an example of how easy it is to determine an interval's quantity.

Figure 10-3:
There are five lines and spaces included in this interval's total quantity, which means this interval is a fifth.

If you start on either the top or bottom note and count all the lines and spaces contained in their interval, including the lines or spaces that contain both notes, you end up with the number five. Therefore, Figure 10-3 has the quantity, or number size, of five, or a fifth. Because the notes are written together, to be played at the same time, it's a *harmonic fifth*, to be exact.

What about Figure 10-4?

Figure 10-4:
The fact that the first note is F sharp doesn't affect the quantity of the interval.

Figure 10-4, as you can see, shows a melodic second. Note that the sharp *accidental* (the # mark) on the F does absolutely nothing to the quantity of an interval. With interval quantity, it's all a matter of simple counting.

Figure 10-5 shows interval quantities from unison (the two notes are the same) to octave (the two notes are exactly an octave apart), and all the intervals in between. Sharps and flats are thrown in for fun, but remember, they don't matter when it comes to interval quantity.

Figure 10-5:
Melodic
intervals in
order from
left to right:
unison,
second,
third, fourth,
fifth, sixth,
seventh,
and octave.

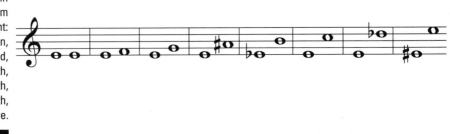

What if an interval spans more than one octave? In that case, it's called a *compound interval*. As with all interval quantities, with a compound interval you just count the lines and spaces, giving the example shown in Figure 10-6 the quantity of ten (not surprisingly, then, it's called a tenth).

Figure 10-6:
A compound
interval with
a total
quantity of
ten — also
called a
tenth.

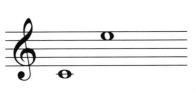

Quality: major, minor, perfect, diminished, and augmented

The *quality* of an interval is a different matter. Interval quality is what gives an interval its distinct sound. Interval quality is based on the number of half steps from one note to another. Accidentals (sharps and flats), which raise or lower a pitch by a half step, *do* matter in interval quality.

Each of the intervals shown in Figure 10-7, while having exactly the same *quantity*, sound different from one another because each one has a different *quality*.

Figure 10-7:
All of these intervals have a quantity of fifths, but the quality of the fifths makes them sound different.

 Play Track 2 on the CD to hear the differences between the intervals that have the same quantity (fifth) but different qualities.

The terms used to describe quality, and their abbreviations, are as follows:

- ✔ **Major (M):** Contains a half step more than a minor interval
- ✔ **Minor (m):** Contains a half step less than a major interval
- ✔ **Perfect (P):** Refers to the harmonic quality of primes, octaves, fourths, and fifths
- ✔ **Diminished (dim):** Contains a half step less than a minor interval
- ✔ **Augmented (aug):** Contains a half step more than a major interval

 Every interval gets its full name from the combination of both the quantity and the quality of the interval. For example, a *major third* or a *perfect fifth*.

Here are the possible combinations that you use when describing intervals:

- ✔ Perfect (P) can only be used with unisons, fourths, fifths, and octaves.
- ✔ Major (M) and minor (m) can only be used with seconds, thirds, sixths, and sevenths.
- ✔ Diminished (dim) and augmented (aug) can be used with any interval, with the exception of unisons, which can be augmented but cannot be diminished.

And that's the end of the vocabulary lesson. Next we go into more detail about each named interval.

Unisons, Octaves, Fourths, and Fifths

Unisons, octaves, fourths, and fifths use the terms perfect, augmented, or diminished to identify their quality. Table 10-1 gives you a summary of these intervals.

Table 10-1:	Intervals in Unisons, Octaves, Fourths, and Fifths
Half Steps Between Notes	**Interval Name**
0	Perfect unison
1	Augmented unison
4	Diminished fourth
5	Perfect fourth
6	Augmented fourth
6	Diminished fifth
7	Perfect fifth
8	Augmented fifth
11	Diminished octave
12	Perfect octave
13	Augmented octave

Perfect unisons

A *perfect melodic unison* is possibly the easiest move you'll ever make on any instrument (except for a rest, of course). You just bang, pluck, or blow the same note twice.

In music written for multiple instruments, a *perfect harmonic unison* is when two (or more) people play exactly the same note, in the exact same manner, on two different instruments.

You can also play unisons on most stringed instruments because the same note occurs more than once on these instruments, such as on the guitar (the fifth fret on the low E string is the same as the open A string, for example).

Augmented unisons

To make a perfect unison augmented, you add one half step between the notes. Alter either of the notes in the pair to increase the distance between the notes by a half step.

The interval from B flat to B is called an augmented unison (or augmented *prime*) — *unison* because the note names are the same (both Bs), *augmented* because the interval is one half step greater than a perfect unison.

There is no such thing as a diminished unison, because no matter how you change the unisons with accidentals, you are adding half steps to the total interval.

Octaves

When you have two notes with an interval quantity of eight lines and spaces, you have an *octave*. A *perfect octave* is a lot like a perfect unison, in that the same note (on a piano, it would be the same white or black key on the keyboard) is being played, the only difference being that the two notes are separated by twelve half steps, including the starting note, either above or below the starting point.

A *perfect melodic octave*, with 12 half steps between the notes, looks like Figure 10-8.

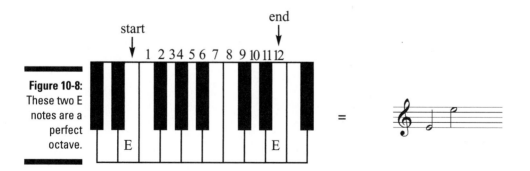

Figure 10-8: These two E notes are a perfect octave.

To make a perfect octave augmented, you increase the distance between the notes by one more half step.

Figure 10-9 shows an augmented octave from E to E#, by raising the top note a half step so that there are 13 half steps from the first note to the last.

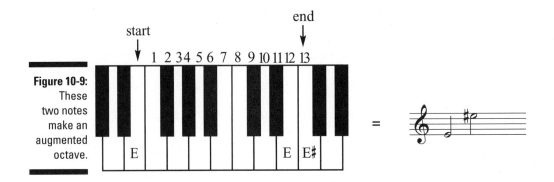

Figure 10-9: These two notes make an augmented octave.

You could also make an augmented octave by lowering the bottom E note a half step to E flat.

To make the same octave a perfect octave diminished, you *decrease* the distance between the notes by one half step.

Figure 10-10 illustrates lowering the top note a half step so that there are only 11 half steps from the first note to the last.

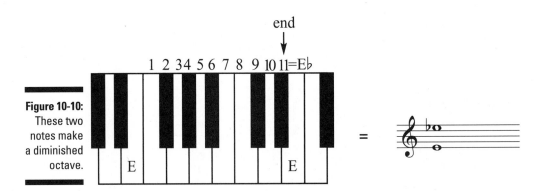

Figure 10-10: These two notes make a diminished octave.

You could also raise the bottom note by a half step to make another diminished octave.

Fourths

Fourths are pairs of notes separated by four lines and spaces. All fourths are perfect in quality, containing five half steps between notes — except for the fourth from F natural to B natural, which contains *six* half steps (making it an *augmented pair*).

Compare the note pairs in Figure 10-11 on the keyboard, and you'll see what we mean.

Figure 10-11: Intervals with the quality of four (in other words, fourths) as seen on the staff. The special (augmented) case of the F and the B is circled.

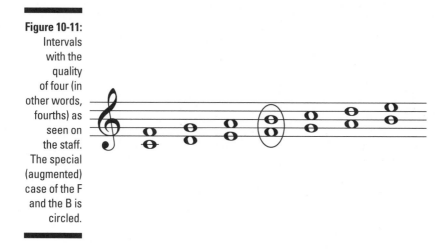

Figure 10-12 shows the connection between each fourth on a keyboard. Note that unlike the rest, the F and B require six half steps.

Figure 10-12: Note how, on the keyboard, every natural fourth is a perfect fourth (except for the interval between F and B).

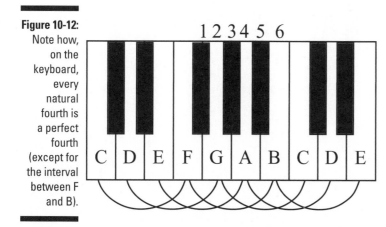

Because augmented fourths are a half step larger than perfect fourths, we can create a perfect fourth between the notes F and B by either raising the bottom note to F sharp, or lowering the top note to B flat.

If the natural fourth is perfect, then adding the same accidental (either a sharp or a flat) to both notes does not change the interval's quality. It stays a perfect fourth. There are the same number of half steps (five) between D natural and G natural as there are between D sharp and G sharp, or D flat and G flat, as shown in Figures 10-13 and 10-14.

Figure 10-13: Adding accidentals to both notes in a perfect fourth interval doesn't change it from being a perfect fourth. There are still five half steps between the first and last notes.

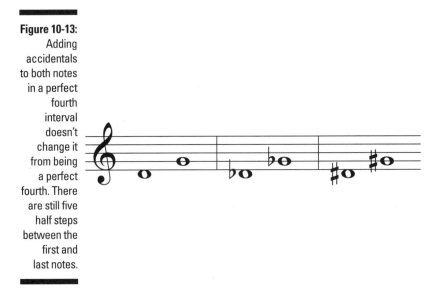

If one note changes but the other doesn't, of course, then the quality of the interval does change.

Fifths

Fifths are pairs of notes separated by five lines and spaces, as shown in Figure 10-15.

Fifths are pretty easy to recognize in notation, as they are two notes exactly two lines or two spaces apart.

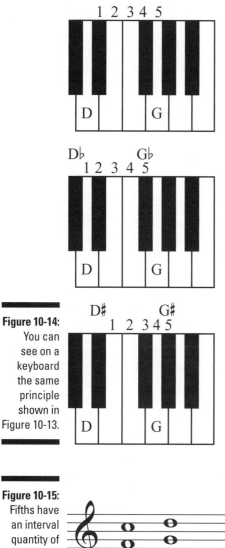

Figure 10-14: You can see on a keyboard the same principle shown in Figure 10-13.

Figure 10-15: Fifths have an interval quantity of five lines and spaces.

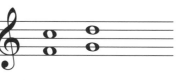

All fifths are *perfect* fifths, meaning that there are seven half steps in the interval, except . . . can you guess? The interval between B to F is a *diminished fifth*, which turns out to have the same sound as an augmented fourth. There are only six half steps between those two notes, no matter if you're going from F to B or B to F.

We can create a perfect fifth between F and B by adding one more half step — either by turning the B to a B flat, or by raising the F to an F sharp. This time, because the notes are flipped around from the order they appeared in the interval of fourths, either change *increases* the size of the interval.

Again, just as in a perfect fourth, if a fifth is perfect (every case except F and B), then adding the same accidentals to both notes in the interval does not change its quality. And, as with fourths, if only one of the notes is altered with an accidental, the quality does change.

Building Intervals

The first step in building any interval is to create the desired quantity, or number size, above or below a given note. Then you determine the quality.

Determining quantity

This part is easy, especially on paper. For, say, a unison interval, just pick a note. Then, right next to the first note, put another one exactly like it.

Want to make your interval an octave? Then put the second note exactly seven lines and spaces above or below the first, making for a total interval quantity of eight lines and spaces, as shown in Figure 10-16.

Figure 10-16:
Octaves of
the note G
(spanning
the two
clefs, with
middle C
indicated).

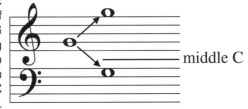

middle C

How about a fourth? Put the second note either three spaces and lines above or below the first note, making for a total interval quantity of four lines and spaces.

And a fifth? Put the second note either four spaces and lines above or below the first note, making for a total interval quantity of five lines and spaces.

Determining quality

The second step to building an interval is to decide what the quality of the interval will be.

Say your starting note is an A flat. And let's say you want your interval to be a perfect fifth above A flat. First, you would count out the *quantity* needed for the fifth interval, meaning you count an additional four spaces above the starting note, making for a total quantity of five lines and spaces, as shown in Figure 10-17.

Figure 10-17:
Figuring out the quantity needed to build a perfect fifth above A flat.

Next we have to alter the second note in order to make it a *perfect* fifth. Because all fifths are perfect so long as both notes have the same accidental (except for that darned B and F), then in order to make this pair a perfect fifth, we flat the second note so that it matches the first, as shown in Figure 10-18.

Figure 10-18:
Flatting the second note to match the first makes a perfect fifth.

If you want to make the second note an *augmented* fifth (aug5, or sometimes A5) *below* A, you count *down* an additional four lines and spaces from A, to make a total quality of five lines and spaces, and write the note, which is D. See Figure 10-19.

Figure 10-19:
Building an augmented fifth below A starts with finding the quantity.

Next, we alter our added note to make the interval augmented. As you now know, a fifth is an augmented fifth when an additional half step is added to the interval (7 + 1 = 8 half steps), so you would lower the bottom note to a D flat, as shown in Figure 10-20.

Figure 10-20:
Adding the accidental makes the interval augmented.

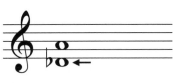

To make the second note a diminished fifth (dim5, or sometimes D5) *above* A, you count *up* an additional four lines and spaces, to make a total quality of five lines and spaces, and write the note, which is E.

Next, we alter our added note to make the interval diminished. A fifth is a diminished fifth when a half step is removed from the perfect fifth (7 – 1 = 6 half steps), so you would lower the top note to a E flat, as shown in Figure 10-21.

Figure 10-21:
Adding the accidental makes the fifth diminished.

Note that a diminished fifth is the same as an augmented fourth — both intervals are made up of six half steps.

Intervals in a nutshell

When a major or perfect interval is increased by a half step, it becomes augmented.

When a minor or perfect interval is decreased by a half step, it becomes diminished.

All fourths and fifths are perfect except for the interval of F sharp to B, which is an augmented fourth (aug4), and the interval of B to F, which is a diminished fifth (dim5).

A perfect fourth between F and B is either F natural to B flat or F flat (same as E) to B natural (five half steps).

A perfect fifth between B and F is either B natural to F sharp or B flat to F natural (seven half steps).

All naturally occurring perfect fourths and fifths stay perfect if both notes are natural or share the same accidental.

Seconds, Thirds, Sixths, and Sevenths

Seconds, *thirds*, *sixths*, and *sevenths* use the terms *major*, *minor*, *augmented*, and *diminished* to identity their quality.

A major interval made *smaller* by one half step becomes minor, whereas a major interval made *larger* by one half step becomes augmented. A minor interval made *larger* by one half step becomes major, and a minor interval made *smaller* by one half step becomes diminished.

Seconds

When you have two notes with an interval quantity of two lines and spaces, you have a second, as you can see in Figure 10-22.

Figure 10-22:
These three sets of notes are all seconds.

Seconds are pretty easy to recognize — they're the two notes perched right next to each other, one on a line and one in a space.

If there is one half step (one piano key or one guitar fret) between seconds, then the interval is a *minor second*. If there are two half steps (one whole step, or two adjacent piano keys or guitar frets) between seconds, then the interval is a *major second*.

For example, the interval between E natural and F natural is a minor second, because there is one half step between those two notes (see Figure 10-23).

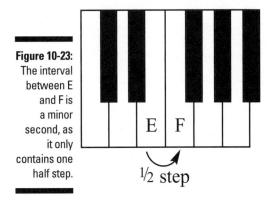

Figure 10-23:
The interval between E and F is a minor second, as it only contains one half step.

½ step

Meanwhile, the interval between F and G is a major second, because there are two half steps (one whole step) between those two notes, as illustrated in Figure 10-24.

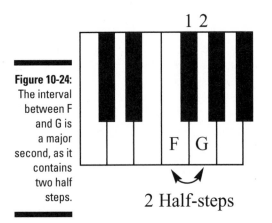

Figure 10-24:
The interval between F and G is a major second, as it contains two half steps.

2 Half-steps

A major second is made minor by decreasing its quantity by one half step. You can do this either by either lowering the top note a half step or raising the bottom note a half step. Both moves reduce the distance between the notes to one half step (one piano key or one guitar fret), as Figure 10-25 shows.

Figure 10-25: Turning a major second (M2) into a minor second (m2).

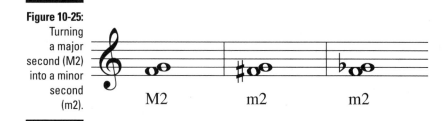

A minor second can, logically enough, be turned into a major second by increasing the interval size by one half step. You can do this by either raising the top note a half step, or by lowering the bottom note a half step. Both moves make the distance between the notes two half steps (two piano keys or three guitar frets).

The only place that half steps occur between seconds is from E to F and B to C — the two spots on the keyboard where there is no black key between two white keys.

Adding the same accidental to both notes of a natural second does not change its quality. All of the seconds shown in Figure 10-26 are major seconds.

Figure 10-26: Major seconds, all.

All of the seconds shown in Figure 10-27 are minor seconds.

Figure 10-27: Minor seconds, all.

An augmented second is one half step larger than a major second. In other words, there are three half steps between each note. You turn a major second into an augmented second either by raising the top note or lowering the bottom note one half step, as shown in Figures 10-28 and 10-29.

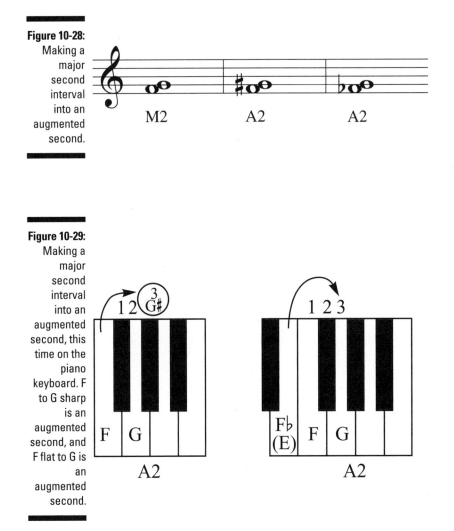

Figure 10-28:
Making a major second interval into an augmented second.

Figure 10-29:
Making a major second interval into an augmented second, this time on the piano keyboard. F to G sharp is an augmented second, and F flat to G is an augmented second.

A diminished second is one half step smaller than a minor second — meaning there are no steps between each note. They are the same note. A diminished second is an *enharmonic* equivalent of a perfect unison. That just means that you're playing the same two notes, but the notation for the pair is different.

Thirds

Thirds occur when you have an interval that contains three lines and spaces, as Figure 10-30 does.

Figure 10-30:
Thirds are located on adjacent lines or spaces.

If there are four half steps in a third, it's called a *major third*. Major thirds (M3) occur from C to E, F to A, and G to B.

If there are three half steps in a third, it's called a *minor third*. Minor thirds (m3) occur from D to F, E to G, A to C, and B to D.

Figure 10.31 shows major and minor thirds on the musical staff

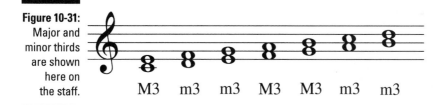

Figure 10-31:
Major and minor thirds are shown here on the staff.

M3   m3   m3   M3   M3   m3   m3

A major third can be turned into a minor third if you decrease its interval size by one half step, making the total three half steps between notes. This can be done either by lowering the top note a half step or raising the bottom note a half step (see Figure 10-32).

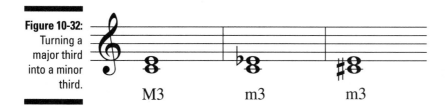

Figure 10-32:
Turning a major third into a minor third.

M3   m3   m3

A minor third can be turned into a major third by adding one more half step to the interval, either by — you guessed it — raising the top note a half step or lowering the bottom note a half step, as shown in Figure 10-33.

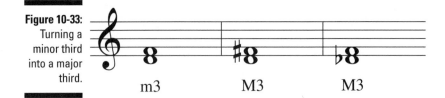

Figure 10-33: Turning a minor third into a major third.

As with seconds, fourths, and fifths, the same accidental added to both notes of a third (both major and minor) does not change its quality; and adding an accidental to just one of the notes of a third does change its quality.

An augmented third is a half step larger than a major third, with five half steps between notes. Starting from a major third, raise the upper note a half step or lower the bottom note a half step. Figure 10-34 shows augmented thirds.

An augmented third is also the enharmonic equivalent of a perfect fourth — they're the same note, but the notation is different.

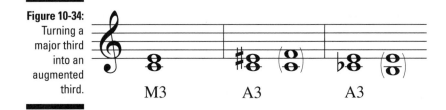

Figure 10-34: Turning a major third into an augmented third.

A diminished third is a half step smaller than a minor third. Beginning with a minor third, either raise the bottom note a half step or lower the upper note a half step, making for an interval of two half steps (see Figure 10-35).

Figure 10-35:
Turning a minor third into a diminished third.

Sixths and Sevenths

When you have two notes with an interval quantity of six lines and spaces, as in Figure 10-36, you have a *sixth*.

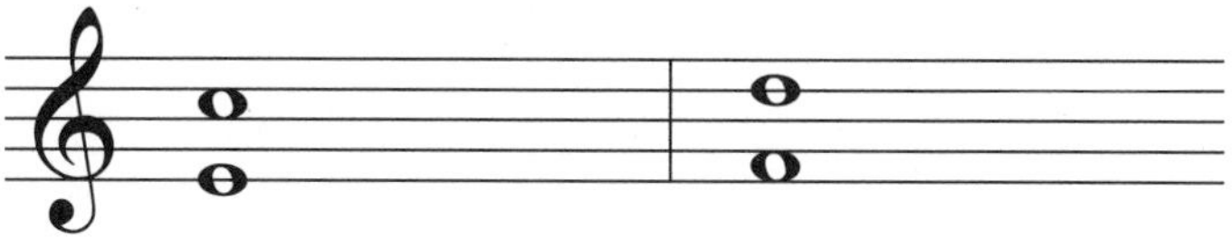

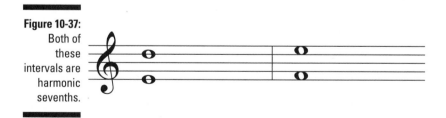

Figure 10-36:
Both of these intervals are harmonic sixths.

The notes in a sixth are always separated by two lines and a space, or two spaces and a line.

When you have two notes with an interval quantity of seven lines and spaces, as in Figure 10-37, you have a *seventh*.

Figure 10-37:
Both of these intervals are harmonic sevenths.

Sevenths always consist of a pair of notes that are both on lines or spaces. They are separated by three lines or three spaces.

Note in Table 10-2 that the identity of the interval itself depends on the quantity of the interval number — that is, how many lines and spaces are included in the total interval.

Table 10-2:	The Whole Caboodle: Intervals, Unison to Octave
Half Steps Between Notes	*Interval Name*
0	Perfect unison/diminished second
1	Augmented unison/minor second
2	Major second/diminished third
3	Augmented second/minor third
4	Major third/diminished fourth
5	Perfect fourth/augmented third
6	Augmented fourth/diminished fifth
7	Perfect fifth/diminished sixth
8	Augmented fifth/minor sixth
9	Major sixth/diminished seventh
10	Augmented sixth/minor seventh
11	Major seventh/diminished octave
12	Augmented seventh/perfect octave
13	Augmented octave

Major and Perfect Intervals in the Major Scale

A *scale* is really nothing more than a specific succession of intervals, starting from the first note of the scale, or the *tonic* note. Getting comfortable with intervals and their qualities is the first step to mastering scales and chords. (See Chapters 11 and 12 for much more on major and minor scales.)

Table 10-3, diagramming the C major scale, illustrates the relationship between the first note and every interval used in a major scale.

Table 10-3:	Intervals in the Major Scale	
Note	*Interval from Tonic*	*Note Name*
First note (tonic)	Perfect unison	C
Second note	Major 2nd (M2)	D
Third note	Major 3rd (M3)	E
Fourth note	Perfect 4th (P4)	F
Fifth note	Perfect 5th (P5)	G
Sixth note	Major 6th (M6)	A
Seventh note	Major 7th (M7)	B
Eighth note	Perfect octave (P8)	C

Figure 10-38 shows the intervals from Table 10-3 on the musical scale.

Figure 10-38:
Simple
intervals in
the C major
scale.

Listen to Track 3 on the CD to hear simple intervals in the C major scale.

The intervals shown in Figure 10-38 are found in the same order in any major scale. In the major scale, only major and perfect intervals occur above the tonic note.

Chapter 11

Key Signatures and the Circle of Fifths

*T*raditionally, when you first begin taking piano lessons — especially classical piano — you're not really taught much about key signatures beyond remembering the one or two sharps or flats you have to play in the piece of sheet music set in front of you. You're taught to play the notes exactly as they occur in that piece, without much thought about what relationship those notes have with one another in the key.

Conversely, guitar players (even bass guitar players) are almost immediately taught about chords, scales, and finding their way around the guitar neck intuitively in their lessons. Note reading is saved for more advanced students who are already familiar with all the sounds of their instrument and where those sounds are located.

This situation is why a lot of classically trained pianists have such a hard time learning how to improvise, and why guitarists and bassists who may not even know how to read music have an edge over such students when it comes to improvising. Knowing which notes go into a specific key is essential when you're playing with other musicians, or even if you're noodling around on your own without the help of sheet music.

However, what happens when a snazzy improviser without a solid classical music background is handed a piece of sheet music and asked to play along with an ensemble? The musician who was raised on reading sheet music will have no problem picking the bones of the song out from a quick glance, but the musician who rarely reads or uses sheet music struggles to figure out even the basic parts of the song.

This is where knowing how to read key signatures comes in handy. When you know, right off the bat, what key the song you're playing is in, it actually helps you read. You're able to anticipate what notes are going to be on the sheet music, based on your knowledge of the scales and the notes in those keys. Also, in a situation where you're playing with other musicians, if you know the key you're playing in, and can anticipate the chords, then you can kind of guess where the melody of the song you're playing is going to go. It's almost like knowing what word is going to come next — or at least what limited selection of words could come next — to fit into a sentence.

But first, indulge us in a brief history lesson.

Pythagoras's Circle

In the sixth century B.C., the Greek scholar and philosopher Pythagoras decided to try to make things easier for everyone by standardizing, or at least dissecting, musical tuning. As he had already discovered pitch frequencies in music instruments by vibrating different lengths of string, and had defined what exactly an octave was, he figured this was the next logical step. As he was partial to triangles *and* circles, but especially triangles, he created something we now call the Pythagorean Circle, which looks like Figure 11-1.

Each of the 12 points around the circle was assigned a pitch value. This roughly corresponds to our present system of an octave with 12 half steps. So far, so good.

In mathematical terms, the unit of measure used in his Circle is *cents*, with 1,200 cents equal to one octave. Each half step, then, is broken up into 100 cents. Due to the fact that Pythagoras was in charge of deciding what unit of measure to use for his formula, his figures, of course, always came out exactly the way he wanted them to.

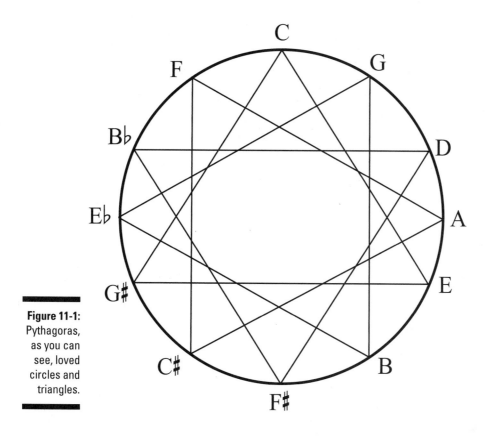

The Circle of Fifths

Western music theorists have since updated Pythagoras's Circle. You saw a version of the Circle of Fifths on the Cheat Sheet inside the front cover of this book, but Figure 11-2 shows slightly different versions of it.

The Circle of Fifths helps you figure out which sharps and flats occur in what key. The name of the key being played is the letter on the outside of the Circle. To figure out how many sharps are in each key, count *clockwise* from C at the top of the Circle.

C major has a number value of 0, so that means it has no sharps. G has a value of 1, so it has one sharp. When you play the G major scale on the piano, you will find that you play only white keys until you come to the seventh interval and land on that one sharp: F sharp, in this case. D has two sharps. A has three. And so on around the Circle. The number value by each letter on the right-hand side of the Circle represents how many sharps are in that key.

Fat Cats Go Down Alleys Eating Birds

But which sharps? There's a trick for that, too. The sharps always appear in a specific order, in every key: F, C, G, D, A, E, B. This pattern of sharps can be easily remembered by the mnemonic *Fat Cats Go Down Alleys Eating Birds*.

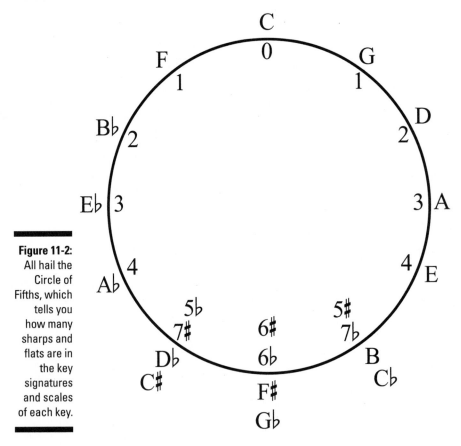

Figure 11-2:
All hail the Circle of Fifths, which tells you how many sharps and flats are in the key signatures and scales of each key.

For example, if you're playing a song in the key of B major, then you know from the Circle of Fifths that there are 5 sharps in B major. And you know from the Fat Cats mnemonic that those sharps are F sharp, C sharp, G sharp, D sharp, and A sharp, because the sharps are always in that order.

If you're playing the key of D major, which has two sharps, you know those sharps are F sharp and C sharp because *Fat Cats . . . .*

If you've got a better mnemonic than the one we give here, feel free to use it.

Battle Ends And Down Goes Charles's Father

For the major scales and keys with flats instead of sharps, you take the same formula and go counterclockwise around the Circle of Fifths, starting again at C, which still has a number value of 0. Therefore, F major has one flat, B flat major has two flats, and so on.

Like the sharps, the flats appear in a specific order in every key: B, E, A, D, G, C, F, or *Battle Ends And Down Goes Charles's Father* — which is, you'll notice, the exact reverse of the order of sharps in the Circle.

So, G flat, for example, which is six steps away from C major on the Circle, has six flats in its scale, and they are B flat, E flat, A flat, D flat, G flat, and C flat. The key of B flat, which is two steps away from C at the top of the Circle, has B flat and E flat in its key.

Notice that the orders of sharps and flats given in the mnemonics are exactly the order in which they are written in key signatures.

There's just no way to emphasize enough how useful knowing the Circle of Fifths is, both as a composer and as a performer and as a student of music theory. All we can do is say it over and over and over: The Circle of Fifths — memorize it and use it.

The creation and use of the Circle of Fifths is the very foundation of Western music theory, which is why we talk about it so much in this book. Along with all the technical things the Circle predicts, it's also your best friend in the world in deciphering key signatures on sight. It's just as essential in writing music, because its clever design is very helpful in composing and harmonizing melodies, building chords, and moving to different keys within a composition.

Just as Pythagoras had it, the Circle of Fifths is divided up into twelve stops, like the numbers on a clock. Each stop is actually the fifth pitch in the scale of the preceding stop, which is why it's called the Circle of Fifths.

For example, the fifth pitch, or the *dominant* note (you'll learn more about the dominant in Chapter 12), of the C scale is G. If you look at the Circle of Fifths in Figure 11-2, you'll see that G is the next letter to the right of C. If you keep going clockwise, you'll see that the dominant note of the G scale, D, is the next stop. And so on.

If you're new to the Circle, the best way to get familiar with it may be to simply tape this book's Cheat Sheet to your wall. The name of all the major keys is on the outside of the Circle, while the relative minor keys (in lower case letters) are all on the inside. (You'll find out more about relative minors later in this chapter and in Chapters 12 and 13.)

Recognizing Major Key Signatures

To figure out how many sharps are in each key signature, count clockwise on the Circle of Fifths from C major. The number of sharps in each successive key goes up by one in that key's key signature — one "stop" from C Major (G), there is one sharp in the key signature, and two stops away from C (D), there are two sharps in the key signature, as shown in Figure 11-3.

Figure 11-3:
The sharps are arranged on the key signature going "up."

Therefore, if you're playing a song in the key of B major, which is located five stops away from the C major on the Circle, you know there will be five sharps in that key. But also, because *Fat Cats Go Down Alleys Eating Birds,* you know that those five sharps in B major are F sharp, C sharp, G sharp, D sharp, and A sharp. If you're playing the key of D major, which has two sharps, you know those sharps are F sharp and C sharp.

For major scales that have flats, you go counterclockwise around the Circle of Fifths. The flats appear in a specific order in every key as you go from C around the Circle counter-clockwise: B flat, E flat, A flat, D flat, G flat, C flat, and F flat (remember: *Battle Ends And Down Goes Charles' Father*). Going counter-clockwise, one stop away from C major, the F has one flat in the key signature; two stops from C major (B flat) has two flats in the key signature, and so on.

Figure 11-4:
The flats are arranged on the key signature going "down."

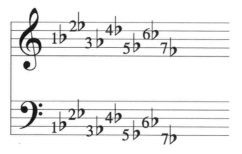

It's easy to remember that the first flat is always B flat because the flat sign itself looks kind of like a lowercase *b*.

So, for example, G flat, which is six steps away from C major on the Circle, has six flats in its key signature. And because the *Battle Ends . . .*, you know that those flats are B flat, E flat, A flat, D flat, G flat, and C flat. B flat, which is two steps away, has two flats, and now you know those flats have to B flat and E flat.

Recognizing Minor Key Signatures and Relative Minors

The Circle of Fifths works exactly the same way for *minor* keys — which are represented by the lowercase letters *inside* the circle (see the Cheat Sheet).

The minor keys on the inside of the Circle are the *relative* minors of the major keys on the outside of the Circle. The *relative minor* and its major key have the same key signature. The only difference is that the relative minor's scale starts on a different tonic, or first note. The tonic, or starting point, of a relative minor is a minor third — or three half steps — lower than its relative major key.

For example, C major's relative minor is A minor (see on the Cheat Sheet's Circle of Fifths where C is on the outside and A is on the inside of the Circle). A minor's tonic note is A, three half steps to the left of C on the piano, or three frets towards the head of the neck on the guitar.

On sheet music, the relative minor is the note one full line or space below the major key note. C is in the third space on the treble clef, and A, its relative minor, is in the second space, below it.

On the piano or guitar, a major chord and its relative minor go together like bread and butter. Many, many songs use this *chord progression* because it just sounds good. (You'll read much more about chords and chord progressions in Chapters 13 and 14.)

The *Fat Cats* . . . and *Battle Ends* . . . mnemonics stay the same when you're dealing with minor keys, because there is no difference whatsoever in the key signature between a major key and its relative minor. The only difference between a major key and its relative minor is where the notes in their scales start. An A minor scale starts on A, of course, but uses the same key signature as C. (More about major and minor scales in Chapter 12.)

The Key Signatures

Following is a run-down of the major and natural minor key signatures and a couple of octaves' worth of notes in those keys, arranged in a scale. Because this chapter is about the Circle of Fifths, we order the key signatures following the Circle, as opposed to alphabetical order.

Don't be thrown by the word *natural* when we use it to describe minor key signatures in this section. Turns out there is more than one kind of minor, and you'll find out about those in Chapter 12.

C major and A minor

Figure 11-5 shows the C major key signature, and Figure 11-6 shows the A minor key signature, C's relative minor.

As you can see, the C Major and the A minor have exactly the same key signature (that is, no sharps and no flats) and exactly the same notes in the scale because A is the relative minor of C. The only difference is that the C major scale starts on C, whereas the A minor scale starts on A.

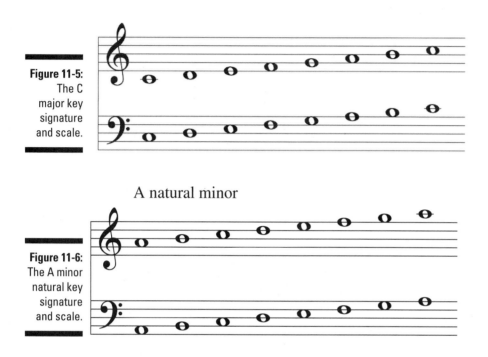

Figure 11-5:
The C major key signature and scale.

A natural minor

Figure 11-6:
The A minor natural key signature and scale.

G major and E minor

Figure 11-7 shows the G major key signature, and Figure 11-8 shows the E minor key signature, G's relative minor.

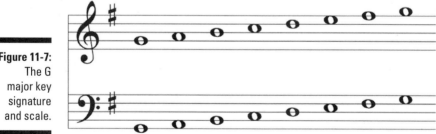

Figure 11-7:
The G major key signature and scale.

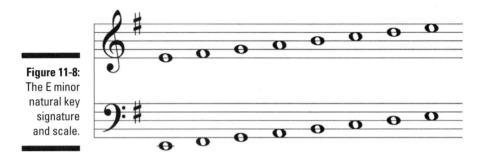

Figure 11-8:
The E minor natural key signature and scale.

We've now added one sharp (F) to the key signature. The next stop (D) will have two (F and C, because *Fat Cats . . .*), and we'll keep adding one more sharp until we get to the bottom of the Circle.

D major and B minor

Figure 11-9 shows the D major key signature, and Figure 11-10 shows the B minor key signature, D's relative minor.

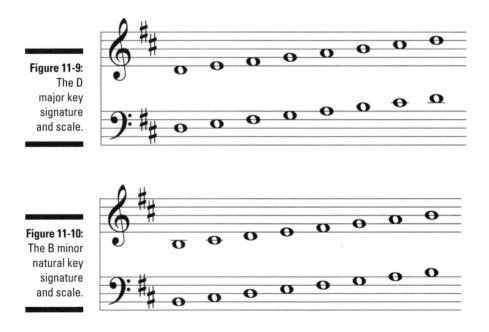

Figure 11-9:
The D major key signature and scale.

Figure 11-10:
The B minor natural key signature and scale.

A major and F sharp minor

Figure 11-11 shows the A major key signature, and Figure 11-12 shows the F sharp minor key signature, A's relative minor.

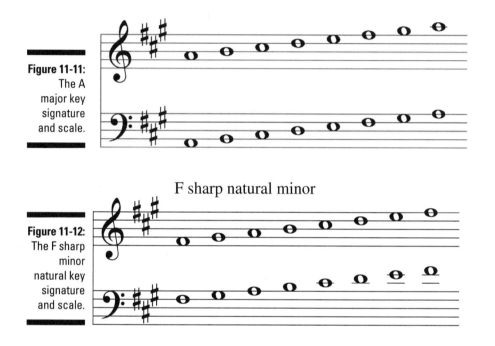

Figure 11-11:
The A major key signature and scale.

F sharp natural minor

Figure 11-12:
The F sharp minor natural key signature and scale.

E major and C sharp minor

Figure 11-13 shows the E major key signature, and Figure 11-14 shows the C sharp minor key signature, E's relative minor.

B/C flat major and G sharp/A flat minor

Figure 11-15 shows the B major key signature and C flat major key signature. Figure 11-16 shows the G sharp minor natural key signature and the A flat minor natural key signature.

Figure 11-13: The E major key signature and scale.

Figure 11-14: The C sharp minor natural key signature and scale.

Figure 11-15: The B major and C flat major key signatures and scales.

B major or
C flat major

Figure 11-16: The G sharp minor natural and A flat minor natural key signatures and scales.

Confused? Take a look at a keyboard, and you'll see that there is no black key for C flat. Instead, there's a white key: B. C flat and B are *enharmonic equivalents* of one another, meaning they are the same but with different names. All of the notes in the key of B major and the key of C flat major sound exactly the same — they just use a little different musical notation.

The same goes for G sharp minor and A flat minor — same notes, just different notation.

As the number of sharps has been going up by one at each stop on the Circle, from this point on, the number of flats will also be going down by one until we get back up to the 12 o'clock (C major/A minor) position.

F sharp/G flat major and D sharp/E flat minor

Figure 11-17 shows the F sharp major key signature and the G flat major key signature. Figure 11-18 shows the D sharp minor natural key signature and the E flat minor natural key signature.

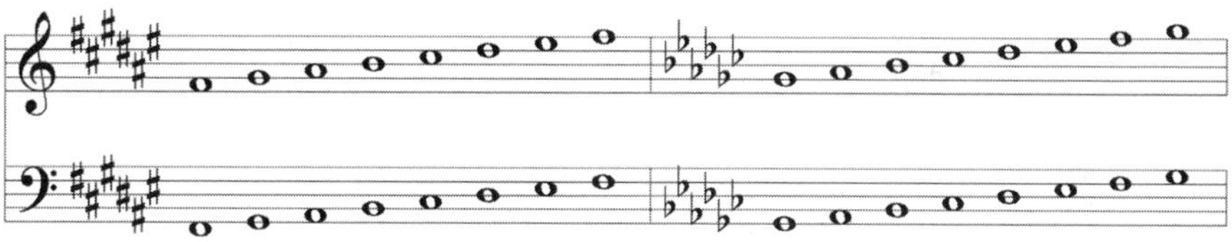

Figure 11-17: The F sharp major and G flat minor key signatures and scales.

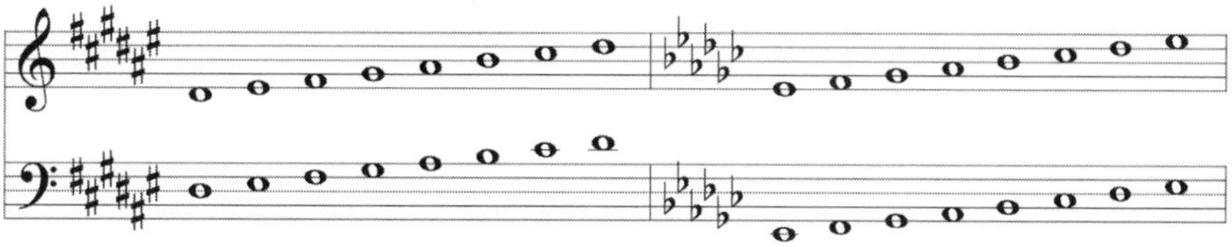

Figure 11-18: The D sharp minor natural and E flat minor natural key signatures and scales.

More enharmonic equivalents!

D flat/C sharp major and B flat/A sharp minor

Figure 11-19 shows the C sharp major key signature and the D flat major key signature. Figure 11-20 shows the A sharp minor key signature and the B flat minor natural key signature.

Figure 11-19:
The C sharp major and D flat major key signatures and scales.

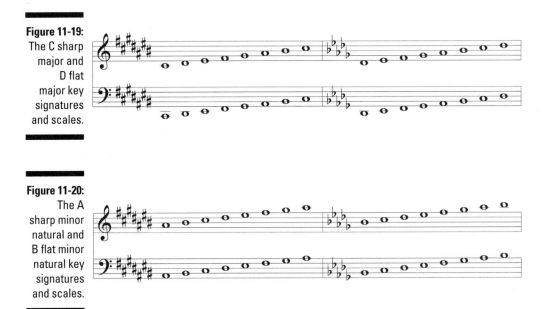

Figure 11-20:
The A sharp minor natural and B flat minor natural key signatures and scales.

These are the last of the enharmonic equivalent key signatures you'll have to remember, we promise. Also, this is the last of the keys with a sharp in its signature — from this point on, we're working with flats alone as we continue going up the left side of the Circle.

A flat major and F minor

Figure 11-21 shows the A flat major key signature and the F minor key signature, A flat's relative minor.

Figure 11-21:
The A flat
major and
F minor
natural key
signature
and scale.

E flat major and C minor

Figure 11-22 shows the E flat major key signature and the C minor key signature, E flat's relative minor.

Figure 11-22:
The E flat
major and
C minor
natural key
signatures
and scales.

B flat major and G minor

Figure 11-23 shows the B flat major key signature and the G minor key signature, B flat's relative minor.

Figure 11-23:
The B flat
major and
G minor
natural key
signatures
and scales.

F major and D minor

Figure 11-24 shows the F major key signature and the D minor key signature, F's relative minor.

Figure 11-24:
The F major and D minor natural key signatures and scales.

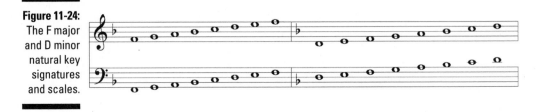

Chapter 12

The Major and Minor Scales

*T*o put it simply, a *scale* is a group of consecutive notes — any group of notes — that provides the material for part or all of a piece of music. We could pretty much write an entire encyclopedia on all the different types of scales used in music from around the world, but because this book is primarily concerned with the Western tradition of music, we're going to have to confine ourselves to the two most-frequently used scales: the major and the minor.

The *diatonic major* scale is the most popular scale and the one that's the easiest to recognize when played. This is the scale that songs like "Happy Birthday" and "Mary Had a Little Lamb" are composed in.

It's impossible to overemphasize just how important knowing your scales back and forth is to playing music. And it isn't just enough to be able to play the scales back and forth and up and down, either. In order to successfully improvise or compose, you need to know how to jump around on your instrument and still land on all the right notes within the scale.

This is exactly why scales are important. Say you're jamming with a group of other musicians. If you know what key the rest of the band is playing in, and you know all the notes that are within that key (for scales are determined by keys — you'll find out a lot more about keys and key signatures in Chapter 11), then it is absolutely impossible to mess up so long as you stick to those notes. In fact, you can noodle all day in the proper key and sound like a regular Carlos Santana or Louis Armstrong.

Scales that share the same starting notes are called *parallel* scales. For example, C major and C minor are parallel scales, because they both start on the same note: C. Same with A and A minor. And Z and Z minor — just kidding.

Major Scale Patterns

Even though every major scale contains a different set of notes, each scale is put together exactly the same way. The specific major-scale pattern of intervals is what lumps every single one of the scales mentioned in this first half of the chapter into the category of *major scale*.

Major scales follow the interval pattern of WWHWWWH. That means: **W**hole step **W**hole step **H**alf step **W**hole step **W**hole step **W**hole step **H**alf step. The first note (and last) in the scale determines the name of the scale.

- **Half step:** Moving one piano key over or one guitar fret up or down.

- **Whole step:** Moving two piano keys or two guitar frets up or down.

Each of the eight notes in a major scale has a name:

- **1st note:** Tonic

- **2nd note:** Supertonic

- **3rd note:** Mediant

- **4th note:** Subdominant

- **5th note:** Dominant

- **6th note:** Submediant

- **7th note:** Leading tone (or leading note)

- **8th note:** Tonic

The first and eighth notes, the *tonic*, determine the name of the scale. Relative to the tonic note, the rest of the notes in the scale are usually attached to the numbers 2–7 (because 1 and 8 are already taken). Each of these numbers represents a *scale degree*, and their pattern of whole steps and half steps determines they key of the scale.

So, for example, if you were playing something in the key of C major, which sequentially has the notes C, D, E, F, G, A, B, C in it, and someone asked you to play the fourth and second notes in the scales, you would play them an F

Mastering scales is all about recognizing patterns on an instrument. If you look at a piano keyboard, or the neck of a guitar, can you *see* where the 1, 2, 3, 4, 5, 6, 7, and 8 of each scale go? If you're given a scale and are asked to play the sequence 5-3-2-1-6-4-5-8, do you know what notes you would play? Eventually, you want to be able to answer yes to these questions for all 12 major scales. How?

First, you need to be able to picture each scale in your head and where it's located on your instrument. Second, you need to know the letter name and number of each note in each scale. Third, you need to be able to play sequences of notes when given the key and number. If you can do all three things, *then* you can stop practicing your scales.

Major Scales on Piano and Guitar

If someone were to ask you to play the scale for C major on the piano, you would put it together like Figure 12-1.

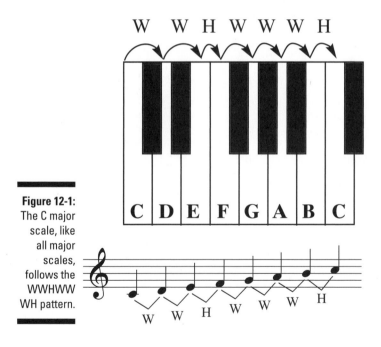

Figure 12-1: The C major scale, like all major scales, follows the WWHWW WH pattern.

Note the marked steps in Figure 12-1 — every single major scale you will ever work with is going to follow this pattern, using different combinations of black and white keys on the piano, depending on the scale.

To play each scale on the piano, begin with the piano key that is the name of the scale. For the A major scale, for example, you begin with the A. (If you still haven't memorized the notes of the piano keyboard, refer to the Cheat Sheet at the front of this book.) Then play the major scale pattern: WWHWWWH. The scale will end on the same note it began with, only an octave higher.

To see the major scale for every key, refer back to Chapter 11, which illustrates key signatures by showing the scale on the staff for each key. To hear all the major scales, listen to the tracks on the CD listed at the end of this chapter.

Playing scales on the guitar is even simpler. Traditionally, guitarists think of the guitar neck as being broken up into blocks of four frets, and, depending on what key you want to play in, your hand is positioned over that block of four frets. Two octaves' worth of every pitch within that scale is located within each four-fret block.

Major scales on the guitar follow the pattern shown in Figure 12-2, playing the notes in the number order they appear below (remember, the 8 of the first octave serves as the 1 of the second octave).

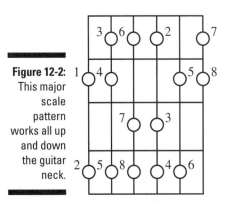

Figure 12-2: This major scale pattern works all up and down the guitar neck.

To play each scale on the guitar, begin with the correct fret on the first string (the top string as you hold the guitar, the low E string), which are as follows:

- ✔ **Open string:** E
- ✔ **1st fret:** F (with the use of open strings for 3, 6, 2, 7)
- ✔ **2nd fret:** F sharp/G flat
- ✔ **3rd fret:** G
- ✔ **4th fret:** G sharp/A flat
- ✔ **5th fret:** A
- ✔ **6th fret:** A sharp/B flat
- ✔ **7th fret:** B
- ✔ **8th fret:** C
- ✔ **9th fret:** C sharp/D flat
- ✔ **10th fret:** D
- ✔ **11th fret:** D sharp/E flat
- ✔ **12th fret:** E
- ✔ **13th fret:** F

To play major scales on the guitar, you just move that pattern along the neck of the guitar to build whatever major scale you'd like. Again, the *key* is determined by the first and last notes of the scale, so if you were asked to play a C major scale on the guitar, you would simply start scale on the eighth fret. No black keys or white keys to fool with here — just the same pattern repeated along the neck, over and over.

Worth noting is that the *actual* pitch of the guitar is one octave (12 half steps) lower than the *written* pitch. This is regularly done in sheet music simply because most sheet music is written for piano. On the piano, the middle octave is the most frequently used and is therefore centered on the grand staff.

Again, to see the major scale for every key, refer back to Chapter 11, which uses scales to illustrate key signatures.

Listening to the Major Scales

Listen to Tracks 4 through 18 to hear each of the major scales played on piano and guitar.

Track	Scale
4	A major
5	A flat major
6	B major

7	B flat major
8	C major
9	C flat major
10	C sharp major
11	D major
12	D flat major
13	E major
14	E flat major
15	F major
16	F sharp major
17	G major
18	G flat major

Minor Scale Patterns

When you hear the term *minor scale*, you might be led to believe that this is a set of scales much less important than the grand collection of *major scales*. Or you might think the minor scale is only for sad, sappy songs. But the truth is that the arrangements and tones, or note sounds, available in the minor scales — divided, according to composition, into the natural, harmonic, and melodic minor scales — can be much more flexible for a composer to use than the major scale alone.

Even though every type of minor scale contains a different set of notes, each type of scale is put together in a very specific way. These specific patterns of intervals are what put the minor scales into their little niche.

Each of the eight notes in a minor scale has a name:

- **1st note:** Tonic
- **2nd note:** Supertonic
- **3rd note:** Minor mediant
- **4th note:** Subdominant
- **5th note:** Dominant
- **6th note:** Minor submediant
- **7th note:** Subtonic
- **8th note:** Tonic

In the harmonic and melodic minor scales, the seventh degree is called the *leading tone*. In the melodic minor scale, the sixth degree is called the *submediant*.

Natural minor scales on piano and guitar

Natural minor scales follow the interval pattern of WHWWHWW. That translates into **W**hole step **H**alf step **W**hole step **W**hole step **H**alf step **W**hole step **W**hole step, with the first note (and last) in the scale determining the scale name.

A *natural* minor scale is taken from the major scale of the same name, but with the third, sixth, and seventh degrees lowered one half step.

So, for instance, if someone were to ask you to play the scale for A minor natural on the piano, you would put it together like Figure 12-3 shows.

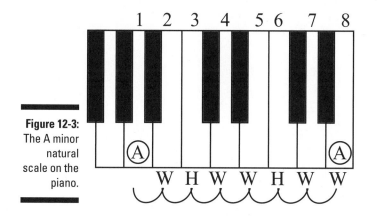

Figure 12-3:
The A minor natural scale on the piano.

Playing minor scales on the guitar is even simpler. Natural minor scales on the guitar follow the pattern shown in Figure 12-4. Play the notes in the number order shown in Figure 12-4. Your first note is indicated by the 1 shown on the first E string.

Just as with major scales, to play natural minor scales on the guitar, you just move the Figure 12-4 pattern along the neck of the guitar to build whatever minor scale you'd like. Whatever note you start with on the top (low E) string is the name of the scale.

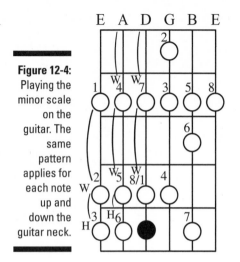

Figure 12-4:
Playing the minor scale on the guitar. The same pattern applies for each note up and down the guitar neck.

If you were asked to play an A minor scale on the guitar, for example, you would play the pattern shown in Figure 12-5.

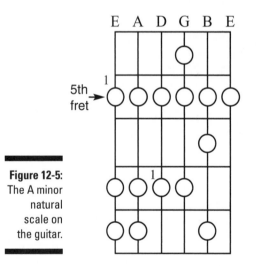

Figure 12-5:
The A minor natural scale on the guitar.

Harmonic minor scales on piano and guitar

The *harmonic* minor scale is a variation of the natural minor scale. It occurs when the seventh note of the natural minor scale is raised a half step. The step is *not* raised in the key signature, but through the use of accidentals (sharps, double sharps, or naturals).

To play the scale for A harmonic minor on the piano, you would put it together like Figure 12-6.

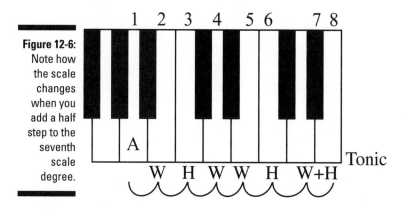

Figure 12-6:
Note how the scale changes when you add a half step to the seventh scale degree.

When you're writing music and you want to use a harmonic scale, it's easiest to write it out, using the natural minor key first, and then go back and add the accidental that raises the seventh degree up a half step.

Again, playing harmonic minor scales on the guitar is simple. You just position the pattern shown in Figure 12-7 over the root (tonic) position you want to play in. Move it around to a different root to play the scale for that note.

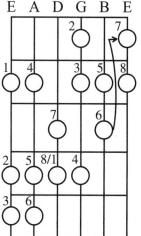

Figure 12-7:
Note how the pattern changes when you add a half step to the seventh scale degree.

As always, the key is determined by the first and last notes of the scale, so if you were asked to play an A harmonic minor scale on the guitar, you would play what is shown in Figure 12-8:

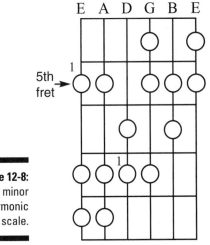

Figure 12-8:
A minor harmonic scale.

Melodic minor scales on piano and guitar

The *melodic* minor scale is also derived from the natural minor scale. In the melodic minor scale, the sixth and seventh notes of the natural minor scale are each raised by one half step when going up the scale, *but return to the natural minor when going down the scale.*

This is a tricky one, so we're going to reiterate: While you're going up in pitch when playing a piece, you add sharps to the six and seventh degrees of the natural minor scale, but during parts of the same piece where the pitch goes *down*, you would play the notes according to the natural minor scale.

To play an A melodic minor scale ascending (going up) on the piano, for example, you would play what is shown in Figure 12-9.

Remember, the A melodic minor scale *descending* reverts to A natural minor.

When writing music in the melodic minor scale, many composers choose to write the song out, using the natural minor pattern, adding the accidentals that modify any ascending sixth and seventh notes afterwards.

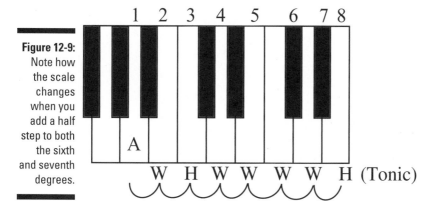

Figure 12-9:
Note how the scale changes when you add a half step to both the sixth and seventh degrees.

Again, the wonderful thing about the guitar is that you really only have to memorize one pattern for each type of scale and you're set. To play the ascending A melodic minor scale, play the pattern shown in Figure 12-10.

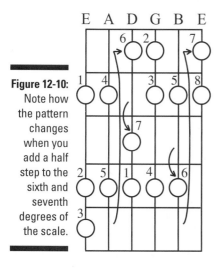

Figure 12-10:
Note how the pattern changes when you add a half step to the sixth and seventh degrees of the scale.

To play an A melodic minor scale ascending on the guitar, you would play it like Figure 12-11.

And of course, for the descending notes you revert to A natural minor.

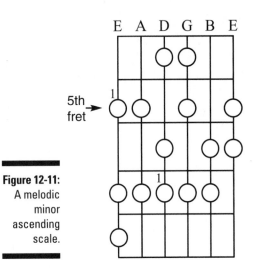

Figure 12-11:
A melodic
minor
ascending
scale.

Listening to the Minor Scales

Listen to Tracks 19 through 63 to hear each of the minor scales played on piano and guitar.

Track	*Scale*
19	A minor natural
20	A minor harmonic
21	A minor melodic
22	A flat minor natural
23	A flat minor harmonic
24	A flat minor melodic major
25	A sharp minor natural
26	A sharp minor harmonic
27	A sharp minor melodic
28	B minor natural
29	B minor harmonic
30	B minor melodic
31	B flat minor natural
32	B flat minor harmonic

33	B flat minor melodic
34	C minor natural
35	C minor harmonic
36	C minor melodic
37	C sharp minor natural
38	C sharp minor harmonic
39	C sharp minor melodic
40	D minor natural
41	D minor harmonic
42	D minor melodic
43	D sharp minor natural
44	D sharp minor harmonic
45	D sharp minor melodic
46	E minor natural
47	E minor harmonic
48	E minor melodic
49	E flat minor natural
50	E flat minor harmonic
51	E flat minor melodic
52	F minor natural
53	F minor harmonic
54	F minor melodic
55	F sharp minor natural
56	F sharp minor harmonic
57	F sharp minor melodic
58	G minor natural
59	G minor harmonic
60	G minor melodic
61	G sharp minor natural
62	G sharp harmonic
63	G sharp melodic

Chapter 13

Building Chords

In This Chapter

▶ Getting a grip on major, minor, augmented, and diminished triads

▶ Looking at all the different kinds of seventh chords

▶ Listening to all the chords so far

▶ Inverting and changing voicing for triads and sevenths

A chord is, quite simply, three or more notes played simultaneously. Using this definition, banging a coffee cup or your elbow on top of three or more keys at the same times makes a chord — it probably doesn't sound particularly musical, but it is still technically a chord.

To the uninitiated and experienced performer alike, chord construction can sometimes seem like magic. There is something absolutely beautiful and amazing about the way the individual notes in a chord work to enhance one another. Most people don't appreciate that until they hear the way the "wrong" notes sound against each other — for example, our coffee cup pushing onto the piano keyboard in a poorly constructed chord.

In most Western music, chords are constructed out of *consecutive intervals of a third* — that is, each note in a chord is a third apart from the one before and/or after it (review Chapter 10 if you've forgotten your intervals). Figure 13-1 illustrates two stacks of thirds to show you what we mean.

With chords based on intervals of a third, all the notes are either going to be line notes or space notes, resting one on top of another like the examples in Figure 13-1.

Figure 13-1:
Two stacks
of thirds,
one on the
lines, and
the other in
the spaces.

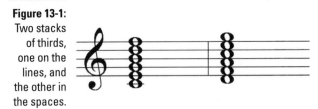

Triads

Triads consist of three pitches and are the most common type of chord used in music. There's a good chance that if people were born with bigger hands or more fingers, this would not be the case. However, because we're stuck with only five fingers and a range of roughly one octave on each hand, chords built with only three closely-spaced notes — that is, triads — have become the basic unit of Western harmony.

Roots, thirds, and fifths

The term *triad* refers to chords that contain three notes and are built of thirds. The bottom note of a triad is called the *root*; many beginning music students are taught to think of a triad as being a tree, with the root of a triad being its, well, root. The root carries the *voicing* of the chord, and chords carry the letter name of the root note, as in a *C chord*, shown in Figure 13-2.

Figure 13-2:
The root of
a C chord
(either
C could be
the root).

Play Track 64 on the CD to hear the root of a C chord.

The second note of a triad is the *third*. The third of a chord is called that because it is a third interval away from the root of the chord.

Figure 13-3 shows the root and major third of a C chord.

Play Track 65 on the CD to hear the root and major third of a C chord.

Figure 13-3:
The root and
major third
of a C major
chord.

The third of a chord is especially important in constructing chords, as it is the *quality* of the third that determines whether you're dealing with a major or minor chord.

A chord is called a *minor triad* if there's a minor third interval between the root and third. A chord is called a *major triad* if there's a major third interval between the root and third.

The third and last note of a triad is the *fifth*. The fifth is called that because it is a fifth interval from the root, as shown in Figure 13-4.

Figure 13-4:
The root and
fifth of a C
major chord.

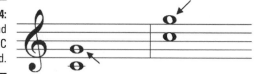

Play Track 66 on the CD to hear the root and fifth of a C major chord.

Put them all together, and you've got the triad shown in Figure 13-5.

Figure 13-5:
C major
triads.

Play Track 67 on the CD to hear a C major triad chord.

Building major triads

Because they are made of intervals, triads are affected by *quality* (see Chapter 10 for a refresher on quantity and quality). The quantity of the notes that make up the triad are intervals of unison, third, and fifth, but it's the interval quality of each note that changes the voicing of the triad.

A major triad, as we mentioned, is made up of a root, a major third above the root, and a perfect fifth above the root. But there are two ways to build major triads.

Half-step counting method

You can count out the half steps between notes to build a major triad, using this formula:

Root position + 4 half steps + 3 half steps (or 7 half steps above root)

Figure 13-6 shows C major on the piano keyboard.

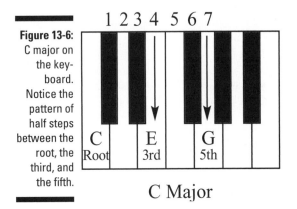

Figure 13-6: C major on the keyboard. Notice the pattern of half steps between the root, the third, and the fifth.

C Major

The pattern stays the same no matter the root, but it looks trickier when you move away from C. As you will see.

First, major third, and fifth method

The second way to construct major triads is to just take the first, major third, and fifth notes from a major scale.

For example, if someone asked you to write down an F major chord, you would first write out the key signature for F major, as shown in Figure 13-7. (Review Chapter 11 for more on key signatures.)

Figure 13-7:
The key
signature
for F major.

Then you would write your triad on the staff, using F as your root position, as seen in Figure 13-8.

Figure 13-8:
Add the F
major triad.

Fmaj

If you were to build an A flat major, you would first write down the key signature for A flat major and then build the triad, as shown in Figure 13-9.

Figure 13-9:
The A flat
major triad.

Building minor triads

A minor triad is made up of a root, a minor third above the root, and a perfect fifth above the root.

Half-step counting method

As with major triads, you can count out the half steps between notes to build a minor chord, using this formula:

Root position + 3 half steps + 4 half steps (7 half steps above root)

Figure 13-10 shows C minor on the piano keyboard, and Figure 13-11 shows it on the staff.

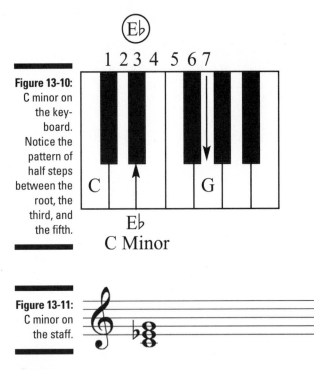

Figure 13-10:
C minor on the keyboard. Notice the pattern of half steps between the root, the third, and the fifth.

Figure 13-11:
C minor on the staff.

As you can see, a minor chord and a major chord have the same root and the same fifth — the only difference is the interval quality of the root to third positions.

First, minor third, and fifth method

The second way to construct minor triads is to just take the first, the minor or *flat third* (which means you lower the third degree of the major third one half step), and fifth intervals from a major scale.

For example, for an F minor chord, you would write down the key signature for F and the notes of the minor triad, as in Figure 13-12.

Figure 13-12:
The F minor triad lowers the third one half step.

If you were to build an A flat minor, you write the A flat key signature and add the notes, flatting the third, as shown in Figure 13-13.

Figure 13-13:
The A flat
minor triad
lowers the
third one
half step.

Building augmented triads

Augmented triads are major triad chords that have had the quality of the
interval between the third and fifth raised a half step.

An augmented triad is just like having a stack of major intervals with four half
steps between each interval.

To build a C augmented triad (written as *Caug*), you could build it by counting out the half steps between intervals, like this:

Root position + 4 half steps + 4 half steps (8 half steps above root)

C augmented is shown in Figures 13-14 and 13-15.

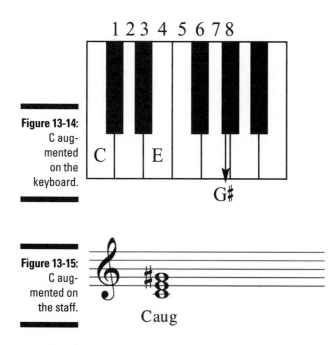

Figure 13-14:
C aug-
mented
on the
keyboard.

Figure 13-15:
C aug-
mented on
the staff.

Using the method of starting with the major key signature first and then building the chord, the formula you want to remember for building augmented chords is this:

Augmented triad: 1, 3, sharp 5

That means first major scale degree, third major scale degree, and then the fifth major scale degree raised a half step.

It's important to note here that *sharp 5* does not mean that the note will necessarily *be a sharp*, but the fifth note occurring in the scale degree raised, or sharped, a half step.

Therefore, if someone asked you to write down an augmented F triad, you would first write the key signature for F and then write your triad on the staff, using F as your root and raising the fifth position one half step, as shown in Figure 13-16.

Figure 13-16:
The F augmented triad.

If you were to build an A flat augmented, you would go through the same process and come up with Figure 13-17.

Figure 13-17:
The A flat augmented triad.

Note that the perfect fifth of A flat major is an E flat — given A flat's key signature, you have to "natural" the fifth to get to that E natural.

Building diminished triads

Diminished triads are minor chords that have had the quality of the interval between the third and fifth *lowered* a half step.

Diminished triads are like having a stack of minor intervals, with three half steps between each interval.

To build a C diminished triad (written as *Cdim*), you could build it by counting out the half steps between intervals, like this:

Root position + 3 half steps + 3 half steps (6 half steps above root)

C diminished is shown in Figures 13-18 and 13-19.

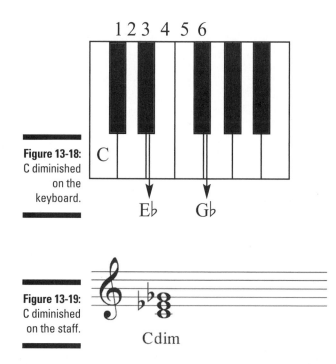

Figure 13-18:
C diminished on the keyboard.

Figure 13-19:
C diminished on the staff.

Using the method of starting with the major key signature first and then building the chord, the formula you want to remember for building diminished chords is this:

Diminished triad: 1, flat 3, flat 5

That means: first major scale degree, third major scale degree lowered one half step, and fifth major scale degree lowered one half step.

It's important to note here that *flat 3* and *flat 5* do not mean that these notes will necessarily *be flats*, but are only the third and fifth notes occurring in the scale degree lowered a half step.

Therefore, if someone asked you to write down an F diminished triad, you would first write the key signature for F and then write your triad on the staff, using F as your root and lowering the third and fifth intervals one half step, as shown in Figure 13-20.

Figure 13-20:
The F diminished triad.

If you were to build an A flat diminished, you would go through the same process and come up with Figure 13-21.

Figure 13-21:
The A flat diminished triad.

Note that the perfect fifth of A flat major is an E flat — flatting the fifth makes it a double flat, or an *enharmonic* (the same note) of a D natural.

Table 13-1 has a handy little chart to help you keep it all straight.

Table 13-1	Building Triads
Building Triads by Counting Half Steps	
Major =	Root position + 4 half steps + 3 half steps (7 half steps above root)
Minor =	Root position + 3 half steps + 4 half steps (7 half steps above root)
Augmented =	Root position + 4 half steps + 4 half steps (8 half steps above root)
Diminished =	Root position + 3 half steps + 3 half-steps (6 half steps above root)
Building Triads with Major Scale Degrees	
Major =	1, 3, 5
Minor =	1, flat 3, 5
Augmented =	1, 3, sharp 5
Diminished =	1, flat 3, flat 5

Seventh Chords

When you add another third above the fifth of a triad, you've gone beyond the land of triads. You've now got a *seventh chord.* Seventh chords are called this because the last third interval is a seventh interval above the root.

There are several kinds of seventh chords. The six most commonly used seventh chords are as follows:

- ✔ Major sevenths
- ✔ Minor sevenths
- ✔ Dominant sevenths
- ✔ Minor 7 flat 5 chords (also sometimes called half-diminished)
- ✔ Diminished sevenths
- ✔ Minor-major sevenths

They may seem scary at first, but the easiest way to really get how sevenths are built is to think of each as a triad with a seventh tagged onto it. Looking at sevenths this way, you'll see that seventh chords are really just variations on the four triads we've already discussed.

As we go over the following types of sevenths, note how the names of the chords tell you how to put the seventh together with the triad.

Building major sevenths

A major seventh chord consists of a major triad with a major seventh added above the root. Let's go back, using our C major example from earlier in the chapter, and build a major triad first, as in Figure 13-22.

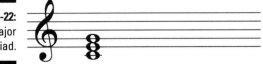

Figure 13-22:
C major
triad.

Now let's add a major seventh to the top of the pile, as in Figure 13-23.

Figure 13-23:
C major
triad + major
seventh
interval =
C major
seventh
(CM7 or
Cmaj7).

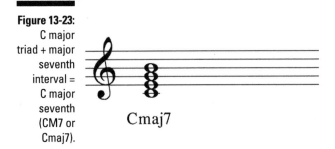

Cmaj7

B natural is a major seventh (in other words, as you saw in Chapter 10, 11 half steps) from the root of the triad. Notice that it's also a major third (four half steps) away from the fifth of the triad.

Minor sevenths

A minor seventh chord consists of a minor triad with a minor seventh added above the root. Using our C minor example, build a minor triad first, as in Figure 13-24.

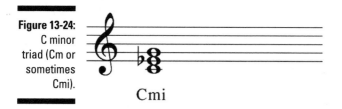

Figure 13-24:
C minor
triad (Cm or
sometimes
Cmi).

Cmi

Then add a minor seventh to the top of the pile, as in Figure 13-25.

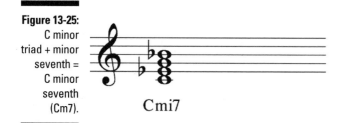

Figure 13-25:
C minor
triad + minor
seventh =
C minor
seventh
(Cm7).

Cmi7

B flat is a minor seventh (ten half steps) from the root of the triad. It's also a minor third (three half steps) away from the fifth of the triad.

To build a minor seventh, using major scale degrees, you would pick the first, flatted third, fifth, and flatted seventh degrees from the scale.

Dominant sevenths

A dominant seventh chord consists of a major triad with a minor seventh added above the root, as in Figure 13-26.

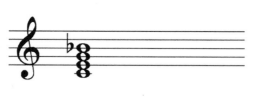

Figure 13-26:
C major
triad + minor
seventh = C
dominant
seventh
(written
as C7).

There are ten half steps between the root and the minor seventh, and three half-steps between the fifth of the triad and the minor seventh.

The dominant seventh is the only seventh chord that doesn't truly give away the relationship between the triad and the seventh in its name. You just have to remember it. And don't get confused between major seventh and dominant seventh chords. The major seventh is always written as M7, whereas the dominant seventh is written simply as 7. For example, GM7 and G7.

To build a dominant seventh, using major scale degrees, you would pick the first, third, fifth, and flatted seventh degrees from the scale.

Minor 7 flat 5 chords

A *minor 7 flat 5 chord* (or *half-diminished seventh*) is a diminished triad with a minor seventh added above the root. Its name, minor 7 flat 5, tells you everything you need to know about how this chord is supposed to be put together.

Minor 7 refers to the seventh being a minor seven, or ten half steps, from the root, as in Figure 13-27.

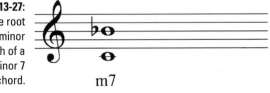

Figure 13-27: The root and minor seventh of a C minor 7 flat 5 chord.

Flat 5 refers to the diminished triad, which shares a flatted third with a minor chord but also has a flatted fifth, as shown in Figure 13-28.

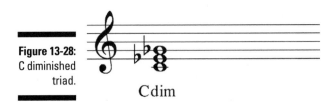

Figure 13-28: C diminished triad.

REMEMBER

Put the two of them together, and you've got the C minor 7 flat 5 chord, as shown in all its glory in Figure 13-29.

The minor 7 flat 5 chord is also sometimes called the *half-diminished seventh.*

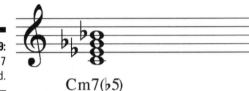

Figure 13-29:
C minor 7
flat 5 chord.

Cm7(♭5)

TIP

To build a minor 7 flat 5, using major scale degrees, you would pick the first, flatted third, flatted fifth, and flatted seventh degrees from the scale.

Diminished sevenths

Essentially, the *diminished seventh* chord is a stack of three consecutive minor thirds.

The name is also is a dead giveaway on how the chord is to be built — just as with the major seventh, which is a major triad with a major seventh, and the minor seventh, which is a minor triad with a minor seventh, a diminished seventh is a diminished triad with a diminished seventh from the root tagged onto it.

So, first you build your diminished triad (as just shown earlier in Figure 13-28). Then you put your diminished seventh on top, as in Figure 13-30.

Figure 13-30:
C diminished
triad +
diminished
seventh = C
diminished
seventh
(Cdim7).

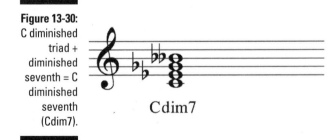

Cdim7

Note that the seventh in a diminished seventh is *double-flatted* from the major seventh, so the diminished seventh of Cdim7 is a double-flatted B.

To build a diminished seventh, using major scale degrees, you would pick the first, flatted-third, flatted-fifth, and double-flatted-seventh degrees from the scale.

Minor-major sevenths

Take another look at the name for this type of seventh. It's actually not supposed to be confusing. The first part of the word is telling you that the first part of the chord, the triad, is going to be a minor chord, and the second part of the word is telling you that the second part of the chord, the seventh, is going to be a major seventh interval above the root.

Therefore, to build a minor-major seventh chord, you start with your minor chord, shown in Figure 13-31.

Figure 13-31:
C minor
triad.

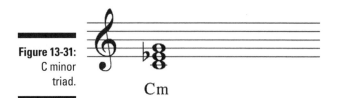

Cm

Then you add your major seventh, as in Figure 13-32.

Figure 13-32:
C minor +
major
seventh
interval = C
minor-major
seventh
(CmiMA7).

CmiMA7

To build a minor-major seventh, using major scale degrees, you would pick the first, flatted third, fifth, and seventh degrees from the scale.

Table 13-2 gathers all this info on how to build sevenths.

Table 13-2	Building Sevenths
Building Sevenths by Counting Half Steps	
Major =	Root + 4 half steps + 3 half steps + 4 half steps (11 half steps above root)
Minor =	Root + 3 half steps + 4 half steps + 3 half steps (10 half steps above root)
Dominant =	Root + 4 half steps + 3 half steps + 3 half steps (10 half steps above root)
Minor 7 flat 5 =	Root + 3 half steps + 3 half steps + 4 half steps (10 half steps above root)
Diminished =	Root + 3 half steps, 3 half steps, 3 half steps (9 half steps above root)
Minor-major =	Root + 3 half steps, 4 half steps, 4 half steps (11 half steps above root)
Building Sevenths with Major Scale Degrees	
Major =	1, 3, 5, 7
Minor =	1, flat 3, 5, flat 7
Dominant =	1, 3, 5, flat 7
Minor 7 flat 5 =	1, flat 3, flat 5, flat 7
Diminished =	1, flat 3, flat 5, double-flat 7
Minor-major =	1, flat 3, 5, 7

Looking at All the Triads and Sevenths

Here's where we just lay out all the types of triads and sevenths we've just discussed, in order of appearance in this chapter, for every key. You can check your own work against the following or use the information for your own quick and handy reference.

Figures 13-33 through 13-47 illustrate the triads and sevenths.

A

Play Track 68 on the CD to hear the triads and sevenths of A.

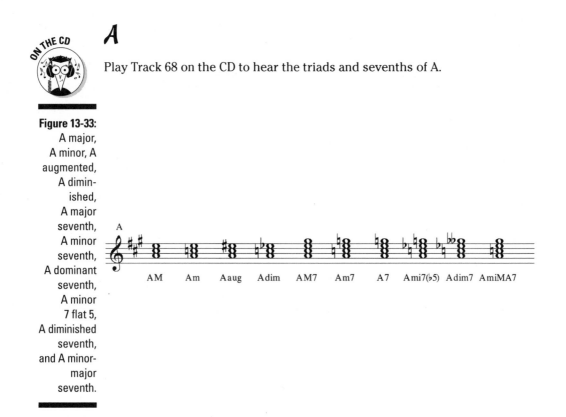

Figure 13-33:
A major,
A minor, A
augmented,
A dimin-
ished,
A major
seventh,
A minor
seventh,
A dominant
seventh,
A minor
7 flat 5,
A diminished
seventh,
and A minor-
major
seventh.

A flat

Play Track 69 on the CD to hear the triads and sevenths of A flat.

B

Play Track 70 on the CD to hear the triads and sevenths of B.

Figure 13-34:
A flat major, A flat minor, A flat augmented, A flat diminished, A flat major seventh, A flat minor seventh, A flat dominant seventh, A flat minor 7 flat 5, A flat diminished seventh, and A flat minor-major seventh.

Figure 13-35:
B major, B minor, B augmented, B diminished, B major seventh, B minor seventh, B dominant seventh, B minor 7 flat 5, B diminished seventh, and B minor-major seventh.

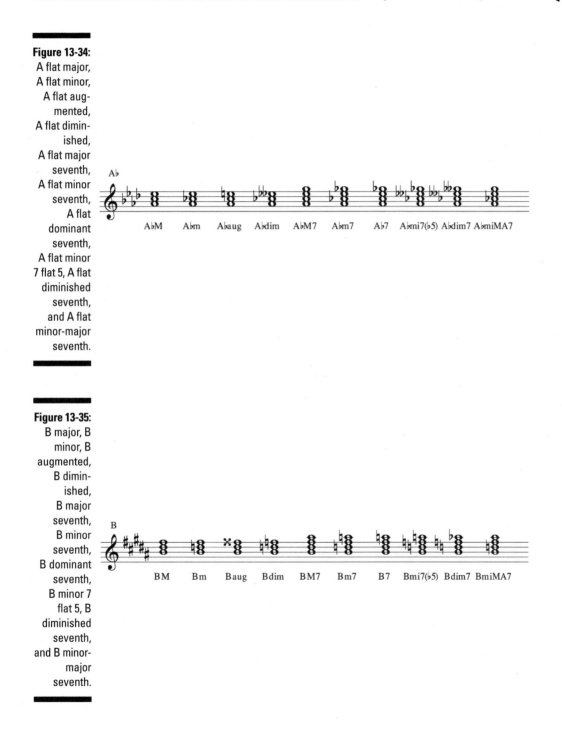

B flat

Play Track 71 on the CD to hear the triads and sevenths of B flat.

Figure 13-36:
B flat major,
B flat minor,
B flat aug-
mented, B
flat dimin-
ished, B flat
major
seventh, B
flat minor
seventh, B
flat dominant
seventh,
B flat minor
7 flat 5, B flat
diminished
seventh,
and B flat
minor-major
seventh.

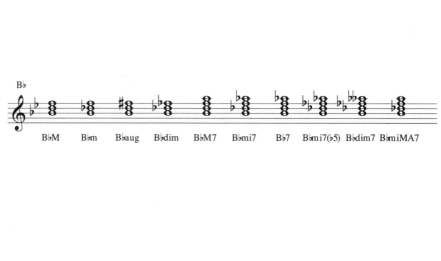

C

Play Track 72 on the CD to hear the triads and sevenths of C.

C flat

Note that C flat is an enharmonic equivalent of B. The chords here will sound exactly like the B chords, but in the interest of being complete, we have included C flat as well.

Play Track 73 on the CD to hear the triads and sevenths of C flat.

Figure 13-37:
C major, C minor, C augmented, C diminished, C major seventh, C minor seventh, C dominant seventh, C minor 7 flat 5, C diminished seventh, and C minor-major seventh.

Figure 13-38:
C flat major, C flat minor, C flat augmented, C flat diminished, C flat major seventh, C flat minor seventh, C flat dominant seventh, C flat minor 7 flat 5, C flat diminished seventh, and C flat minor-major seventh.

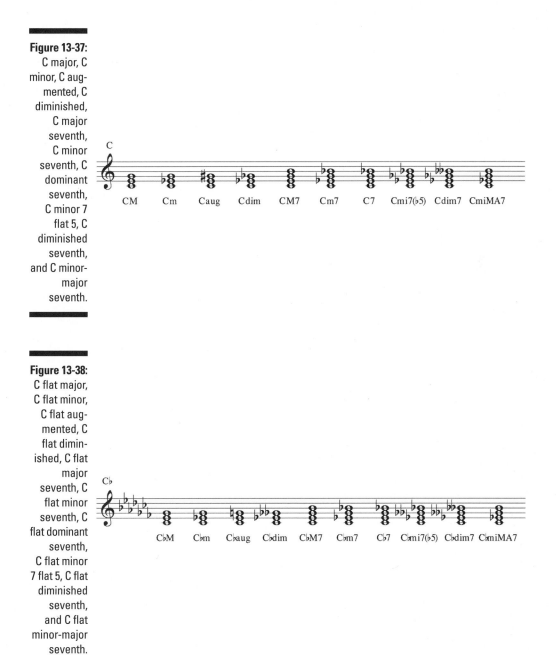

ON THE CD

C sharp

Play Track 74 on the CD to hear the triads and sevenths of C sharp.

Figure 13-39:
C sharp major, C sharp minor, C sharp augmented, C sharp diminished, C sharp major seventh, C sharp minor seventh, C sharp dominant seventh, C sharp minor 7 flat 5, C sharp diminished seventh, and C sharp minor-major seventh.

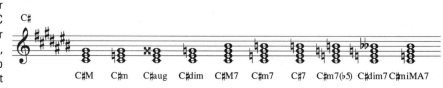

C#M   C#m   C#aug   C#dim   C#M7   C#m7   C#7   C#m7(♭5)   C#dim7 C#miMA7

ON THE CD

D

Play Track 75 on the CD to hear the triads and sevenths of D.

ON THE CD

D flat

Play Track 76 on the CD to hear the triads and sevenths of D flat.

Figure 13-40:
D major,
D minor, D
augmented,
D dimin-
ished,
D major
seventh,
D minor
seventh,
D dominant
seventh,
D minor
7 flat 5, D
diminished
seventh, and
D minor-
major
seventh.

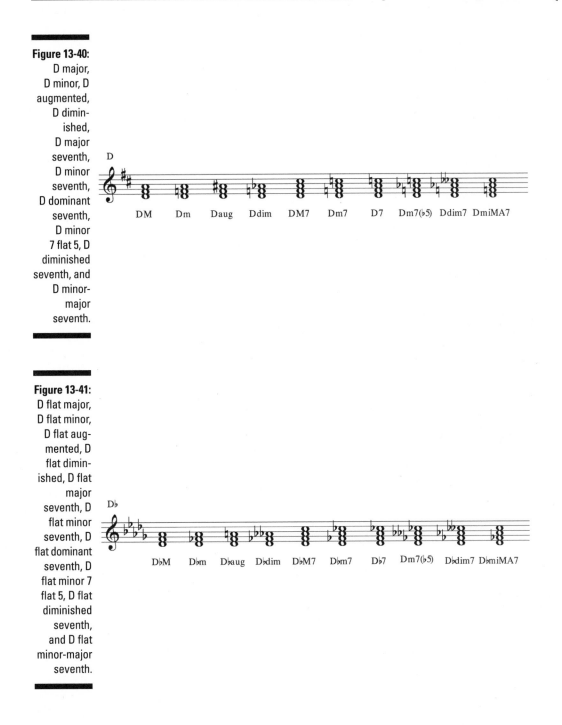

Figure 13-41:
D flat major,
D flat minor,
D flat aug-
mented, D
flat dimin-
ished, D flat
major
seventh, D
flat minor
seventh, D
flat dominant
seventh, D
flat minor 7
flat 5, D flat
diminished
seventh,
and D flat
minor-major
seventh.

E

Figure 13-42:
E major,
E minor, E
augmented,
E dimin-
ished,
E major
seventh,
E minor
seventh, E
dominant
seventh, E
minor 7 flat 5,
E diminished
seventh, and
E minor-
major
seventh.

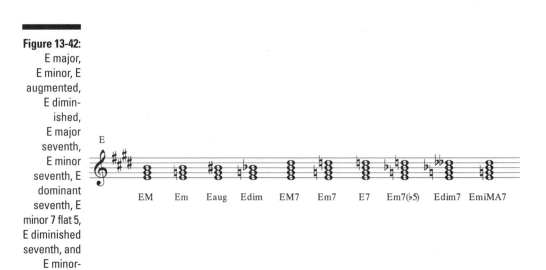

Figure 13-42: E major, E minor, E augmented, E diminished, E major seventh, E minor seventh, E dominant seventh, E minor 7 flat 5, E diminished seventh, and E minor-major seventh.

EM   Em   Eaug   Edim   EM7   Em7   E7   Em7(♭5)   Edim7   EmiMA7

Play Track 77 on the CD to hear the triads and sevenths of E.

E flat

Play Track 78 on the CD to hear the triads and sevenths of E flat.

F

Play Track 79 on the CD to hear the triads and sevenths of F.

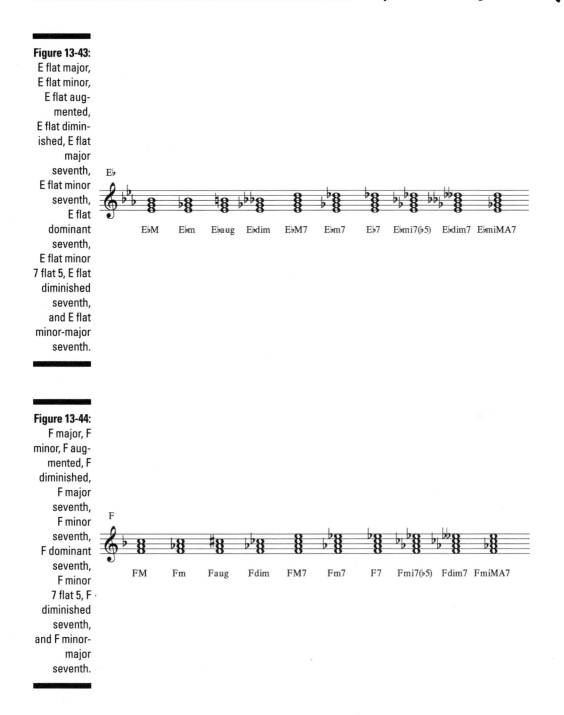

Figure 13-43:
E flat major, E flat minor, E flat augmented, E flat diminished, E flat major seventh, E flat minor seventh, E flat dominant seventh, E flat minor 7 flat 5, E flat diminished seventh, and E flat minor-major seventh.

Figure 13-44:
F major, F minor, F augmented, F diminished, F major seventh, F minor seventh, F dominant seventh, F minor 7 flat 5, F diminished seventh, and F minor-major seventh.

F sharp

Figure 13-45:
F sharp major, F sharp minor, F sharp augmented, F sharp diminished, F sharp major seventh, F sharp minor seventh, F sharp dominant seventh, F sharp minor 7 flat 5, F sharp diminished seventh, and F sharp minor-major seventh.

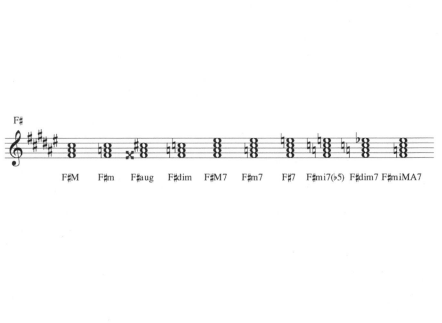

F#M   F#m   F#aug   F#dim   F#M7   F#m7   F#7   F#mi7(♭5)   F#dim7   F#miMA7

Play Track 80 on the CD to hear the triads and sevenths of F sharp.

G

Play Track 81 on the CD to hear the triads and sevenths of G.

G flat

Play Track 82 on the CD to hear the triads and sevenths of G flat.

Figure 13-46:
G major, G minor, G augmented, G diminished, G major seventh, G minor seventh, G dominant seventh, G minor 7 flat 5, G diminished seventh, and G minor-major seventh.

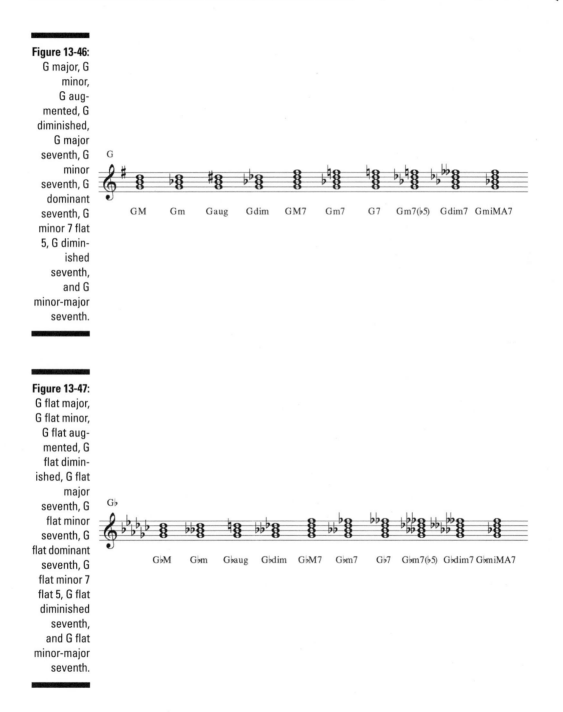

Figure 13-47:
G flat major, G flat minor, G flat augmented, G flat diminished, G flat major seventh, G flat minor seventh, G flat dominant seventh, G flat minor 7 flat 5, G flat diminished seventh, and G flat minor-major seventh.

Voicing and Inversion

Here's a riddle: When is a triad not a perfect little stack of thirds built on top of a root?

Answer: when its *voicing* is *open*, or when it's *inverted*.

Open and close voicing

Sometimes, the notes of a triad are spread out over two or more octaves, with the different parts rearranged so that, for example, the root may carry the highest sounding note, or the third, or the fifth can carry the lowest sounding note. The notes are still the same (C, E, G, for example) — they're just located an octave or even octaves above or below where you would expect them in a normal triad.

When all the notes of a chord are in the same octave, the chord is considered to be in a *closed voicing*.

Figure 13-48 shows a C major chord with closed voicing.

Figure 13-48:
C major
chord with
closed
voicing.

CM

The chord in Figure 13-49, however, is *also* a C major chord, but with *open voicing*.

Both chords in Figures 13-48 and 13-49 have the same notes contained in the triad, but in the latter case the third has been raised a full octave from its closed position. Both chords are still considered to be in the *root position*, because the root note, C, is still the lowest note of the triad.

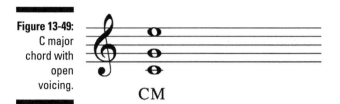

Figure 13-49:
C major
chord with
open
voicing.

Inverted chords

If the lowest-sounding pitch of a chord is *not* the root, then the chord is considered to be *inverted*.

First inversion

If the third of a chord is the lowest-sounding note, then the chord is in *first inversion*.

Figure 13-50 shows our C major chord in first inversion, with closed (same octave) and open (different octaves) voicing.

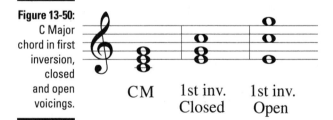

Figure 13-50:
C Major
chord in first
inversion,
closed
and open
voicings.

Second inversion

When the fifth of a chord is the lowest-sounding note, the chord is in *second inversion*.

Here's our C Major chord in second inversion (Figure 13-51).

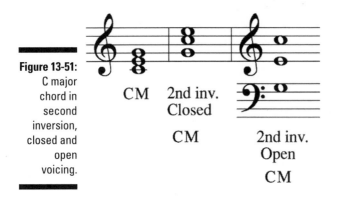

CM   2nd inv.
      Closed

      CM

2nd inv.
Open

CM

Third inversion

When a seventh of a chord is the lowest-sounding note, then that chord is in *third inversion.*

So, how do you identify inverted chords? Simple: they are not arranged in stacks of thirds. To find out which chord it is, you have to rearrange the chord into thirds again. There's only one way to rearrange a chord into thirds, so there's no real guessing on the order of the notes. It just may take a little patience.

Look at, for instance, the three inverted chords shown in Figure 13-52.

If we try moving the notes up or down octaves, to rearrange them so that they're all suddenly in stacks of thirds, they end up looking look like Figure 13-53 instead.

Figure 13-53:
Rearranging
the inverted
chords
shows them
to be an F
sharp major
triad, a G
diminished
seventh,
and a D
major triad.

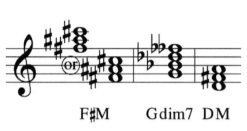

F♯M   Gdim7 DM

From rearranging the chords, you can tell that the first example was an F sharp major in second inversion, because the fifth was the lowest-sounding note in the chord. The second example was a G diminished seventh, also in second inversion, because the fifth of the chord was at the bottom of the stack. The third example was a D major triad in first inversion, because the third of the chord was the lowest-sounding note.

This chapter covered a lot, we know. But look at it this way: now you know how to build chords! Or at least you know where to come back to when you're scratching your head over them.

But building chords is only half the battle. You have to know where to put which ones, which is what Chapter 14 is all about.

Chapter 14

Chord Progressions

*U*p until now, we've talked a lot about the building blocks of music: rhythm, reading notes, the scales, key signatures, and finally, building chords. But although all this stuff is really handy for reading other people's music, it doesn't really tell you anything about how all these things come together to make music, or how you can go about writing your own.

Well, hold on — we're almost there. Here's where we start to put it all together for you, after giving you just one more set of tools.

Diatonic Triads

One key point you should be able to get from previous chapters is that the key signature of a piece of Western music governs everything within that piece. You could, theoretically, have dozens of octaves' worth of notes on the instrument in front of you, but only the notes allowed by the key signature can be used in that piece of music.

Therefore, if you have a song written in C major, the only eight notes that will appear in any order or assemblage in the song are C, D, E, F, G, A, and B (with the odd sharp or flat thrown in as rare exceptions allowed by accidentals). If your song is written in A major, the only notes appearing in that song will be A, B, C sharp, D, E, F sharp, and G sharp (again, with possible accidentals). The chords will also be made of some combination of these seven notes for each key.

Diatonic chords, chromatic chords, and minor scale modes

Chords built on the seven notes of a major key signature are called *diatonic chords*. Chords that are built out of notes *outside* of the key signature are called *chromatic chords*.

Minor keys get a little trickier, because there are potentially *nine* notes that fit under a single minor key signature, when you take the melodic and harmonic minor scales into consideration (review Chapter 12 if you're unclear on these kinds of minor scales).

Because the natural, melodic, and harmonic scales are taught as separate scales for musicians to practice, there's often the misconception that you have to stick to *one* of these types of minor scales when composing music. Alas, for those of us who like nice, simple rules to build our music against, this just isn't so.

The easiest way to think about chords built on minor keys is to recognize there really is just one minor scale per key signature, but one facet of minor keys is the flexible nature of the sixth and seventh degrees of the scale.

There are two ways, called *modes*, that the sixth and seventh degrees can be in the scale, depending on the composer's whimsy. Often, those two different versions of those degrees, or modes, will appear in the same piece of music. The minor scale therefore has potentially nine notes in it, as shown in Figure 14-1.

Figure 14-1:
The A minor
scale,
including
harmonic
and melodic
mode steps.

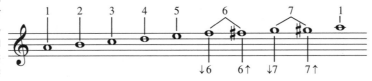

Notice how the use of arrows indicates where the sixth and seventh degrees are either raised (up arrow) or unaltered (down arrow).

Major triad progressions within a key

When triads are used in an organized series, they're called *progressions*. And it's chord progressions that make up pretty much all of Western harmonic music.

Because the name of a chord comes from its root note, it's only natural that the root of each chord located within a scale would also carry the scale degree with its name. In other words, a chord's name tells us what the chord is, based on the root note, whereas a chord's *number* tells us what the chord does, based on key.

For example, let's take our handy C major scale again. Each note of the C major scale is assigned a scale degree number and name, like so:

Scale degree number and name	Note
1 Tonic	C
2 Supertonic	D
3 Mediant	E
4 Subdominant	F
5 Dominant	G
6 Submediant	A
7 Leading tone	B
8/1 Tonic	C

When you build triads within the C major scale, each triad is assigned the scale degree of the root in its name, as shown in Figure 14-2.

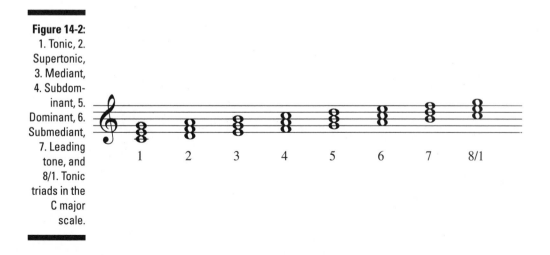

Figure 14-2: 1. Tonic, 2. Supertonic, 3. Mediant, 4. Subdominant, 5. Dominant, 6. Submediant, 7. Leading tone, and 8/1. Tonic triads in the C major scale.

As you can see in Figure 14-2, the *subdominant* triad is called that because the chord is built on the fourth scale degree. The *leading tone* triad is called that because the chord is built on the seventh scale degree.

When breaking down a piece of music based on chord progressions, roman numerals are used to represent the different scale degrees. Major chords in the progression have their roman numerals capitalized, and minor chords have their roman numerals lowercased. There are also special characters that indicate whether the chord is diminished (°) or augmented (+), as the following table shows:

Triad type	Roman numeral	Example
Major	Uppercase	V
Minor	Lowercase	ii
Diminished	Lowercase with °	vii°
Augmented	Uppercase with a +	III+

So, using roman numerals, our chart for chord progressions in the C major scale would actually look like this:

Scale degree number/name	Note
I Tonic	C
ii Supertonic	D
iii Mediant	E
IV Subdominant	F
V Dominant	G
vi Submediant	A
vii° Leading tone	B
(I) Tonic	C

Because the leading tone is a diminished triad, it has the little ° symbol next to its roman numeral.

Figure 14-3 takes a look at that C major scale again, this time with the chords' names according to the root of each triad written underneath them. Note the capital *M* in the chord's shorthand name (such as CM) stands for major, and the lowercase *m* (such as Em) stands for minor.

Figure 14-3:
Triads
contained
within the
key of C
major.

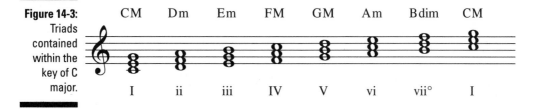

As you can see in Figure 14-3, the chord progression naturally follows the pattern of ascending the scale starting with the tonic note, in this case C. Figure 14-4 tests this on another major key, this time E flat.

Figure 14-4:
Triads
contained
within the
key of E flat
major.

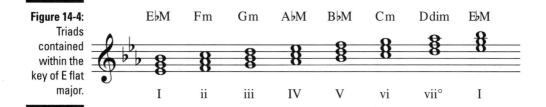

The eight notes that make up the key of E flat major are used produce the eight chords shown in Figure 14-4.

Minor triad progressions within a key

When dealing with minor keys, unfortunately, the construction of triads is a lot more involved. Recall (from Chapter 12) the fact that the sixth and seventh degrees of the scale are variable, depending on whether the music's in the natural minor, harmonic minor, or melodic minor keys. This means that for nearly all minor triads, there are more possibilities for building chords in the sixth and seventh degrees than in the major scale.

Therefore, if you're looking at a piece of music written in C minor, the possible chords within that key are the ones in Figure 14-5.

Figure 14-5:
Possible
triads within
the key of
C minor.

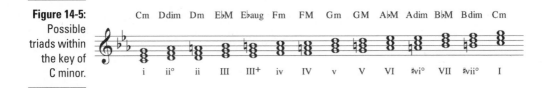

Although any of the chords from Figure 14-5 are *possible*, the most common choices made by traditional composers are those shown in Figure 14-6.

Figure 14-6:
The most
common
scale
degrees
used in
C minor.

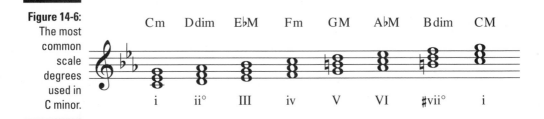

Notice in Figure 14-6 that the supertonic and the leading tone triads are diminished, resulting in a combination of the natural, harmonic, and melodic scales in coming up with this set of chords.

You may find it helpful to remember that, with the raised seventh degree, the fifth (V) and seventh (vii°) degrees of both major and minor scales of the same letter name are identical.

Sevenths

Of course, we can't forget all the seventh chords (you may want to peek back at Chapter 13 for a refresher on seventh chords). When you add the additional seventh above the regular triad, you end up with a combination of the triad's chord symbols *and* the seventh's.

There's one more symbol that you need to learn when dealing with seventh progressions (Figure 14-7). This symbol is used to indicate a *minor 7 flat 5 chord*, also sometimes called a *half-diminished seventh*.

Figure 14-7:
This symbol means the chord is a minor 7 flat 5 chord.

Ø

The roman numerals we use to describe sevenths chords are as follows:

Seventh chord type	Roman numeral	Example
Major 7th	Uppercase with M7	IM^7
Major minor 7th	Uppercase with a 7	IV^7
Minor 7th	Lowercase with a 7	iii^7
Minor 7 flat 5	Lowercase with ø	$ii^ø$
Diminished 7th	Lowercase with °	$vii°$

Figure 14-8 shows the seventh chords based on C major.

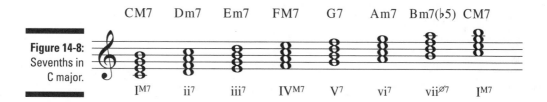

Figure 14-8:
Sevenths in C major.

CM7   Dm7   Em7   FM7   G7   Am7   Bm7(♭5)   CM7

I^{M7} ii^7 iii^7 IV^{M7} V^7 vi^7 $vii^{ø7}$ I^{M7}

There are a possible 16 *minor* seventh chords in a key, taking into consideration the natural, harmonic, and melodic scales. The seven shown in Figure 14-9 are the most commonly used.

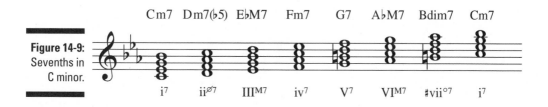

Figure 14-9:
Sevenths in C minor.

Cm7   Dm7(♭5)   E♭M7   Fm7   G7   A♭M7   Bdim7   Cm7

i^7 $ii^{ø7}$ III^{M7} iv^7 V^7 VI^{M7} $♯vii^{°7}$ i^7

Table 14-1 collects in one place the major, minor, and seventh chord symbols.

Table 14-1	Major and Minor Scale Triads and Seventh Chords						
Major scale triads:	I	ii	iii	IV	V	vi	#vii°
Minor scale triads:	i	ii°	III	iv	V	VI	vii°
Rare minor chords:		ii	III+	IV	v	#vi°	VII
Major 7th chords:	IM7	ii7	iii7	IVM7	V7	vi7	viiø
Minor 7th chords:	i7	iiø7	IIIM7	iv7	V7	VIM7	#vii°7

Lead Sheets, Fake Books, and Tabs

If you've ever picked up a *fake book* (and there are thousands and thousands of these out there), then you've seen lead sheets. They provide just enough information for a performer to play a song competently by providing the lead melody line and noting the basic chords beneath the melody lines to fill out the harmony, either with a straight chord or with improvisation.

Figure 14-10 shows a short example.

Figure 14-10: A sample of a lead sheet.

EM   Em   Edim   EM7

Fake books are great for both working on note reading and improvising within a key. Often, for guitar fake books, the lead sheets go so far as to even draw the chords out for you by the use of *tablature*, or *tabs*.

You've been looking at guitar tabs in this book already. Figure 14-11 shows the guitar tab for an E major chord.

When reading guitar tabs, you just put your fingers on the guitar fret board where the little black dots are, and presto — you've got your chord. Guitar tabs in lead sheets also have the name of the chord written right next to the tab, making it even easier to either improvise or anticipate the notes that might logically be in the melody line.

E

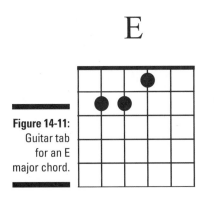

Figure 14-11:
Guitar tab
for an E
major chord.

Putting It All Together: Chord Progression

We've probably thrown more numbers at you in this chapter than any other single chapter, and for this, we apologize. Unless, of course, you *like* numbers, and to those who harbor a deep, Pythagorean love of all things mathematical, then this is your lucky day.

As you may have guessed, maybe while reading this book, constructing music is about as far from randomly throwing notes together as writing a book is from randomly pulling letters out of a Scrabble bag. There are about as many rules to putting a song together as there are to putting a sentence together, and we're about to show you a few more.

When you analyze the bulk of Western harmonic music, you start to see certain patterns emerge in the ways chord progressions are built. It is *possible* for any one chord to progress to any one of the other chords in a key; however, certain chord progressions are used more frequently than others. Why? Because they sound better. These are obviously natural patterns that are pleasing to listeners and composers alike, because the same patterns continuously appear in popular music, classical, rock, jazz, and so on.

You can bet music theorists have taken note of those patterns and come up with a set of rules concerning chord progressions. These rules are immensely helpful in songwriting. Tables 14-2 and 14-3 show common chord progressions for major and minor chords.

Don't forget: major key signatures can contain minor chords, and minor key signatures can contain major chords.

Table 14-2	Common Major Key Chord Progressions
Chord	**Leads to**
I	Can appear anywhere and lead anywhere
ii	V or vii° chords
iii	IV or vi chords
IV	ii, V, or vii° chords
V	vi chords
vi	ii, iii, IV, or V chords
vii°	I chord

Table 14-3	Common Minor Key Chord Progressions
Chord	**Leads to**
i chords	Can appear anywhere and lead anywhere
ii° (ii) chords	V(v) or vii°(VII) chords
III(III+) chords	iv (IV), VI (#vi°), or vii°(VI) chords
iv (IV) chords	V(v) or vii°(VII) chords
V(v) chords	VI (#vi°) chords
VI (#vi°)chords	III(III+), iv(IV), V(v), or vii°(VII) chords
vii° (VII) chords	i chord

Any of the triads in Tables 14-2 and 14-3 with a seventh added on is also acceptable in that triad's numbered place as well.

The parenthetical chords in the preceding tables are the less-commonly used, but still acceptable, chords that would work in the progression.

Let's take a look at some musical examples so you can see these rules in action. Take note that when we talk about *chords* in music, we're not only talking about the stacked triads and sevenths; we're talking about the individual notes that make up the chords as well.

Our first example is Brahms's "Lullaby," a portion of which is shown in Figure 14-12.

Figure 14-12:
First four measures of Brahms's "Lullaby."

Notice that the first three measures of the song use the notes found in the D major triad (D, F sharp, and A), making D major our I chord.

In the fourth measure, the first chord of the measure is a D Major (two Ds, treble and bass clef). The second beat of the measure, the notes C sharp, A, and F sharp come up in an open triad, meaning that we've now progressed to a iii chord. The third beat of the fourth measure is made up of the three of the four notes of a B minor seventh chord, or a vi7 chord.

Judging from the common chord progression we saw in Table 14-2, our next chord would have to be either a ii, iii, IV, or a V chord. See Figure 14-13 to find out what Brahms did.

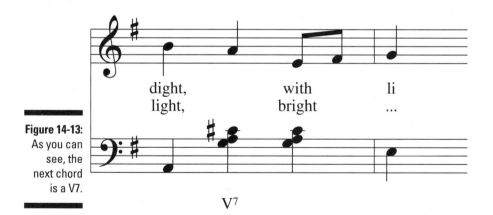

Figure 14-13:
As you can see, the next chord is a V7.

Remember, seventh chords work, too. In this case a V7 is just as acceptable as a V chord would be.

The next example (Figure 14-14) is a lead sheet for the traditional English folk song "Scarborough Fair." Less traditional versions of some of the chords in the minor scale are used here: the II, III, IV, and VII chords. The pattern of progression still holds, though: The i chord leads to the VII chord, the II to the III to the IV, and then another II to the VII chord. The I/i chord can appear anywhere in a piece of music — and, in this one, it certainly does.

Like everything in music and art in general, you are the creator of your work, and you can decide whether you want to follow the rules are try something completely different. However, Tables 14-2 and 14-3 do make a very good launch pad for familiarizing yourself on how chords fit against one another. Just for fun, try playing, or just listening to, the chord progressions on the CD listed below to get a feel of how easy it can be to build a great song — or at least a halfway decent pop song.

Play Track 83 to hear the I-V-I (G Major-D Major-G Major) chord progression in G major.

Play Track 84 to hear the I-ii-V-I-iii-V-vii°-I (CM-Dm-GM-CM-Em-GM-Bdim-CM) chord progression in C major.

Figure 14-14: Lead sheet for "Scarborough Fair."

Play Track 85 to hear the i-iv-V-VI-iv-vii°-i (Fm-Bflatm-CM-DflatM-Bflatm-Edim-Fm) chord progression in F minor.

Play Track 86 to hear the i-III-VI-III-VII-i-v7-i (Am-CM-FM-CM-GM-Am-Em7-Am) chord progression in A minor.

A Quick Word on Modulation

Sometimes a piece of music temporarily moves into a new key. This is called *modulation*. It is very common in traditional classical music, and long symphony and concerto movements almost always spend at least some time in a different key, usually a closely related key such as the relative minor or relative major of the original key. The key signature of these pieces of music will remain the same, of course, but the I/I, II/ii, III/iii (and so on) chords will be completely different, leading to a completely different set of chord progressions.

If you find that the a piece of music suddenly contains chord progressions that you would not expect in that key, it may be that the piece has modulated. Lots of accidentals, or even an new key signature stuck in the middle of a piece, are other clues that the music has modulated.

A favorite way for modulating current pop music is to simply move the key up one whole step, for example, from F major to G major. So long as you remember to keep your key signatures straight, dealing with modulation within a piece is usually not a problem.

Chapter 15

Cadence

In This Chapter

▶ Getting the real story on authentic cadences

▶ Playing with plagal cadences

▶ Uncovering deceptive cadences

▶ Knowing the half of it: half-cadences

*J*ust as most music follows a basic pulse set forth by the time signature, most Western music also follows a pulse of tension and release through changing chord progressions. A *cadence* is any place in a piece of music that has the feel of an ending. This can be either a strong, definite stopping point, like at the end of a song, or even just a movement or section, but cadence also refers to the short pause that comes at the end of individual musical phrases.

A piece of music can come to an end by simply stopping, of course, but if that stopping position doesn't "make sense" to the listeners, they're not going to be very happy with it. Ending a song on the wrong note or notes is like ending a conversation mid-sentence, and most listeners react with dissatisfaction at a song simply stopping instead of ending properly.

A more universally satisfying ending is usually provided by giving clues in the music, through chord progressions (see Chapter 14), that let the listener know the end is coming up. Like the ending of a story (or a sentence, paragraph, chapter, or book), an ending in music "makes sense" if it follows certain constraints in "grammar" and delivery. As with the customs for storytelling, these expectations can be different in different musical genres or traditions.

Of course, if you're writing music, you don't *have* to follows any of the rules of cadence, including the rules designed to provide a certain level of comfort and satisfaction for your listeners. But if you don't, be prepared for angry, torch-wielding mobs to follow you home after your performances, and don't say we didn't warn you.

The basic foundation of most music is what we call a *harmonic goal*, where a phrase starts at a I chord and follows a series of chord progressions to end up at an IV or a V chord, depending on the type of cadence used in the song (see Chapters 13 and 14 for more on the different types of chords).

A song can have two chords or a hundred chords; it can be a 3-second song or a 45-minute song, but eventually, it *will* reach that harmonic goal of the IV or V chord before going back down to the I chord.

There is a continuum of tension and release that moves through music, with the I chord being the point of rest or release, and every chord leading up to the return to the I chord being points of tension.

The two-chord progression between the V chord, or the IV chord, and the I chord, is the *cadence*.

There only four types of cadences commonly used in Western harmonic music:

- ✔ Authentic cadence
- ✔ Plagal cadence
- ✔ Deceptive cadence
- ✔ Half cadence

When you really think about it, the entire history of Western music can be summed up by I-V-I or I-IV-I. From the Baroque period to rock and roll, this formula holds pretty darned true. What's really amazing is that this simple formula has resulted in so many songs that sound so different from one another. That's because the notes and chords in a key signature can be arranged in so many different ways.

Authentic Cadences

Authentic cadences are the most obvious-sounding cadences and are therefore considered the strongest. In an authentic cadence, the harmonic goal of a musical phrase, or section of music that starts with a I/i chord and ends with a cadence, is the V chord (or v, depending on whether the song's in a major or minor key), and cadence occurs when you move from that V/v chord to an I/i chord. The phrase involved in the authentic cadence essentially ends at the V/v chord, and the song either ends completely there or starts a new phrase with the I/i chord.

Beethoven was particularly keen on using authentic cadences in his music, as shown in Figure 15-1, a section from his "Ode to Joy."

Listen to Track 87 on the CD for an example of an authentic cadence.

There are two types of authentic cadences that are used in music:

✔ Perfect authentic cadence (PAC)

✔ Imperfect authentic cadence (IAC)

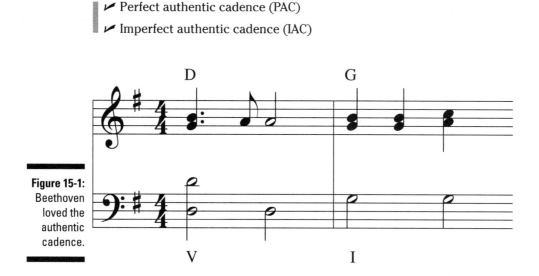

Figure 15-1:
Beethoven
loved the
authentic
cadence.

Perfect authentic cadence

In a PAC, as it's often called by acronym-loving music theorists, the two chords that make up the cadence are both in their *root* positions, meaning (as we discuss in Chapter 13) that the note on the bottom of the stack is the root, the note the chord is named after.

The very strongest PAC occurs when the second chord, the I/i chord, has the root of the chord on both the bottom *and* the top of the stack of notes — this makes for a very high-impact sort of end to a song. Beethoven's "Ode to Joy" ends with just that type of cadence (Figure 15-2).

Figure 15-2:
A perfect
authentic
cadence
(PAC).

Listen to Track 88 on the CD for an example of a perfect authentic cadence.

Note in Figure 15-2 how the top note on the I chord is the same as the bottom note in the bass clef, making the root of the chord both the highest and lowest-pitched note of the chord. Also note that there is no fifth in that final chord, which means it isn't really a triad. The first and third, though, still make it sound almost like a major triad.

Imperfect authentic cadence

Every other V-I chord progression is called an *imperfect authentic cadence* (IAC), and it's basically anything that isn't a perfect authentic cadence.

For example, the V/v chord could be in some inversion. In the I/i chord shown in Figure 15-3, or there's a melody note moving between the chords. The difference between a PAC and an IAC is illustrated in Figure 15-3.

Figure 15-3: Difference between a PAC and an IAC. Note how the PAC ends with the root of the chord in the root position, whereas the IAC ends with an inverted chord.

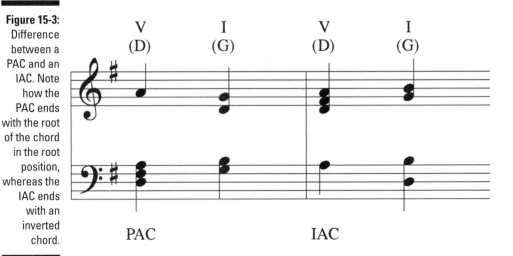

Listen to Track 89 on the CD to hear the difference between a perfect authentic cadence and an imperfect authentic cadence.

Plagal Cadences

The harmonic goal of a *plagal* cadence is ultimately the 4 (IV/iv) chord, with cadence occurring when that chord moves to the 1 (I/i) chord. Possibilities include IV-I, iv-i, iv-I, and IV-i.

This structure originated with medieval church music, mostly vocal music, and is therefore often referred to as the *Amen cadence*. If you're familiar with Gregorian chants at all, or even many modern hymns, then you've heard the Amen cadence in action. It usually happens, not surprisingly, at the point where the chanters sing the two-chord "A-men."

"Amazing Grace" contains a great example of a plagal cadence (Figure 15-4). Where would *American Idol* be without this classic gem?

Listen to Track 90 on the CD to hear an example of a plagal cadence.

Figure 15-4:
A plagal cadence in "Amazing Grace."

Plagal cadences are usually used within a song to end a phrase, instead of at the very end of a song, because they're not as decisive-sounding as perfect cadences are.

Figure 15-5 shows two more examples of plagal cadences.

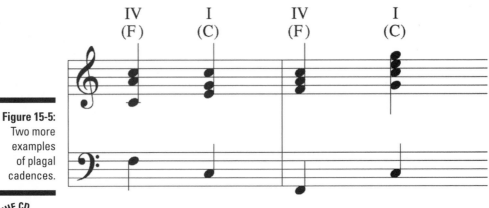

Figure 15-5:
Two more
examples
of plagal
cadences.

Listen to Track 91 to hear two more examples of plagal cadences.

Deceptive Cadences

A *deceptive* cadence (sometimes called an *interrupted* cadence) essentially reaches an ultimate point of tension on a V/v chord, just like the authentic cadence, but then it resolves to something other than the tonic (I/i) chord. Hence the name *deceptive*. You think you're about to return to the I chord, but then you don't.

The most common deceptive cadence, used 99 times out 100, is when you have a V/v chord that moves up to a VI/vi chord. The phrase looks and feels like it's about to end and close with the I chord, but instead it moves up to the VI instead, as shown in Figure 15-6.

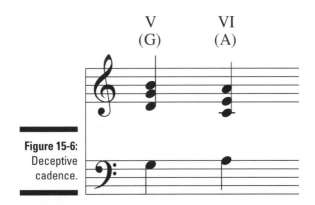

Figure 15-6:
Deceptive
cadence.

Listen to Track 92 to hear an example of a deceptive cadence.

A deceptive cadence can lead from the V/v chord to any other chord *other* than an I/i chord. The VI or vi is just the most common second chord used in deceptive cadences. Deceptive cadences are considered one of the weakest cadences because they invoke a feeling of incompleteness.

Half-Cadence

With a *half-cadence*, the musical phrase ends *at* the point of tension, the V/v chord itself. It basically plays to a V chord and stops, resulting in a musical phrase that feels unfinished. This is why it's called a half-cadence, because it just doesn't feel like it's done yet.

Steve Reich, composer, on knowing when a song is done

Steve Reich (composer): When I start out, I always have a rough idea of how much time I have to work with a piece of music, whether it's going to be a long piece of a short piece of music. And that's often dependent on whoever's commissioning the piece. Exactly how long it is, how many minutes it ends up being — that's worked out by musical intuition, which is the rock-bottom foundation of composing music for me, and, I think, for most composers. In other words, you sketch out the number of movements you're going to have, and the basic harmonies you're going to be using to get through the movements, and the rest is worked out in detail largely by intuition, by listening to the music itself.

Barry Adamson (Nick Cave and The Bad Seeds): I guess there's a point where all the criteria are satisfied, and also, sometimes there's an immediate feeling that you didn't write the song, that it's something perfect and separate from yourself, because now you're hearing the finished thing and you can't remember how it was put together.

Momus (a.k.a. Nick Currie): I work very quickly. Concept, lyrical notes, chord structure, bass line, percussion, more arrangement, vocal, mix. It's usually all done in one ultra-concentrated session of perhaps eight hours. A day's work. It's finished when you get the mix you like, simple as that. It's important to me not to leave things open. I like to make quick decisions, and bring things to a conclusion. This is probably one reason I'm so prolific.

John Hughes III (soundtrack composer): With me? I don't know. I think that's the biggest problem for me. I know, with other musicians, too, it's just sort of not knowing when to stop. So, usually, I usually feel my best stuff is the stuff I don't feel like I have to keep working on. Usually, if there's something that I keep on adding stuff to, and changing it over and over, it's probably already dead, and the core of it just isn't right. Usually, my favorite stuff, I'll get done really quick, and the longer I dwell on it — I don't know if it's just because I get sick of it or what — but you just kind of know when something's done.

Mika Vainio (Pan Sonic): When we feel that the song is bearable.

The most common form of half- cadence occurs when the V chord is preceded by the I chord in second inversion. This pattern produces two chords with the same bass note, as seen in Figure 15-7.

Listen to Track 93 to hear an example of a half-cadence.

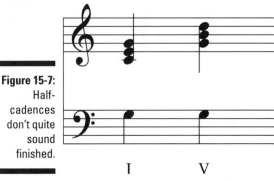

Figure 15-7:
Half-
cadences
don't quite
sound
finished.

I   V

Part IV
Form: How It's Shaped

"Jake never knew how to end a song."

In this part . . .

In this part, you discover how and why different kinds of music are structured as they are. From the smallest phrases of music through whole symphonies, structure is very important. In the big picture, from classical to rock, blues, and jazz, music comes in numerous, distinct forms and genres, and here is where you get acquainted with them.

Chapter 16

The Elements of Form

Contemplate the doily. Many types of stitches and knots are used to construct a whole doily, with perhaps hundreds of different techniques being responsible for the invention and evolution of each piece of the pattern. However, unless you're really into constructing doilies yourself, you really don't care, or care to know, that more than 600 years of history and shared knowledge went into constructing that round, lacy thing your grandmother sets under her coffee cup to protect the woodwork.

As you may have gathered from previous chapters, a piece of music is a lot like that doily. (If you're uncomfortable with the doily analogy, try a fine-tuned diesel engine instead, and all the little metal bits that work together to make those big trucks go.)

The casual pianist who pounds out Christmas carols once a year prob-ably doesn't think much about how every single piece of written music contains more that 7,000 years worth of speculation, theory, and technique. The notation of pitches and rhythm on the musical staff, the concepts of harmony and melody, and even the tuning system we use to synchronize our instruments has been a long, massive undertaking of science, art, and aesthetics. Understanding and notating music has been as much a part of the human experience as the development of the written word.

Form versus Genre

When we talk about musical *form*, what we're talking about is the blueprint used to create a specific type of music. For example, if you wanted to write a sonata, there is a very specific blueprint you would use to construct that piece of music. Although things like the basic melody, theme, and key signature would be entirely up to you, the way the sonata as a whole fits together — the beginning, middle, and ending — is set right from the very beginning by the constraints of the sonata *form* itself.

In many ways, knowing how form works makes things extremely easy for a composer. After all, the pattern's already there — you just have to fill in the blanks. The downside is that is that there is a real challenge to making your *particular* sonata, fugue, or concerto stand out from every other piece of music written in that form.

Classical music is usually classified by form, and most of the forms used in classical music were established by the middle of the 19th century.

The true exceptions to this are the New Classical forms invented between 1900 and 1950, such as musique concrete and minimalism.

There's a lot of crossover between the definitions of form and genre. *Genre* is usually used to describe modern music, especially when it comes to breaking down the different types of rock and jazz. It's all a matter of perspective, because when you really think about it, hip-hop, gospel, heavy metal, country, and reggae are as specific in "form" as minuets, fugues, sonatas, and rondos.

The problem with classifying modern "forms" is that new music is still evolving, whereas pre-1950 classical forms are pretty much established. It is entirely possible that students of music form in the 21st century will be studying anti-4/4 math-rock pioneers like Steve Albini alongside the composers Philip Glass and Beethoven.

Before we begin discussing the actual building blocks of musical form — phrases, periods, themes, and so on — let's take a look at some of the generative forces behind music.

Rhythm

Yes, there's a whole part of this book already on this subject, but you can't talk about form without talking about rhythm one more time. Rhythm is the most basic element of musical form. You can write a piece of music without a melody line or without harmonic accompaniment, but there's just no way around writing a piece of music with rhythm — unless, of course, your "music" is one single, sustained note with no variations in pitch.

Often, it's the rhythm that differentiates one form from another — such as the difference between alternative rock and punk rock, say. Put a faster tempo to any Son Volt or Wilco song, and you can file the result in the same section of the record store as The Ramones and The Sex Pistols. Change the inherent rhythm patterns of a song, even a Sex Pistols song, and you can make it into anything from a tango to a waltz. Rhythm is *that* important.

Rhythm moves through music as a generative force in several different ways. First of all, of course, it creates the basic pulse of a song, as discussed in Part I of this book. Rhythm is the part of the song your toes tap along to, your head nods to, your feet move to. Meter helps organize notes into groups by use of a time signature and defines the repetitive pattern of strong and weak beats that noticeably move a song along. This pulse creates a feeling of familiarity and expectation for the listener, so that, theoretically, you can throw a pile of unexpected, jangly notes and chords at the listener and still retain a feeling of connection with your audience by holding onto them with the same, steady beat.

The actual rhythm that you hear when you listen to a song is usually referred to as the *surface rhythm*. For example, when people say they like the *beat* of a pop song, they mean they enjoy the surface rhythm, which may simply be a rhythmic pattern on the drums. Sometimes the surface rhythm matches the underlying pulse of a song — often it does, especially in pop music, where the drums and the bass lines usually follow the basic beat. But sometimes, because of *syncopation* (which emphasizes the "off" beats), the surface rhythm and the pulse don't match up.

Tempo comes into play when we discuss the speed of the piece. Is it going to move along quickly and lively? Or along somber and slowly? The speed at which a piece of music is played determines the overall feeling of the music for the audience. Rarely do you have a super-happy song played slowly and quietly, nor do you hear a super-sad song played at "Flight of the Bumblebee" speeds.

Melody

Most often, the melody is the part of the song we can't get out of our heads. The melody is the lead line of a song, the part that the harmony is built around, and the part of the song that gives as much glimpse into the emotion of a piece as the rhythm does.

Much of melody's expressive power comes from the upward or downward flow of pitch. The pitch of a song goes up, and it can make the song sound like it's either getting more tense or more lively; the pitch of a song goes down, and it can give that part of the song an increased melancholic or dark feel. The shape of the pitch's travels is called its *contour*.

There are four common *melodic contours*:

- ✔ Arch
- ✔ Wave
- ✔ Inverted arch
- ✔ Pivotal

Contour simply means that the melody is shaped a certain way; the shape of a melody is especially easy to pick out when you've got the sheet music right in front of you. The possibilities for building melodic phrases (that is, starting at the I chord, going up to the IV or V chord, and ending at the I chord) with just four basic contours are virtually infinite.

Figure 16-1 shows a stretch of music with an arch contour.

Figure 16-1: In the arch contour, the pitch of notes goes up and then down.

Note how the melody line in the treble clef first goes up in pitch from a low point to a high point, then goes back down again. Hence, *arch*. When music goes up in pitch so gradually like this, it results in an increase in tension in that section of the composition. The lower the pitch gets in such a gradual arch, the more the level of tension decreases.

Figure 16-2 shows some music with a wave contour.

Note how the melody line goes up, and down, and up again, and down — just like a series of waves. The wave contour permeates most happy-sounding pop music.

Figure 16-2:
In the wave contour, pitch goes up and down and up and down, like waves on the sea.

Figure 16-3 shows music with an inverted arch contour.

Figure 16-3 looks a lot like Figure 16-1, except the melody line is going down in pitch and then up to the end of the phrase. The phrase will therefore start out sounding relaxed and calm, but contain an increase in tension as the arch rises towards the end of the phrase.

Figure 16-3:
In the inverted arch contour, the pitch starts out high, goes down, and then up again.

Figure 16-4 shows an example of music with a pivotal contour.

Figure 16-4:
The pivotal contour revolves around a certain pitch.

A pivotal melody line essentially pivots around the central note of the piece — in the case of Figure 16-4, the E. It's a lot like a wave melody, except that the movement above and below the central note is very minimal and continuously returns to that central note. Traditional folk music uses this melodic pattern a lot.

Any melody line in a piece of music will generally fall into one of these categories of contour — try randomly picking up a piece of sheet music and trace out the melody pattern yourself, and you'll see what we mean.

The *range* of a melody is determined by the interval between the highest and lowest pitches of the song. The rise and fall of tension in a melody is often proportional to its range. Melodies with a narrow pitch range tend to have only a slight amount of musical tension in them, whereas melodies with a wide range in pitches are more likely to have a wider expressive range. As the range of pitches in a song is widened, the potential for greater levels of tension increases.

Harmony

Harmony is the part of the song that fills out the musical ideas expressed in the melody. Often, when you build a harmony based on a melodic line, you're essentially filling in the missing notes of the chord progressions used in the song.

For example, take a look at the very simple melody line shown in Figure 16-5.

Figure 16-5:
A simple melody line in the key of C.

You could fill out the harmony in Figure 16-5 by simply grabbing the notes of the I and V chords and placing them in the bass line, as shown in Figure 16-6.

To put it really simply, harmony is concerned with the building of chords, which are tones derived from the scale on which the music is based played together. Harmony also stems from the order of the chord progressions themselves, and also how a phrase resolves itself through the V-I or IV-I cadence.

Figure 16-6:
Harmony for
a melody
line in the
key of C.

Additional tension can be created in a song through harmony by creating *dissonance*, often by adding extra third intervals on top of a triad to build sevenths, ninths, and so on.

Consonant harmonies (harmonies that are aurally pleasing) are those that sound stable, such as the I chord at the end of a phrase, whereas *dissonant* harmonies (harmonies that just sound "wrong") sound unstable or seem to clash until they're resolved into consonant harmonies. Composers also use the tension between consonance and dissonance to establish a sense of a beginning and ending in a song.

Musical Phrases

A *musical phrase* is the smallest unit of music with a defined beginning that ends with a cadence.

As discussed in Chapter 15, most musical phrases consist of a beginning I chord progressing to a IV or a V chord and ending again on the I chord. Theoretically, there could be thousands of chord progressions between that first I chord and the IV or V chord — however, there's a good chance you would lose your audience in that time.

Musical phrases are like sentences in a paragraph — just as most readers don't want to wade through a thousand lines of text to find out the point of a sentence, most music audiences are listening for the musical idea expressed in a phrase and get bored if it sounds like you're just meandering between chords and not coming to a resolution.

So how long should a musical phrase be? It's really up to the composer, but generally, a phrase is usually two to four measures long. Within that space, a phrase begins, works through one or more chord progressions, and resolves itself back to the I chord.

When a composer really wants you to understand that a group of measures are to be linked together in a phrase and played as an important unit — kind of like a topic sentence in an essay — he or she links the phrase together with a curved line called a *phrase line*, as shown in Figure 16-7.

Figure 16-7:
Note the
phrase line
in the bass
clef.

Notice how the phrase both begins and ends on the I chord, or the G Major chord.

Don't confuse phrase lines with ties and slurs. A phrase line ties an entire musical phrase together, whereas slurs and ties only tie together a small part of a phrase.

Musical Periods

As we mentioned, the phrase represents the smallest unit ending with a cadence in a piece of music. The next larger unit used in musical form is the period.

Musical *periods* are created when two or three musical phrases are linked together. Generally, the first musical phrase is one that ends in a half-cadence (ending *at* the V/v chord), and the second phrase ends with an authentic cadence (ending with the V/v chord resolving to the I/i chord).

The half-cadence comes across like a comma in a sentence, with the authentic cadence, or consequent, ending the linked phrases like a period.

Figure 16-8 shows an example of a musical period.

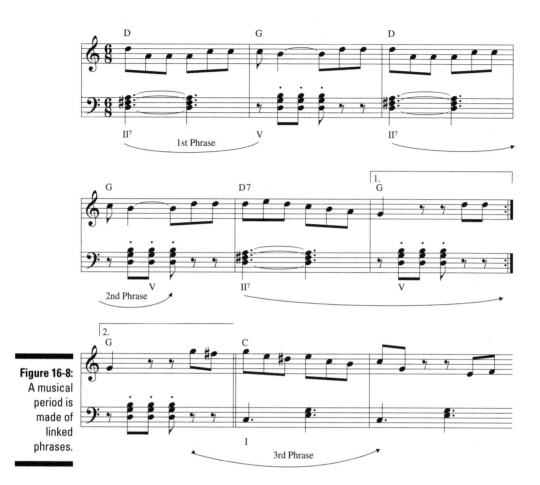

Figure 16-8: A musical period is made of linked phrases.

Musical Parts and Forms

The division of music into *parts* happens when you link two or more periods that tonally sound like they belong together. They share major harmonic focal points, similar melody lines, similar rhythm structure, and may have other resemblances.

Parts can be further linked together to create musical *forms*.

We conventionally give alphabetic labels to the musical parts within a composition: A, B, C, and so forth. If a part is repeated in a song, its letter is repeated: for example, ABA is a familiar layout in classical music, where the opening theme (labeled A), after vanishing during part B, is repeated at the end of the song.

As the *contrast form*, AB forms come in a boundless array of possibilities. There may be recurring sections, unique ones, or any combination of both. For example, a rondo — a popular form in classical music — consists of an alternation of a recurring section and others that occur one time each. A rondo, then, would be labeled ABACADA . . . (and so on).

An ongoing form, with no recurrence whatsoever, is also possible: ABCDE. . . . Any sequence of recurring and unique sections may occur.

One-part form (A)

The *one-part*, or A, form is the most primitive song structure, and is also sometimes referred to as the *air* or *ballad* form. In a one-part form, a simple melody is repeated with slight changes to either accommodate different words, as in a *strophic* song such as in "Old McDonald Had a Farm," which repeats the same musical line but changes the words with each verse.

The one-part form is mostly found in folk songs or carols or other songs that are pretty short with a limited theme and movement. As the unbroken form, A forms come only in a single variety. They may be long or short, but they are always described as A (or AA, or even AAA).

Binary form (AB)

Binary form consists of two contrasting sections that function as statement and counterstatement. The pattern may be a simple AB, as in "My Country, 'Tis of Thee," or by variation, as in the tune "Greensleeves" (AABB, with the second A meaning "variation of A").

In the binary form used in the Baroque period, the pattern can involve a change of key, usually to the key of the fifth of the original key. Section A begins in one key, and the second version of A is played in a new key; section B begins in the new key and ends in the original key. Each section is repeated, giving the pattern AABB.

Song form (ABA)

Songs frequently take the form ABA (or *three-part* form, or *ternary/tertiary* form). One of the simplest forms is produced by varying and repeating the melody. For example, "Twinkle, Twinkle, Little Star" states a tune, varies it, and then restates it (ABA form).

Rachel Grimes, composer, on the limits of form

In school, there's the tendency to get didactic about theory, so you get into this mindset that only certain chord progressions are allowed, and all the rest aren't. Pop music is very didactic that way. There are certain expected standards, like you're not allowed to go to a VI chord after resolving to a IV or a V — you're just expected to go to the I, and there really isn't much deviation from that pattern. I think the biggest challenge for students and users of music theory is to accept that certain groundwork has been laid out for them, so far as what sounds "right" in Western music, but that deviations from that groundwork and those patterns are still allowed.

Pop music is frequently a variation on ABA, called AABA, while blues is often AAB. AABA form is used in songs like "Over the Rainbow" (the B section here may be called the *bridge*, or the link between the two A parts). In song form, the first section (A) may be played once or repeated immediately following, the middle section (B) is a contrasting episode, and the last section is the same or very similar to the first section (A). Song form extends the idea of statement and departure by bringing back the first section. Both contrast and repetition are used in this form.

Arch form (ABCBA)

Music written in arch form is made up of three parts: A, B, and C. In arch form, the A, B, and C are played sequentially, then the B section is played for a second time, directly following the C, and the song ends with the replaying of the A part.

Chapter 17

Classical Forms

*A*s stated in Chapter 16, the difference between form and genre has as much to do with how long a very specific type of music has been around than anything else. If you've got a half-dozen composers playing music built on the repetition of certain intervals — à la John Cage and Philip Glass — you've got a genre (in this case, *serialism*). A hundred years later, if thousands have written music along those guidelines, you've got a form.

During the Golden Age of classical music, from the late 1700s to the mid 1800s, composers were competing viciously with one another to create new and more vibrant types of music. With the adoption of the piano by classical artists, more complicated ways of playing music could be invented, the most famous and useful of which was *counterpoint*, initially introduced by Johann Sebastian Bach. Prior to the Classical period, the left hand of a pianist was fairly limited to banging out one or two whole notes per measure. This was a carryover from the music of the Catholic Church, where the organ provided simple bass lines (figured bass) to accompany vocalists.

Bach, not content with this arrangement, began writing music for the left hand that was just as complicated as the music written for the right and often mirrored closely what the right hand had been playing. His invention, which he called *counterpoint*, may have had to do with the fact that Bach was left-handed himself and was therefore pretty nimble with both paws on the piano keys.

Counterpoint not only enhanced the melody of his songs, but blurred exactly where the melody ended and the harmony began. Almost every classical composer since has used counterpoint in their own music — even the right-handed ones. Figure 17-1 shows an example of counterpoint.

Figure 17-1:
Example of counterpoint from J.S. Bach's "Aus meines Herzens Grunde" ("From the Depths of My Heart").

The Sonata

The *sonata* was the most popular form used by instrumental composers from the mid 18th century until the beginning of the 20th. It is considered by many to be the first true break from the liturgical music that had made such an impact on Western music from the Medieval period on up through the Baroque period.

The true genius of the sonata is that not only does its structure allow many of the rules of basic music theory to be broken — it *encourages* such defiance. With a sonata, it's perfectly allowable to switch to a new key and time signature in the middle, which is pretty unthinkable in your standard folk music tune.

Exposition

Sonatas are based on the song (ternary) form, ABA, which means they have three defined parts. The first part, or *exposition*, presents the basic thematic material of the movement, which is also often broken up into two thematic groups, the second being a reflection of the first.

Generally, the first part of the exposition presents the main theme of the song, or the musical "thread" that ties the piece together and will probably be the line that sticks the most in your head.

The second part of the exposition is a "reflection" of the first part, in that it sounds a lot like the first part but is slightly changed. Put on Beethoven's Sonata No. 8 to get a good example of these two defined parts, or look at the excerpts shown in Figures 17-2 and 17-3 from the same sonata.

Figure 17-2: Excerpt from opening theme, first part, of Beethoven's Sonata No. 8.

Figure 17-3:
Excerpt from
second part
of Sonata
No. 8,
which is a
reflective
theme of
the first.

Development

The second section of the sonata form, called the *development*, often sounds like it belongs to a completely different piece of music altogether. In this section, you're allowed to move through different key signatures and explore completely different musical ideas than the original theme. Often this part of the sonata is the most exciting. It's where you put your big, banging chords and increase tension through use of stronger rhythm and greater interval content, or number of interval steps between each note.

Figure 17-4 shows an excerpt from the development of Sonata N. 8.

Figure 17-4:
Excerpt from second part, or development, of Beethoven's Sonata No. 8.

Recapitulation

After the excitement of the second section, it feels only natural to come to rest where we began. The third and final part of a sonata is the *recapitulation*, where we return to the original key and the musical theme expressed in the first section and bring it all to a final close, as Figure 17-5 shows.

Figure 17-5:
Excerpt from third part of Beethoven's Sonata No. 8.

The Rondo

Rondos expand on the freedom of expression inherent in the sonata form by allowing even more disparate pieces of music to be joined together by a common musical section. The formula for a rondo is ABACA. . . . Technically, with a rondo you can continue to add brand new pieces — featuring different keys or time signatures — to a particular piece indefinitely, so long as you keep linking them together with the opening (A) theme.

In the example shown in Figure 17-6, which includes only the first of many pages, Mozart ties more than six different musical ideas together by use of this form.

Figure 17-6:
Excerpt
from
Mozart's
Rondo Alla
Turca.

The Fugue

The third major musical form to come out of the Classical period was the *fugue*. It was the first form to fully utilize the counterpoint method. Fugues are defined by the way the notes in the treble clef and the notes in the bass clef switch off carrying the melody line and driving the rhythm of the piece.

Note in Figure 17-7 how the eighth notes and sixteenth notes appear first in one clef and then in the other, making both clefs alternately responsible for carrying the harmony (eighth notes) and melody (sixteenth notes) of the music.

Figure 17-7: Excerpt from Fugue in C Major, by Bach, of course.

Symphony

Literally, a *symphony* is a harmonious melding of elements. In music, a symphony is a piece of music that combines several different musical forms, usually performed by an orchestra.

Traditionally, a symphony consists of four movements:

- ✔ Sonata allegro, or fast sonata
- ✔ Slow movement (free choice)

> ✔ Minuet (a short, stately piece of dance music set in 3/4 time)
> ✔ Combination of sonata and rondo (generally) that is a thematic repeat of the first movement

WARNING!

However, the idea of a symphony is that it combines a multitude of musical forms harmoniously, so the aforementioned pattern is absolutely not set in stone.

TIP

The symphony form leaves the field for musical experimentation wide open, and some pieces that have come from this form are the most enduring and recognizable classical music ever recorded. The most famous one, of course, is Beethoven's Symphony No. 5 (Opus 67), whose opening line, "Bu-bu-bu-BUM," is possibly the most universally known intro line of any type of music.

Figure 17-8 shows you the music for this legendary intro.

Figure 17-8:
Bu-bu-bu-
BUM. . . .

Toy companies such as Baby Einstein have begun including stuffed animals that play the No. 5 in their toy line. Six-month-olds that don't even know what classical music is are familiar with the first few bars of this particular symphony.

Other Classical Forms

A number of other classical forms are also enduring and important.

Concerto

A concerto is a composition written for a solo instrument backed by an orchestra. It's with the concerto that we often get our superstars of classical music, such as pianist Lang Lang and violinist Itzhak Perlman. The soloists often carry as much weight as the long-dead composers themselves do.

Duet

Anybody who's ever sat through a piano lesson has probably played one of these. A *duet* is simply a piece of music written for two people, generally two pianists or a pianist and a vocalist.

When other instrumentation is used, such as a bass and a violin, or some other combination, the term *duo* is most commonly applied.

Piano duets are most often used as teaching devices, with the student handling the basic melody line and the more advanced pianist handling the trickier accompaniment.

Etude

An *etude* is a brief musical composition based around a particular technical aspect of music, such as building scales, designed to help instruct the performer through musical exercise.

Fantasia

The modern equivalent of the *fantasia* is free jazz. Fantasias are freeform and try to convey the impression of being completely improvised and divinely inspired, and are most often written for a solo instrument or a small ensemble.

Chapter 18

Popular Forms

Discussing *form* when talking about popular music is tricky, simply because new "forms" — and non-forms, if you take into consideration noise rock and contemporary free jazz — are being created and old ones are being adapted all the time. You can't really call a here-today-gone-tomorrow style of music a form. It is a genre. A significant amount of time has to pass for us to see whether a genre has any lasting power or influence. Only then can we even begin to think of it in terms of possibly one day becoming a form.

However, there are some popular, modern genres of music that have been around long enough that specific patterns can be seen in their overall construction, making them candidates on the road to becoming forms.

They are:

✔ Blues/Early Country

✔ Folk/Rock

✔ Pop

✔ Jazz

The Blues

The blues is the first truly American folk music — not counting the Native Americans, who had their own music before the European invasion. The blues is the common ancestor of pretty much all other forms of American popular music and has been influential around the world. Around the turn of the 20th century, field holler, church music, and African percussion had all melded into what we know now as the blues, and by 1910 the word *blues* to describe this music was in widespread use.

Blues music is a *song*, or *ternary*, form (three-part form, as in ABA) that follows an AABA pattern of I, IV, and V chords in a given scale, with the B section here being the *bridge* — a contrasting section that prepares the listener or performer for the return of the original A section.

Of course, we've all heard people complain that rock music only uses three chords: the I, IV, and V chords. Well, that all started with the blues.

12-bar blues

The name is pretty self-explanatory: in 12-bar blues, you have 12 bars, or measures, of music to work with. The blues are almost always played in 4/4 time, with the rhythm either beat out in regular quarter notes or eighth notes, and with strong accents given on both the first and third beats of each measure.

In each verse of the 12-bar blues, the third 4-bar segment works to resolve the previous 4 bars. The resolution to the I chord at the end of the song may signal the end of the song, or, if the 12th bar is a V chord, then you go back to the beginning of the song to repeat the progression for another stanza. If the song continues on to a new verse, the V chord at the end of the song is called the *turnaround*.

The most commonly used pattern for 12-bar blues looks like the following:

I	I	I	I
IV	IV	I	I
V	IV	I	V/I (turnaround)

This means that if you were playing a 12-bar blues song in the key of C, you would play it like this:

C	C	C	C
F	F	C	C
G	F	C	G/C (turnaround)

Hit those chords in that order, and you've got the bare bones for Muddy Water's classic "You Can't Lose What You Ain't Never Had." Change the tonic (I) chord to an A (AAAA DDAA EDAE/A), and you've got Robert Johnson's "Crossroads Blues."

If you're playing the 12-bar blues in a *minor* key, the common pattern to use is this:

i	iv	i	I
iv	iv	i	i
ii	V	i	V/i (turnaround)

Count Basie's famous and much-loved variation on the 12-bar blues form took elements of both the major and minor keys:

I	IV	I	v
IV	IV	I	VI
ii	V	I	v/I (turnaround)

8-bar blues

8-bar blues is very similar to 12-bar blues — it's just got shorter verses in it. The pattern used for 8-bar blues is this:

I	IV	I	VI
ii	V	I	V/I (turnaround)

16-bar blues

Another variation on the basic 12-bar blues is the 16-bar blues. Where the 8-bar blues is four bars shorter than the 12-bar blues, the 16-bar blues, as you can probably guess, is just that much longer.

The 16-bar blues uses the same basic chord pattern structure as the 12-bar blues, with the 9th and 10th measures repeated three times, like so:

I	I	I	I
IV	IV	I	I
V	IV	V	IV
V	IV	I	V/I

24-bar blues

The 24-bar blues progression is similar to a 12-bar traditional blues progression except each that each chord progression is doubled in duration, like so:

I	I	I	I
I	I	I	I
IV	IV	IV	IV
I	I	I	I
V	V	IV	IV
I	I	I	V/I (turnaround)

32-bar blues ballads and country

The 32-bar blues pattern is where we see the true roots of rock and jazz music. This extended version of the 12-bar blues has the AABA structure, also called *song form*, that was adopted by rock bands in the 1960s.

A typical 32-bar blues layout can look something like this:

(A1)	I	I	VI	VI
	ii	V	IV	V
(A2)	I	I	VI	VI
	ii	V	IV	I
(B)	I	I	I	I
	IV	IV	IV	IV
(A3)	I	I	VI	VI
	ii	V	IV	V/I

32-bar blues wasn't nearly as popular a form with "true" blues performers as the 12-bar form was, partly because it didn't work as well with the short call-and-response form of lyricism that earmarked the blues. It *did* work well for the country music genre, though, and Hank Williams (Sr.) used it in songs like "Your Cheating Heart" and "I'm So Lonesome (I Could Cry)," while Freddy Fender used this form in his hits "Wasted Days and Wasted Nights" and "Before the Next Teardrop Falls."

Discussing popular "forms"

One problem with discussing popular form is that whereas almost all classical music, or at least all classical music from the Classical period, is in the *public domain* (no licensing fees required to perform, record, or rewrite passages from those pieces of music), very little blues, jazz, and absolutely no rock is in the public domain. In order for a piece of written music to be released into the public domain, the composer has to have been dead for 70 years. Therefore, in discussing this chapter, we're crippled by legal limitations on what music we can use to illustrate points. If we were to print in these pages a partial score of the Muddy Water's song used in one example, we'd have to raise the cover price of the book a titch. If we were to reprint several scores, the price would have to go up that many more titches.

However, when this particular form was picked up by people like Irving Berlin and George Gershwin, a lot — perhaps all — of the true heart of blues disappeared from the resulting music. The 32-bar blues form transitioned into popular songs like "Frosty the Snowman" and "I Got Rhythm."

The 32-bar blues form also was significantly altered by the intervention of other classically-trained composers, who mixed the ideas of the sonata and the rondo (see Chapter 17) with the traditional American blues. The result was the eventual creation of very non-blues-sounding songs that utilized such aspects of classical music as the ability to change keys during the bridge section of a song.

Rock

The real break between blues and rock came when Leo Fender invented the first electric guitar in his Orange County garage. A far better inventor than he was a businessman, Fender released his solid-body design to the public in 1948, and by the early 1950s, instrument manufacturers all over the world were creating knock-offs of the Fender guitar. The electric guitar provided the opportunity to use such musical devices as *sustain* and *distortion*, previously unavailable to your average bluesman with an acoustic guitar.

The Beach Boys were masters of the 32-bar form, utilizing it such songs like "Good Vibrations" and "Surfer Girl." The Beatles' also used this form in many of their songs, including "From Me to You" and "Hey Jude." Jerry Lee Lewis's "Great Balls of Fire," The Righteous Brothers' "You've Lost that Loving Feeling," and Led Zeppelin's "Whole Lotta Love" also all use the AABA 32-bar form.

Compound *AABA* form should almost be called AABAB2 form (but it isn't, so just think of it as *compound AABA form*), because in this form, after you play the first 32 bars, you move into a second *bridge* section (B2) that sends you right back to the beginning of the song to repeat the original 32 bars of the song. The Beatles' "I Want to Hold Your Hand," The Police's "Every Breath You Take," Boston's "More Than a Feeling," and Tom Petty and the Heartbreakers' "Refugee" all follow this pattern.

Pop: Verse-Chorus

The *verse-chorus* form is the most widely used form of rock and pop music today. As you can tell from the name, verse-chorus form follows the structure of the lyrics attached to it. You can, of course, write an instrumental piece that follows the same pattern as a verse-chorus pop song, but the structure itself gets its name from the way the words in a song fit together.

Verse-chorus pop songs are laid out like this:

- ✔ Introduction (I): The introduction sets the mood and is usually instrumental, although sometimes it may include a spoken recitation, like in Prince's "Let's Go Crazy."
- ✔ Verse (V): Begins the story of the song.
- ✔ Chorus (C): The most memorable lyrical points of the song. The song's *hook*.
- ✔ Verse (V): Another verse continuing the story.
- ✔ Chorus (C): Reinforcing the hook.
- ✔ Bridge (B) This may be instrumental or lyrical.
- ✔ Chorus (C) Repeat chorus to fade, or just stop at the I chord.

The typical pop song form, then, as we have described it here, is: IVCVCBC. And just as in the 12-bar blues form, the chords of choice are the I, IV, and V chords.

Thousands, perhaps even millions, of pop songs follow this structure. The really amazing thing is how different from one another, either by virtue of lyrics or the music itself, one song can sound from the next.

Jazz

In 32-bar pop music, the music is divided up into four 8-bar sections. Songs like Fats Waller's "Ain't Misbehavin'" and Duke Ellington's "It Don't Mean a Thing" follow the AABA 32-bar form, whereas Charlie Parker took the rondo approach (ABAC) to the 32-bar form in songs like "Ornithology" and "Donna Lee."

The true spirit of jazz has always been improvisation, which makes calling jazz a *form* most difficult. The goal in jazz is to create a new interpretation of an established piece (called a standard), or to build on an established piece of music by changing the melody, harmonies, or even the time signature. It's almost like the point of jazz is to break *away* from form.

The closest thing to defining jazz as a form is to take the basic idea behind blues vocalizations — the call-and-response vocals — and replace the voices with the various instruments that make up the jazz sound: brass, bass, percussive (including piano), and wind instruments, with a more recent inclusion being the electric guitar. In Dixieland jazz, for example, musicians take turns playing the lead melody on their instruments while the others improvise countermelodies.

The one predictable element of a piece of jazz music — with the exclusion of *free jazz*, where there are no real discernable rules, but jazz instrumentation is used — is the rhythm. All jazz, with the exception of free jazz, uses clear, regular meter and strongly-pulsed rhythms that can be heard through the music.

Mark Mallman, musician, on the rules

Don't let theory bring you down. Theory is the tool that you use to get where you want to go. Just remember, you're the boss of your music. But at the same time, theory is a language that will enable you to communicate more decisively and more easily with other musicians. Sometimes, I'll find the need to bring in an extra bassist, and I'll get these guys whose technique is great, and they know all these tunes, but they have no theory training. I'll yell out, "Let's go up to the 5!" during the course of a song, and it takes them forever to figure out what we're doing, and I can't use someone like that. Every musician should know the basics of music theory, like scales, and how rhythm works, the really simple stuff that you can learn in a week. Knowing this stuff is like having all the secrets to making it through Super Mario Brothers. There's this magic that happens in a band setting when everyone knows where the other person is going with a song, and you can't have that magic without knowing theory.

Part V
The Part of Tens

The 5th Wave   By Rich Tennant

"I'm pretty sure this is the part labeled,
'Allegro con Boring.'"

In this part . . .

Here's where you can wade through frequently asked questions, check out some of the wide variety of other music resources available, and read up on some of history's most important contributors to music theory.

Chapter 19

Six Most Frequently Asked Questions About Music Theory

*T*here are some who have, no doubt, skipped to this part just to see if your top six questions match the ones listed here. Without the benefit of a write-in campaign, we can't possibly know exactly what's ticking away in all those musically minded heads out there, but we gave it a shot, and here's what we've got.

Why Is Music Theory Important?

Music theory helps people understand music. The more you know about it, the better your comprehension of music is, and the better you will play it. It's like learning to read and write: it helps you can communicate better. Is it absolutely necessary? No. Is it tremendously helpful? Yes.

Just to take one example, by knowing music theory you can know *exactly* what a composer wanted you to hear in the piece of music he or she wrote down, no matter how many years separate the two of you.

If I Can Already Play Some Music Without Knowing Music Theory, Why Bother Learning It?

There are plenty of people in the world who can't read or write, yet they can communicate their thoughts and feelings verbally. And there are plenty of intuitive, self-taught musicians who have never learned to read or write music. Many of them find the whole idea of music theory tedious and unnecessary.

However, the issue is educational. Leaps and bounds come from learning to read and write. Music theory can help musicians learn new techniques and new styles that they would never stumble upon on their own. It gives them confidence to try new things. In short: learning music theory makes you smarter about music.

Why Is So Much Music Theory Concerned with the Piano Keyboard?

The advantage a keyboard instrument has over other instruments — so far as composing goes, anyway — is that the tuning of the keyboard is such that the ascending and descending notes are laid out right in front of you, in a no-nonsense straight line. From the piano's very beginning, the notes also matched the pitch notations already being used in sheet music. In order to go up a half step, you simply had to go over one key from where you started. This simple clarity is extremely helpful in the composition process.

A second advantage is that anyone can make musical noise on a keyboard from day one — there is no practicing with a bow, no learning how to properly blow over or into a mouthpiece, and no fingertip calluses that need to be built up.

A third advantage is the keyboard's huge range. There is almost no limit to how many octaves you can pile on a keyboard. The two to three octaves of the piano's predecessor, the harpsichord, were adequate to cover the range of music being performed in the 16th century. As the harpsichord spun off into the virginal, the spinet, the clavichord, and eventually the piano, more octaves were added on to the basic form, until it became the eight-octave, concert-ready monster we have today.

How Do You Look at a Key Signature and Identify What Key It Is?

This is a real doozie, especially for musicians who aren't comfortable following a piece of sheet music note-for-note but who want to be able to *sound* like they know what they're doing right out of the gate — as opposed to noodling around until they figure out what the other guys are playing.

There are a few quick ways to tell what key a piece of music is in, *if* you know whether a piece of written in a major or minor key. With a little practice, you can usually figure that out after hearing just one or two measures of a song. Here are some quick rules:

1. If there are no sharps or flats in the key signature, then the piece is in C major (or A minor).

2. If there is one flat in the key signature, then the piece is in F major (or D minor).

3. If there is more than one flat in the key signature, then the piece is written in the key of the next-to-last flat in the key signature.

4. If there are sharps in the key signature, take the note of the last sharp and go up one note. If the last sharp is D sharp, then the key is E. If it's F sharp, the key is G.

5. The relative minor of a key is a minor third down from the major. That means three moving adjacent keys, black or white, to the left; on the guitar, move three frets up the guitar neck (toward the tuning pegs). The note you land on is the relative minor.

Will Learning Music Theory Hinder My Ability to Improvise?

Absolutely not! Learning proper grammar didn't keep you from swearing, did it?

Is There a Quick and Easy Way to Learn to Read Music?

Of course. Every first-year music student is given a couple of cheesy mnemonics to help them memorize the lines and spaces of the treble and bass clefs.

Here are just a few (and if coming up with your own phrases works better, then go, man, go!).

Treble clef (from bottom to top of staff)

Notes on the lines: **E**very **G**ood **B**oy **D**eserves **F**udge (EGBDF).

Notes on the spaces: **FACE**. That's it — everyone uses this one.

Bass clef (from bottom to top of staff)

Notes on the lines: **G**o **B**uy **D**onuts **F**or **A**lan (GBDFA).

Notes on the spaces: **A**ll **C**ows **E**at **G**rass (ACEG).

Chapter 20

Ten Cool and Useful Resources

So, where do you go from here? Lots of places. Music theory is more than learning how to read notes and keep a steady beat — it's also an exploration of the relationship between man and music, about why some things sound really cool and others sound really bad, and about trying to find new ways to communicate with the language of music. This chapter gives you a taste of just a few Web sites and books to get you started down the path of total music theory immersion. Once you get started, you may never come back.

Dolmetsch Online

www.dolmetsch.com

The Dolmetsch site, named after performer, composer, and music historian Arnold Dolmetsch, is an extremely detailed music theory, instruction, and history site. Just about every musical term and concept you can think of is defined and discussed on this site. Plus you'll find classical composers' biographies and a rundown on the evolution of classical music. There are essays, both speculative and factual, on the effect the invention of the piano and the guitar has had on music theory; chord charts for guitars; fingering charts for woodwinds; and a breakdown of the evolution of music notation from the ancient Greeks to the present.

The site also has dozens of music and video files to go along with the notation charts on the site, playable with a free download of the browser plug-in Scorch. Maybe it's not exactly like having a music teacher at your desk, but it does work well as a supplement to the novice-to-intermediate musician trying to learn more about an instrument.

Comparative Arts: A Cyber-Ed Course

www.uml.edu/Dept/History/arthistory/compart/songs.html

Run by Dr. Liana Cheney of the University of Massachusetts, Lowell, this site covers almost the entire known history of human music — from the ancient Greeks up through classical and experimental classical composers in the 20th century. There is enough material and information on this site to easily make up a good-sized book, and the writing style is engaging enough that if it was a book, it'd be a lot of fun to read. The site compares art and literature examples of the different periods of time to the types of music being created by those peoples and really tries to get to the core of why certain types of music were made at certain periods of time. There are also more than a dozen music files from antiquity and the more recent past to download, as well as lots of pictures of archaic instruments and their owners playing them.

Open Directory Project

www.dmoz.org/Arts/Music/Theory/

If there is a Heaven specially made for die-hard music theorists, then the ODP Music Theory site is a glimpse of it. The ODP is a huge group of editor-monitored links about every subject imaginable.

The ODP Music Theory links range from very basic music tutorial sites to incredibly wild and speculative sites concerning the effect of music on the brain and the very origins of music itself. There are discussion groups full of vigorous arguments on why we should toss out the 5-lined music staff and rework music notation to fit a 6-lined staff instead, as well as sites dedicated to composers' take on atonal tunings and samples of some of their compositions. Because it is just a list of music theory-related links, the list changes on a fairly regular basis — it's worth dropping by every few weeks just to see what new sites have joined the list.

ClassicalWorks.com

www.classicalworks.com

The ClassicalWorks.com site has an excellent global history of music in timetable form, spanning nearly 4,000 years of music history (click on the History of Music link). The entries are all pretty short and sweet, but so far as dates, events, and names go, all the information you need is right there.

There's a fair amount of historic artwork to go along with specific groups of entries, such as pictures of Gregorian chants drawn on illuminated manuscripts and excerpts from Egyptian murals commemorating some of the oldest known musical ensembles. There's also a Google search engine on the site, so if there's an event or name you specifically need to look up, chances are it'll be there and will be easy to get to.

Smithsonian Folkways Series

`www.folkways.si.edu`

The Smithsonian Folkways music series is an amazing project run by the Smithsonian Institute. Folkways Records was founded in 1948 in New York City by Moses Asch and Marian Distler, who sought to record and document the entire world of sound. During the 40 years that Asch owned the label, between 1948 and his death, Folkways' tiny staff released 2,168 albums, which included traditional, ethnic, and contemporary music from around the world; poetry, spoken word, and instructional recordings in numerous languages; and documentary recordings of individuals, communities, current events, and natural sounds. After Asch's death in 1987, the Smithsonian Institution Center for Folklife and Cultural Heritage in Washington, D.C., acquired Folkways Recordings.

As a condition of the acquisition, the Smithsonian agreed that virtually all Asch's 2,168 titles would remain in print forever. Considering how much music and culture have changed all over the world in the past 60 years, this amazing collection has more significance today than ever. Folkways has also released 300 new titles since the Smithsonian's acquisition of the label, adding rock, hip-hop, and electronic music recordings. Whether they sell 8,000 copies each year or only one copy every five years, every Folkways title ever released will *forever* remain available for purchase.

The Rough Guide to Classical Music

Edited by Joe Staines and Jonathan Buckley, published by Rough Guides, distributed by Penguin

This book is a wonderful guide to classical music. Not only does it profile a little over 160 classical composers with full biographical sketches, but it provides coherent and believable reviews of the best (and worst) recordings of those composers' works. Each entry is divided into types of music the composer delved into, where their influence is most felt in later composers' works, and even the political pressures that made them write the types of music that they did. It's fun to both read straight through and to jump around in as a reference book. This is an indispensable guide to anyone who wants to learn more about classical music without getting bogged down by the snobbery that can accompany the genre.

The Virgin Directory of World Music

By Philip Sweeney, Owl Books/Henry Holt & Company

This is an extremely well-organized summary of traditional music from around the world. It's divided into regions of the world: Africa (North, West, Central, South, and East), Europe (North, South, and East), The Middle East and India, and so on. Each division is then broken down into the states and countries of those regions, with descriptions of their traditional music. There's even detailed mention of notable performers who have recorded and released albums of the music of their region, from Ladysmith Black Mambazo to Jamaica's The Jolly Boys.

American Mavericks

Edited by Susan Key and Larry Roethe, published by University of California Press

This book is gorgeous enough to be a coffee table book. If you're as obsessed with music as we are *and* you have a coffee table, you really should pick up a copy. It's loaded with fantastic photographs of unique American composers and their equally unique choices of instruments. It features in-depth profiles of composers as varied and dissimilar as John Cage, Aaron Copland, Steve Mackey, and Carl Ruggles. The book also comes with a CD containing 18 tracks of music — one for every composer — many from albums that are just about impossible to find in your local record store.

Parallels and Paradoxes: Explorations in Music and Society

By Daniel Barenboim and Edward W. Said, Pantheon Books

This book is a collection of conversation transcripts between Daniel Barenboim, Music Director of the Chicago Symphony Orchestra and the Deutsche Staatsoper Berlin, and Edward W. Said, literary critic, political analyst, and all-over expert on Middle Eastern culture. In these conversations, Barenboim and Said discuss the effect of music on global and national politics, and vice versa, to incredibly minute detail, from the difficulties of conducting Wagner in post-Hitler Germany to comparisons between Jane Austen and Verdi. The book is full of the type of really brilliant and deep conversations musicians and music lovers dream about getting to have with their peers, but don't usually happen due to the fact that most of us are not world-class musicians and political analysts.

The Art of Practicing: A Guide to Making Music from the Heart

By Madeline Bruser, Bell Tower/Crown Books

In some ways, the book is as goofy as the title suggests. There is definitely some stuff in here that seems better suited for a book in the New Age section of the bookstore. However, its strength is that it covers something that's not usually talked about in music instruction books — namely, training your body to learn how to play music. It's really not enough to just know how to read notes and tap out a rhythm. Learning to endure the many hours of training necessary to truly master an instrument is another thing entirely. The book covers everything from breathing exercises to help you relax before practicing, ergonomically correct hand and body positions for playing instruments for an extended period of time, and a variety of stretching exercises for working out all the kinks and knots that form during practice.

Chapter 21

Nine Music Theorists You Should Know About

*T*he evolution of music theory and notation is almost more amazing than the evolution of human writing. When you really think about it, modern music notation is like Esperanto that lots of people can actually speak. People all over the Western world, and much of the Eastern world as well, know how to communicate with each other effectively through sheet music, chord theory, and the Circle of Fifths. Here are ten music theorists who have helped define how we look at music or have changed our view of music entirely.

Pythagoras: 582–507 B.C.

Anybody who's ever taken a geometry class has heard of this guy. Obsessed with the idea that everything in the world could be broken down into a mathematical formula, and that numbers themselves were the ultimate reality, Pythagoras came up with equations that could theoretically calculate everything from determining the size of a mountain by measuring its shadow to his famous Pythagorean Theorem.

The beautiful thing about ancient Greek culture is that the study of science, art, music, and philosophy were really considered one great big pursuit. It wasn't that strange for someone like Pythagoras to turn his attention to music and try to come up with mathematical theories to define exactly what it was.

As the lyre was the most popular instrument of the day, it's only natural that Pythagoras used the lyre, and stringed instruments in general, to come up with his working model for what would eventually be called the Pythagorean Circle, and which eventually evolved into the Circle of Fifths. According to legend, he took a piece of string from a lyre, plucked it, measured its tone and vibration rate, and then cut that string in half and made a new set of measurements. He named the difference between the rate of vibration of the first length of string and the second an *octave*, then went to work breaking the octave up into twelve evenly divided units with each unit equivalent to 100 "cents." Every point around the circle was assigned a pitch value, with each pitch value exactly 1/12 octave higher or lower than the note next to it.

The problem with Pythagoras's Circle was that, first of all, he wasn't a musician. Even though the Circle was mathematically sound, and really, just an amazing conceptual leap altogether, some of the "tunings" he proposed weren't particularly pleasing to the ear. Also, due to variations in the size of sound waves that he wasn't privy to — and really, nobody was 2,500 years ago — his octaves quickly fell out of tune the further you went from the starting point. A high C, tuned to his perfect fifths, was definitely not in tune with a low C, for example, because in his system you moved just a bit out of pitch with each new octave in between.

For the next 2000 years, musicians and theorists alike concentrated on "tempering" this Circle, with its twelve spots and shape left intact, but retuning some of his "perfect fifths" by the use of "Pythagorean commas" to create a Circle that was much more musician- and audience-friendly.

Boethius: 480–524 A.D.

If it hadn't been for the Roman statesman and philosopher Anicius Manlius Severinus Boethius, the Greek contribution to music theory might have been completely lost, along with much of Europe's own musical history. Boethius was a remarkable man who dedicated his short life to studying Greek mathematics, philosophy, history, and music theory. He was the first scholar since Pythagoras to try to connect the pitch of a note with the vibration of sound waves.

Not content to sit at home writing books, Boethius' most ambitious project was also one of his most enduring. He began venturing out into the Western European countryside with music scribes who transcribed the folk music of the different groups of people that made up the landscape. Because of this work, we can still hear what sort of music rural people were playing and singing about from this time period. Formal music traditionally did not have lyrics; music with lyrics was considered low-brow and aesthetically in bad taste. Ironically, this study of "common music" led to Boethius' exploration of writing songs with lyrics that told a story — an idea that would one day lead to a high-brow genre of music: the opera.

Sadly, before Boethius could write his own fully formed opera, or translate the entire works of Plato and Aristotle, or come up with a unifying theory to explain all of the known body of Greek philosophy (all three were lifetime goals of his), he was thrown in prison under charges of practicing magic, sacrilege, and treason. The third charge probably came from his efforts to peaceably unite the Church in Rome and the Church in Constantinople.

Despite a death sentence, Boethius continued to write in prison. His last work was the *De consolatione philosophia* (*The Consolation of Philosophy*), a novella-sized treatise about how the greatest joys in life came from treating other people decently and from learning as much as possible about the world while we're here. Well into the 12th century, Boethius' many texts were standard reading in religious and educational institutions all over Europe.

Gerbert d'Aurillac/Pope Sylvester II 950–1003

Gerbert of Aurillac, later known as Pope Sylvester II, was born around the year 945 in Aquitaine. He entered the Benedictine monastery of St. Gerald in Aurillac when he was a child and received his early education there. Highly intelligent and a voracious reader, Gerbert rose up among the ranks of the monastery quickly so quickly that there were rumors that he had received his genius from the Devil.

From 972 to 989, Gerbert was the abbot at the royal Abbey of St. Remi in Reims, France, and at the Italian monastery at Bobbio (Italy). There, he taught mathematics, geometry, astronomy and music, incorporating Boethius's method of teaching all four at once in a system called the *quadrivium*. At the time, the laws of music were considered to be divine and objective, and it was important to learn the relation between the musical movement of the celestial spheres, the functions of the body, and the sounds of the voice and musical instruments.

Gerbert created an instrument called a monochord for his students, from which it was possible to calculate musical vibrations. He was the first European since the fall of Rome to come up with a standard notation of notes in tones and semitones (half steps). He wrote extensively about the measurement of organ pipes and eventually designed and built the first hydraulically-powered musical organ (as opposed to the hydraulically-powered siren of the Roman arenas) that exceeded the performance of any other previously-constructed church organ.

Guido D'Arezzo: 990–1040

Guido D'Arrezo was a Benedictine monk who spent the first part of his religious training at the monastery of Pomposa, Italy. While there, he recognized the difficulty singers had in remembering the pitches to be sung in Gregorian chants and decided to do something about it. He reworked the *neumatic* notation (early music markings) used in Gregorian chant and designed his own musical staff for teaching Gregorian chants much faster. He attracted much positive attention from his higher-ups because of it. However, he also attracted the animosity of the other monks in his own abbey and soon left the monastic life for the town of Arezzo, which had no official religious order but did have a lot of decent singers that desperately needed training.

While in Arezzo, he improved his musical staff. He added a time signature at the beginning to make it easier for performers to keep up with one another. He also devised *solfege*, a vocal scale system that used six tones, as opposed to the four tones used by the Greeks: *ut* (later changed to *do*), *re*, *mi*, *fa*, *so*, and *la*, to be placed in specific spots on the staff. Later, when the diatonic scale was combined with the "Guido Scale," as it's sometimes called, the *ti* sound finished the octave (making *The Sound of Music*, much later, become possible). The *Micrologus*, written at the cathedral at Arezzo, contains Guido's teaching method and his notes regarding musical notation.

Nicola Vicentino: 1511–1576

Nicola Vicentino was an Italian music theorist of the Renaissance period whose experiments with keyboard design and equal-temperament tuning rival those of many 20th century theorists. He moved from Venice to Ferrara, which was like 1970s Berlin (except it was in 16th-century Italy) in that it was a hotbed of experimental music. He served briefly as a music tutor for the Duke of Este to support himself while writing treatises on the relevance of ancient Greek music theory in contemporary music, and why, in his opinion, the whole Pythagorean system should be thrown out the window. He was both adored and reviled by contemporaries for his distain for the 12-tone system and was invited to speak at international music conferences on his beliefs.

Vicentino amazed the music world even more when, to further prove the inadequacies of the *diatonic scale*, he designed and built his own microtonal keyboard that matched a music scale of his own devising, called the *archicembalo*. On the archicembalo, each octave contained 36 keys, making it possible to play acoustically satisfactory intervals in every key — predating the well-tempered *meantone* keyboard in use today by nearly 200 years. Unfortunately, he only built a few of the instruments, and before his work could catch on, he died of the plague.

Christiaan Huygens: 1629–1695

Christiaan Huygens did as much for science and the scientific revolution of the 17th century as Pythagoras did for mathematics. Huygens was a mathematician, astronomer, physicist, and music theorist. His discoveries and scientific contributions are staggering and well known.

In his later years, he turned his immense brain to the problem of meantone temperament in the musical scale and devised his own 31-tone scale in his books *Lettre Touchant le Cycle Harmonique* and *Novus cyclus harmonicus*.

Here, he developed a simple method for calculating string lengths for any regular tuning system, worked out the use of logarithms in the calculation of string lengths and interval sizes, and demonstrated the close relationship between meantone tuning and 31-tone equal temperament. Since the standard system of tuning at that time was *quarter-comma meantone*, in which the fifth was tuned to 5 ¼, the appeal of this method was immediate, as the fifth of 31-et, at 696.77 cents, is only a fifth of a cent sharper than the fifth of quarter-comma meantone.

As much as people in the scientific community applauded his genius, people in the musical world were not yet ready (and still aren't) to give up their Pythagorean 12-tone scale, so aside from a few experimental instruments built on his calculations, the main principle adopted from his theories was to rebuild and retune instruments so that twelve tones could finally build a true octave.

Harry Partch, 1901–1974

At age 29, Harry Partch gathered up 14 years of music he had written, based on what he called the "tyranny of the piano" and the twelve-tone scale, and burned it all in a big iron stove. For the next four-and-a-half decades, Partch devoted his entire life to producing sounds found only in microtonal scales— the tones found between the notes used on the piano keys. By the time he died in 1974, he had built around 30 instruments and had devised complex theories of intonation and performances to accompany them, including a 43-tone scale, with which he built most of his compositions.

Because there were no available instruments with which to perform 43-tone scale on, Partch built his own instruments for both him and his orchestras to play on. Some of his remarkable instruments include the Kitharas I & II, lyre-like instruments made of glass rods that produced gliding tones on four of the chords; two Chromelodeons, reed pump organs tuned to the complete

43-tone octave with total ranges of more than five acoustic octaves; the Surrogate Kithara, with two banks of eight strings and sliding glass rods under the strings as dampeners; two Adapted Guitars that used a sliding plastic bar above the strings, with one string tuned to a six-string 1/1 unison, the other tuned to ten-string chord whose higher three notes are a few microtonal vibrations apart.

Partch's orchestras also incorporated unusual percussive instruments, such as the sub-bass Marimba Eroica, which utilized tones that vibrate at such a low frequency that the listener can "feel" the notes more than hear them; the Mazda Marimba, made up of tuned light bulbs severed at the socket; the Zymo-Xyl, which creates loud, piercing shrieks by vibrating suspended liquor bottles, auto hubcaps, and oar bars; the Spoils of War, which consisted of artillery shell casings, Pyrex chemical solution jars, a high wood block, a low marimba bar, spring steel flexitones (Whang Guns), and a gourd.

Karlheinz Stockhausen: 1928–2007

Stockhausen's greatest influence as a theorist can best be felt in the genres of music that came directly out of his teachings. During the 1950s, he helped develop the genres of *minimalism* and *serialism*. Much of the 1970s "krautrock" scene was created by his former students at the National Conservatory of Cologne, Germany, while his teachings and compositions greatly influenced the musical renaissance of 1970s West Berlin (notable characters included David Bowie, Brian Eno). In the long run, Stockhausen can be seen as the father of *ambient music*, and the concept of *variable form*, in which the performance space and the instrumentalists themselves are considered a part of a composition, and changing even one element of a performance changes the entire performance.

He is also responsible for *polyvalent form* in music, in which a piece of music can be read upside-down, from left-to-right or right-to-left, or, if multiple pages are incorporated in a composition, the pages can be played in any order the performer wishes. As former student and composer Irmin Schmidt said, "Stockhausen taught me that the music I played was *mine*, and that the compositions I wrote were for the *musicians* who were to play it."

Robert Moog: 1934–2005

Although we don't know who built the first fretted guitar, or who truly designed the first real keyboard, we do know who created the first pitch-proper, commercially available synthesizer. Robert Moog is widely recognized as the father of the synthesizer keyboard, and his instrument revolutionized the sound of pop and classical music from the day it hit the streets in 1966. He specially designed keyboards for everyone from Wendy Carlos to Sun Ra to the Beach Boys, and even worked with groundbreaking composers like Max Brand. Unfortunately, Moog wasn't the greatest businessman — or perhaps he was just very, very generous with his ideas — and the only synthesizer-related patent he ever filed was for something called a low-pass filter.

When he first began building synthesizers, his goal was to create a musical instrument that played sounds completely different than any instrument that came before. However, as people began to use synthesizers to recreate "real" instrument sounds, he became disillusioned with the instrument and decided that the only way to get people to work with "new" sounds was to break away from the antiquated keyboard interface altogether. His North Carolina–based company, Big Briar, began working on Leon Theremin's theremin design to create a MIDI theremin, which was designed to eliminate the interval steps between each note but still keep the tonal color of each individual instrument's MIDI patch.

Outside of building instruments, Moog also wrote hundreds of articles speculating on the future of music and music technology for a variety of publications, including *Computer Music Journal*, *Electronic Musician*, and *Popular Mechanics*. His ideas were way ahead of their time, and many of his predictions, such as those from his 1976 article in *The Music Journalist* that predicted the advent of MIDI instruments and touch-sensitive keyboards, have already come true.

Appendix A

How to Use the CD

*M*any music examples discussed in *Music Theory For Dummies* are performed on the CD that comes with this book — over 60 of them! This makes *Music Theory For Dummies* a true multimedia experience. You have text explaining the techniques used, visual graphics of the music often in more than one form — piano diagrams, guitar tablature, or standard music notation — and lots of audio performances of music (playable on your CD or MP3 players).

One fun way to experience *Music Theory For Dummies* is to just scan the text, looking for the "On the CD" icon and listening to the corresponding performances on the CD. Or pop in the CD and when you hear something you like, read the text that goes into detail about that particular piece of music, by referencing the track list in Table A-1 later in this chapter. Or go to a particular chapter that interests you (say, Chapter 14 on chord progressions), skip to the appropriate tracks on the CD, and see if you can hack it.

Whenever you see the "On the CD" icon, just play the track on the CD mentioned in the text for that icon. Table A-1, later in this chapter, lists all track numbers, chapter references, and track times (in minutes and seconds). Use the *track skip* control on your CD or MP3 player to go to the desired track.

Always keep the CD with the book, rather than mixed in with your rack of CDs. The plastic envelope helps protect the CD's surface from scuffs and scratches, and whenever you want to refer to *Music Theory For Dummies* (the book), the CD will always be right where you expect it. Try to get in the habit of following along with the printed music whenever you listen to the CD, even if your sight-reading skills aren't quite up to snuff. It helps. You absorb more than you expect just by moving your eyes across the page in time to the music, associating sound and sight. So store the CD and book together as constant companions and use them together as well for a rich visual and aural experience.

System Requirements

Here is the least you need to be able to play the CD.

Audio CD player

The CD included with this book will work just fine in any standard CD player. Just put it into your home stereo system or boom box and check out Table A-1 in the section "What's on the CD?," later in the chapter, for the track descriptions.

Computer CD-ROM drive

If you have a computer, you can pop the accompanying CD into your CD-ROM drive to play the CD. Make sure that your computer meets the minimum system requirements shown here:

- A computer running Microsoft Windows or Mac OS
- Software capable of playing MP3s and CD audio
- A CD-ROM drive
- A sound card for PCs (Mac OS computers have built-in sound support)

1. **Put the CD in your computer's CD-ROM drive.**

2. **Rip the tracks to your hard drive as you normally do with an audio CD.**

3. **If you have a digital music player such as an MP3 player or iPod, transfer the tracks to it as you normally do.**

The specific steps you go through to transfer tracks to your hard drive and/or digital music player depend on your OS platform and software. See your software documentation for help.

What's on the CD

Here is a list of the tracks on the CD along with the chapter numbers, where applicable, that they correspond to in the book. Use this as a quick reference to finding more about interesting-sounding tracks on the CD.

Table A-1		Tracks on the Book's CD	
Track	*(Time)*	*Chapter*	*Description*
1	(0:36)	6	80, 100, and 120 beats per minute
2	(0:09)	10	Intervals with a quality of fifths
3	(0:10)	10	Simple intervals in the C major scale
4	(0:45)	12	A major scale, piano and guitar
5	(0:45)	12	A flat major scale, piano and guitar
6	(0:45)	12	B major scale, piano and guitar
7	(0:45)	12	B flat major scale, piano and guitar
8	(0:45)	12	C major scale, piano and guitar
9	(0:45)	12	C flat major scale, piano and guitar
10	(0:45)	12	C sharp major scale, piano and guitar
11	(0:45)	12	D major scale, piano and guitar
12	(0:45)	12	D flat major scale, piano and guitar
13	(0:45)	12	E major scale, piano and guitar
14	(0:45)	12	E flat major scale, piano and guitar
15	(0:45)	12	F major scale, piano and guitar
16	(0:45)	12	F sharp major scale, piano and guitar
17	(0:45)	12	G major scale, piano and guitar
18	(0:45)	12	G flat major scale, piano and guitar
19	(0:45)	12	A minor natural scale, piano and guitar
20	(0:45)	12	A minor harmonic scale, piano and guitar
21	(0:45)	12	A minor melodic scale, piano and guitar
22	(0:45)	12	A flat minor natural scale, piano and guitar
23	(0:45)	12	A flat minor harmonic scale, piano and guitar

(continued)

Table A-1 *(continued)*

Track	*(Time)*	Chapter	Description
24	(0:45)	12	A flat minor melodic scale, piano and guitar
25	(0:45)	12	A sharp minor natural scale, piano and guitar
26	(0:45)	12	A sharp minor harmonic scale, piano and guitar
27	(0:45)	12	A sharp minor melodic scales, piano and guitar
28	(0:45)	12	B minor natural scale, piano and guitar
29	(0:45)	12	B minor harmonic scale, piano and guitar
30	(0:45)	12	B minor melodic scale, piano and guitar
31	(0:45)	12	B flat minor natural scale, piano and guitar
32	(0:45)	12	B flat minor harmonic scale, piano and guitar
33	(0:45)	12	B flat minor melodic, piano and guitar
34	(0:45)	12	C minor natural scale, piano and guitar
35	(0:45)	12	C minor harmonic scale, piano and guitar
36	(0:45)	12	C minor melodic scale, piano and guitar
37	(0:45)	12	C sharp minor natural scale, piano and guitar
38	(0:45)	12	C sharp minor harmonic scale, piano and guitar
39	(0:45)	12	C sharp minor melodic scale, piano and guitar
40	(0:45)	12	D minor natural scale, piano and guitar

Track	(Time)	Chapter	Description
41	(0:45)	12	D minor harmonic scale, piano and guitar
42	(0:45)	12	D minor melodic scale, piano and guitar
43	(0:45)	12	D sharp minor natural scale, piano and guitar
44	(0:45)	12	D sharp minor harmonic scale, piano and guitar
45	(0:45)	12	D sharp minor melodic scale, piano and guitar
46	(0:45)	12	E minor natural scale, piano and guitar
47	(0:45)	12	E minor harmonic scale, piano and guitar
48	(0:45)	12	E minor melodic scale, piano and guitar
49	(0:45)	12	E flat minor natural scale, piano and guitar
50	(0:45)	12	E flat minor harmonic scale, piano and guitar
51	(0:45)	12	E flat minor melodic scales, piano and guitar
52	(0:45)	12	F minor natural scale, piano and guitar
53	(0:45)	12	F minor harmonic scale, piano and guitar
54	(0:45)	12	F minor melodic scale, piano and guitar
55	(0:45)	12	F sharp minor natural scale, piano and guitar
56	(0:45)	12	F sharp minor harmonic scale, piano and guitar
57	(0:45)	12	F sharp minor melodic scale, piano and guitar

(continued)

Table A-1 *(continued)*

Track	(Time)	Chapter	Description
58	(0:45)	12	G minor natural scale, piano and guitar
59	(0:45)	12	G minor harmonic scale, piano and guitar
60	(0:45)	12	G minor melodic scale, piano and guitar
61	(0:45)	12	G sharp minor natural scale, piano and guitar
62	(0:45)	12	G sharp minor harmonic scale, piano and guitar
63	(0:45)	12	G sharp minor melodic scale, piano and guitar
64	(0:02)	13	The root of a C major chord
65	(0:02)	13	The root and the first third of a C major chord
66	(0:02)	13	The root and fifth of a C major chord
67	(0:02)	13	C major triad
68	(0:19)	13	AM, Am, Aaug, Adim, AM7, Am7, A7, Am7(b5), Adim7, AmiMA7 on piano
69	(0:19)	13	AbM, Abm, Abaug, Abdim, AbM7, Abm7, Ab7, Abm7(b5), Abdim7, AbmiMA7 on piano
70	(0:19)	13	BM, Bm, Baug, Bdim, BM7, Bm7, B7, Bm7(b5), Adim7, AmiMA7 on piano
71	(0:19)	13	B flat M, B flat m, B flat aug, B flat dim, B flat M7, B flat m7, B flat 7, B flat m7(b5), B flat dim7, B flat miMA7 on piano
72	(0:19)	13	CM, Cm, Caug, Cdim, CM7, Cm7, C7, Cm7(b5), Cdim7, CmiMA7 on piano
73	(0:19)	13	C flat M, C flat m, C flat aug, C flat dim, C flat M7, C flat m7, C flat 7, C flat m7(b5), C flat dim7, C flat miMA7 on piano

Track	(Time)	Chapter	Description
74	(0:19)	13	C#M, C#m, C#aug, C#dim, C#M7, C#m7, C#7, C#m7(b5), C#dim7, C#miMA7 on piano
75	(0:19)	13	DM, Dm, Daug, Ddim, DM7, Dm7, D7, Dm7(b5), Ddim7, DmiMA7 on piano
76	(0:19)	13	D flat M, D flat m, D flat aug, D flat dim, D flat M7, D flat m7, D flat 7, D flat m7(b5), D flat dim7, D flat miMA7 on piano
77	(0:19)	13	EM, Em, Eaug, Edim, EM7, Em7, E7, Em7(b5), Edim7, EmiMA7 on piano
78	(0:19)	13	E flat M, E flat m, E flat aug, E flat dim, E flat M7, E flat m7, E flat 7, E flat m7(b5), E flat dim7, E flat miMA7 on piano
79	(0:19)	13	FM, Fm, Faug, Fdim, FM7, Fm7, F7, Fm7(b5), Fdim7, FmiMA7 on piano
80	(0:19)	13	F#M, F#m, F#aug, F#dim, F#M7, F#m7, F#7, F#m7(b5), F#dim7, FmiMA7 on piano
81	(0:19)	13	GM, Gm, Gaug, Gdim, GM7, Gm7, G7, Gm7(b5), Gdim7, GmiMA7 on piano
82	(0:19)	13	G flat M, G flat m, G flat aug, G flat dim, G flat M7, G flat m7, G flat 7, G flat m7(b5), G flat dim7, G flat miMA7 on piano
83	(0:04)	14	Key of G major chord progressions
84	(0:05)	14	Key of C major chord progressions
85	(0:15)	14	Key of F minor chord progressions
86	(0:14)	14	Key of A minor chord progressions
87	(0:07)	15	Authentic cadence
88	(0:07)	15	Perfect authentic cadence
89	(0:04)	15	Difference between a PAC and an IAC
90	(0:02)	15	Plagal cadence

(continued)

Table A-1 *(continued)*

Track	(Time)	Chapter	Description
91	(0:03)	15	Two more plagal cadences
92	(0:02)	15	Deceptive cadence
93	(0:02)	15	Half cadence

Total time: 59:23 minutes

Troubleshooting

If you have trouble with the CD that came with this book, please call the Wiley Product Technical Support phone number: 877-762-2974. Outside the United States, call 1-317-572-3994. You can also contact Wiley Product Technical Support at www.wiley.com/techsupport. Wiley Publishing will provide technical support only for installation and other general quality control items.

Appendix B

Chord Chart

● ●

*T*his appendix functions as a quick reference to chords on the piano and guitar. It covers all the keys and shows each key's chords to the seventh degree. First, we list the piano chords, and then the guitar chords.

The tricky thing about diagramming guitar chords is that the same chord can be built in many ways, in many different places on the neck. To make things easier, we only included chords that don't go beyond the upper seven frets of the guitar neck.

For piano, the keys to be played in the chord are shown in gray.

For the guitar, big black dots show where to put your fingers on the frets. An X above a string means you don't play that string. Also, for each guitar chord diagram, the pitches for each open (non-fretted) string are, from left to right, (low) E, A, D, G, B, (high) E.

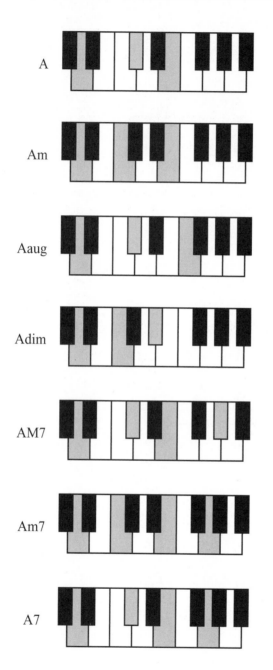

A

Am

Aaug

Adim

AM7

Am7

A7

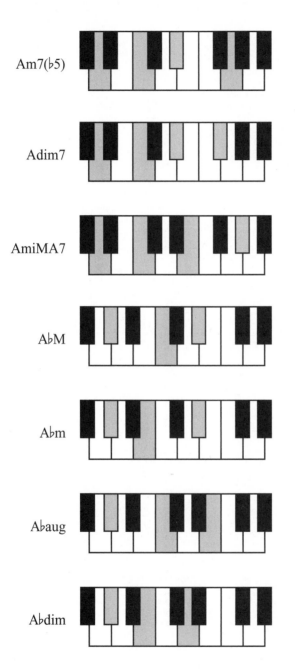

Am7(♭5)

Adim7

AmiMA7

A♭M

A♭m

A♭aug

A♭dim

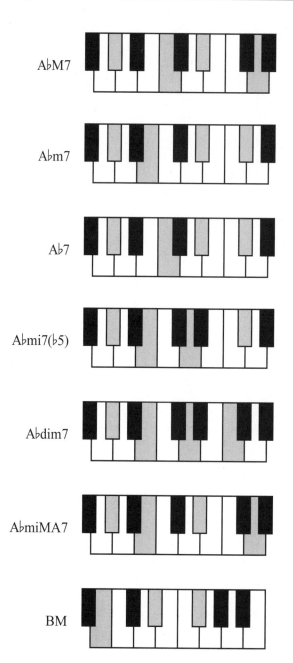

A♭M7

A♭m7

A♭7

A♭mi7(♭5)

A♭dim7

A♭miMA7

BM

Bdim7

BmiMA7

BbM

Bbm

Bbaug

Bbdim

BbM7

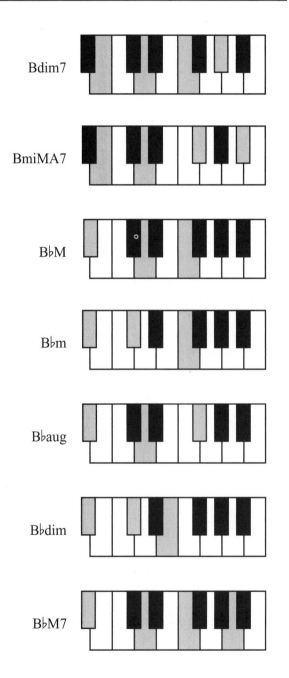

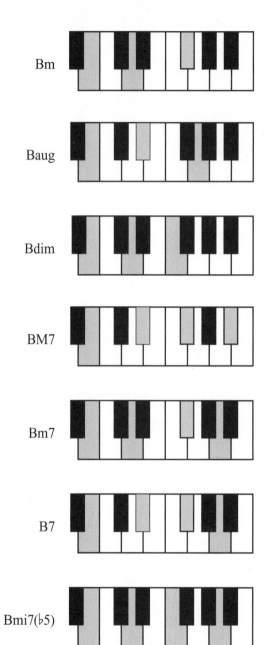

Bm

Baug

Bdim

BM7

Bm7

B7

Bmi7(♭5)

B♭mi7

B♭7

B♭mi7(♭5)

B♭dim7

B♭miMA7

CM

Cm

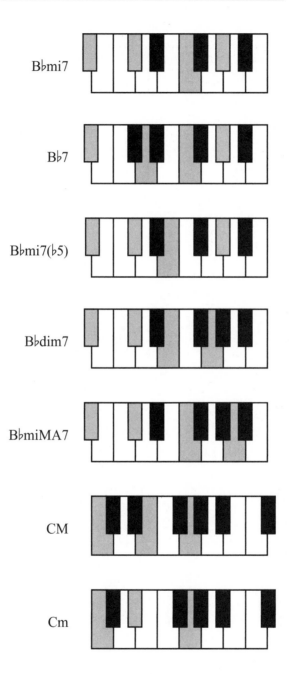

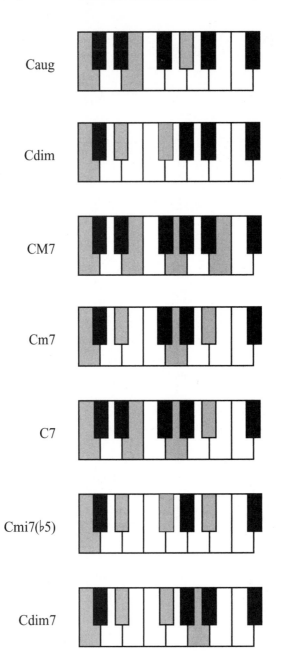

Caug

Cdim

CM7

Cm7

C7

Cmi7(♭5)

Cdim7

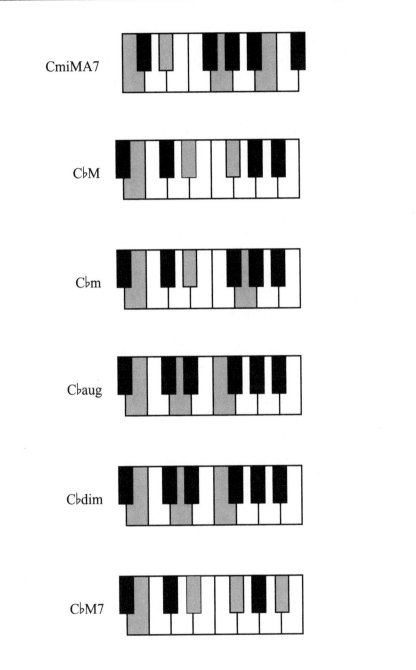

CmiMA7

CbM

Cbm

Cbaug

Cbdim

CbM7

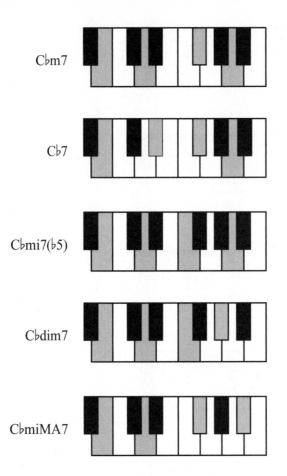

C♭m7

C♭7

C♭mi7(♭5)

C♭dim7

C♭miMA7

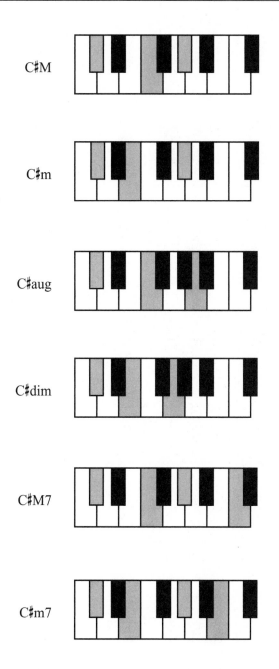

C#M

C#m

C#aug

C#dim

C#M7

C#m7

C#7

C#m7(♭5)

C#dim7

C#miMA7

DM

Dm

Daug

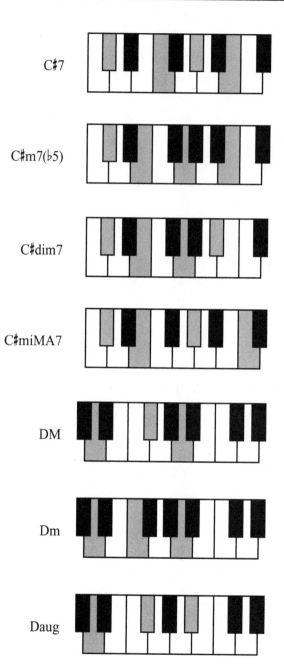

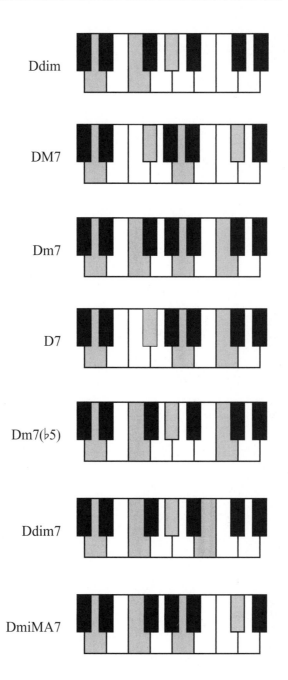

Ddim

DM7

Dm7

D7

Dm7(♭5)

Ddim7

DmiMA7

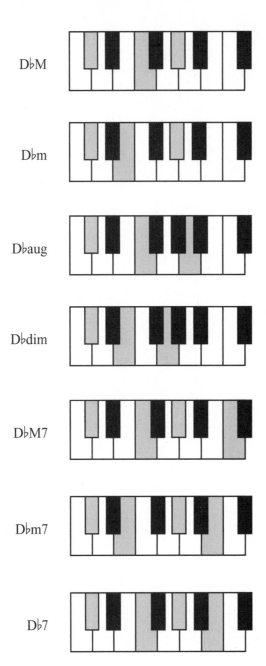

D♭M

D♭m

D♭aug

D♭dim

D♭M7

D♭m7

D♭7

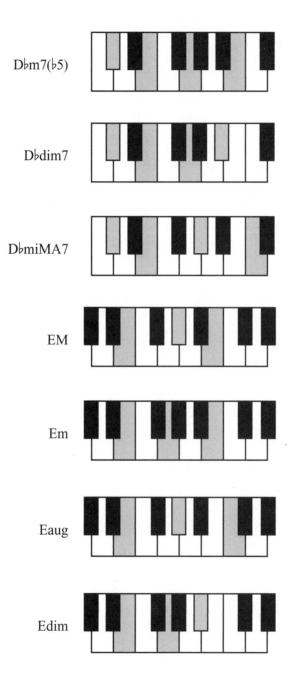

D♭m7(♭5)

D♭dim7

D♭miMA7

EM

Em

Eaug

Edim

EM7

Em7

E7

Em7(♭5)

Edim7

EmiMA7

E♭M

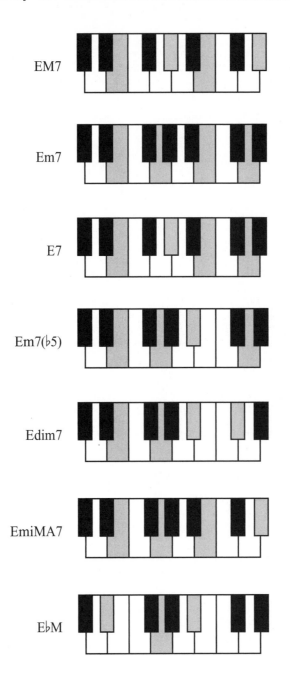

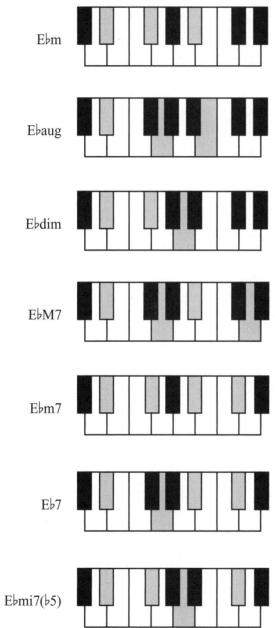

E♭m

E♭aug

E♭dim

E♭M7

E♭m7

E♭7

E♭mi7(♭5)

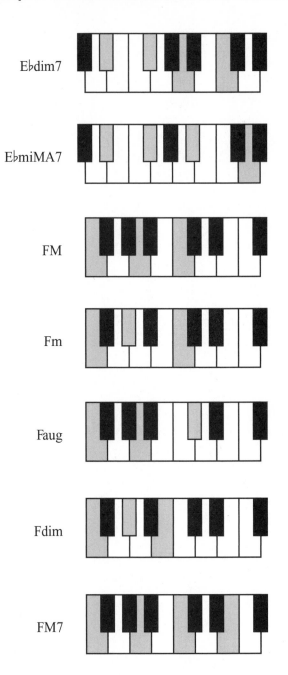

E♭dim7

E♭miMA7

FM

Fm

Faug

Fdim

FM7

Fm7

F7

Fmi7(♭5)

Fdim7

FmiMA7

F♯M

F♯m

F♯aug

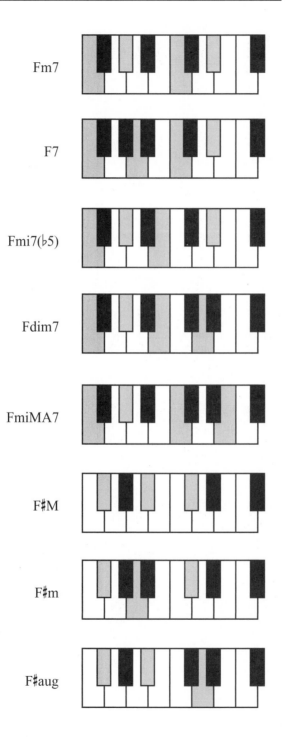

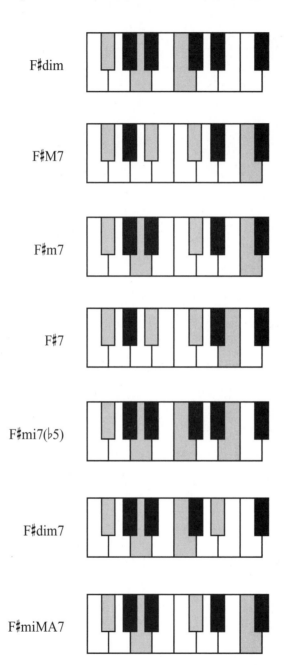

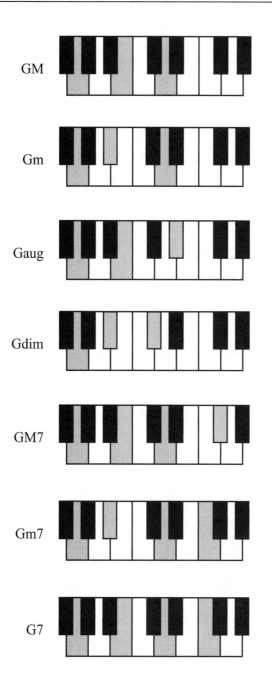

GM

Gm

Gaug

Gdim

GM7

Gm7

G7

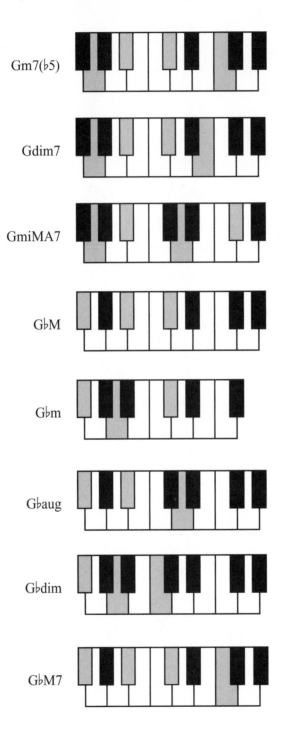

Gm7(♭5)

Gdim7

GmiMA7

G♭M

G♭m

G♭aug

G♭dim

G♭M7

G♭m7

G♭7

G♭m7(♭5)

G♭dim7

G♭miMA7

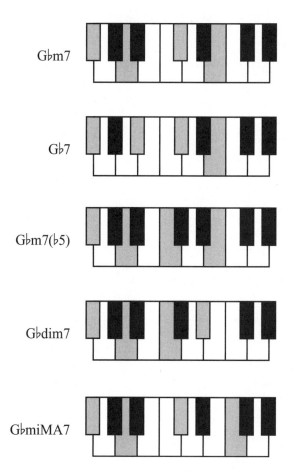

AM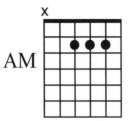

Am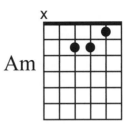

Aaug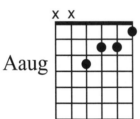

Adim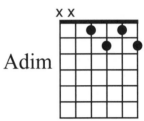

AM7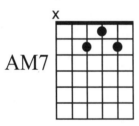

Am7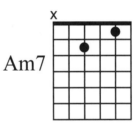

A7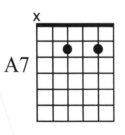

Am7(♭5)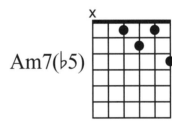

AmiMA7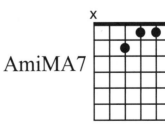

BM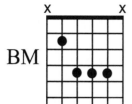

Bm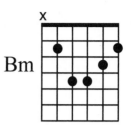

Baug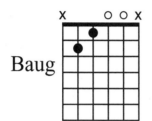

Bdim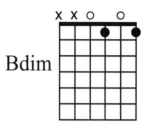

BM7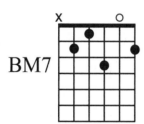

Bm7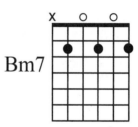

B7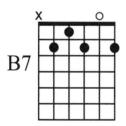

Bmi7(♭5)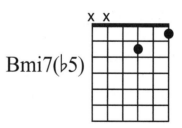

Bdim7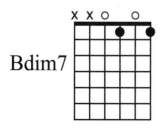

BmiMA7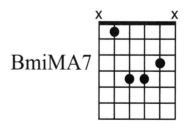

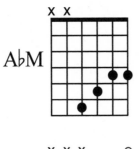

AbM

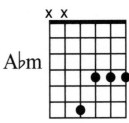

Abm

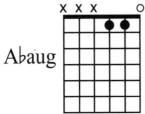

Abaug

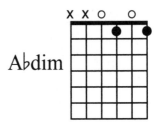

Abdim

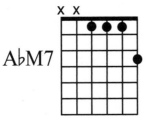

AbM7

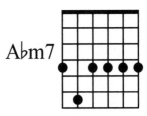

Abm7

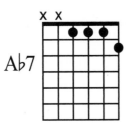

Ab7

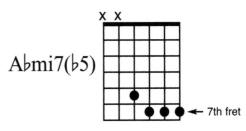

Abmi7(b5)

← 7th fret

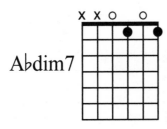

Abdim7

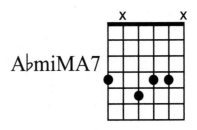

AbmiMA7

B♭M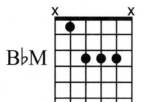

B♭m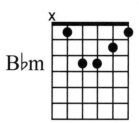

B♭aug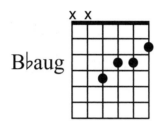

B♭dim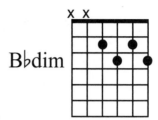

B♭M7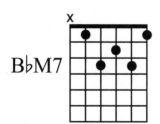

B♭mi7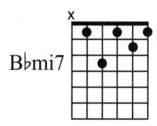

B♭7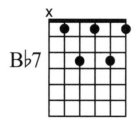

B♭mi7(♭5)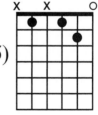

B♭dim7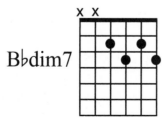

B♭miMA7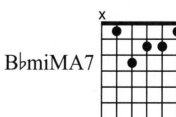

CM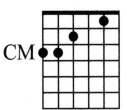

Cm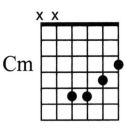

Caug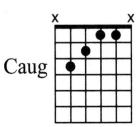

Cdim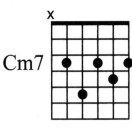

CM7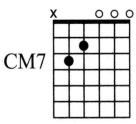

Cm7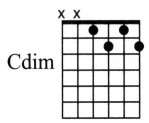

C7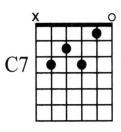

Cmi7(♭5)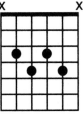

Cdim7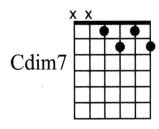

CmiMA7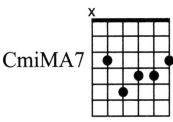

C♭M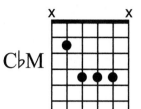

C♭m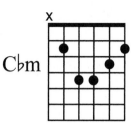

C♭aug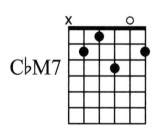

C♭dim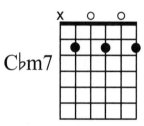

C♭M7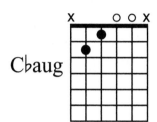

C♭m7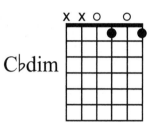

C♭7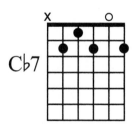

C♭mi7(♭5)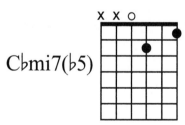

C♭dim7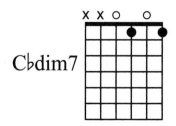

C♭miMA7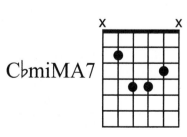

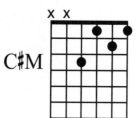

C#M

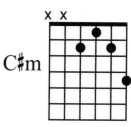

C#m

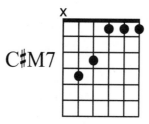

C#aug

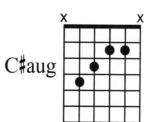

C#dim

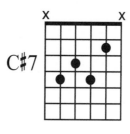

C#M7

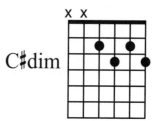

C#m7

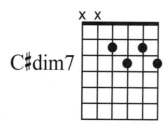

C#7

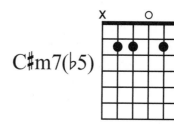

C#m7(♭5)

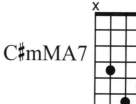

C#dim7

C#mMA7

DM

Dm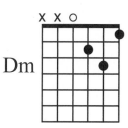

Daug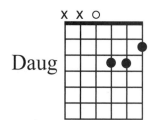

Ddim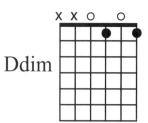

DM7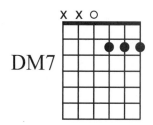

Dm7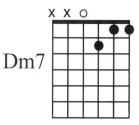

D7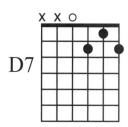

Dm7(♭5)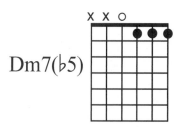

Ddim7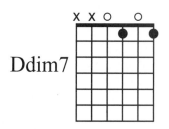

DmiMA7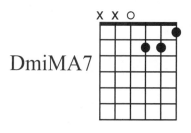

DbM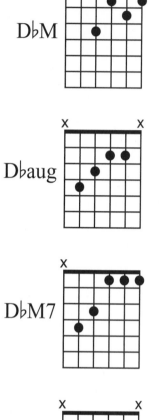

Dbm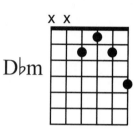

Dbaug

Dbdim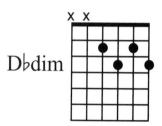

DbM7

Dbm7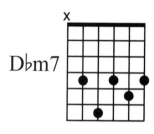

Db7

Dbm7(b5)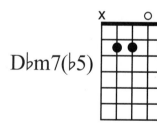

Dbdim7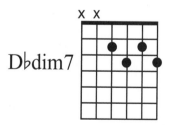

DbmiMA7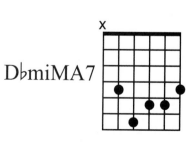

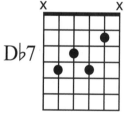

EM

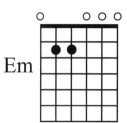

Em

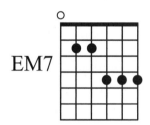

Eaug

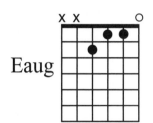

Edim

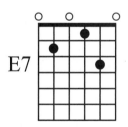

EM7

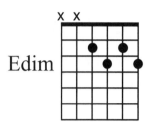

Em7

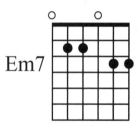

E7

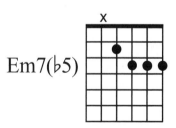

Em7(♭5)

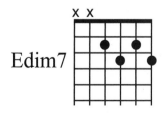

Edim7

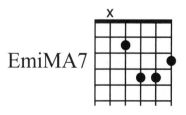

EmiMA7

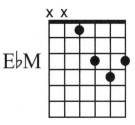

E♭M

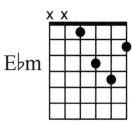

E♭m

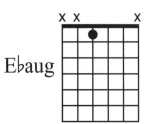

E♭aug

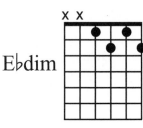

E♭dim

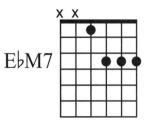

E♭M7

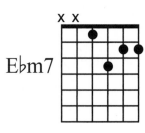

E♭m7

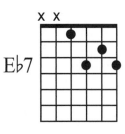

E♭7

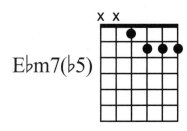

E♭m7(♭5)

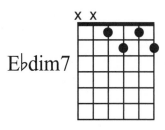

E♭dim7

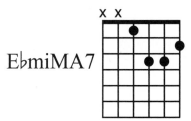

E♭miMA7

FM

Fm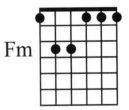

Faug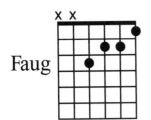

Fdim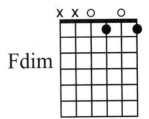

FM7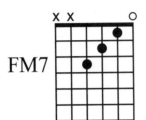

Fm7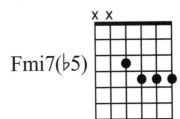

F7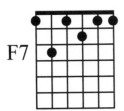

Fmi7(♭5)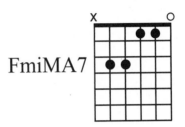

Fdim7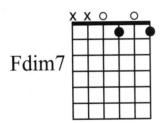

FmiMA7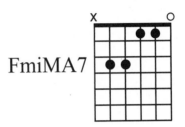

F#M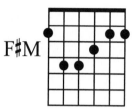

F#m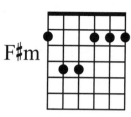

F#aug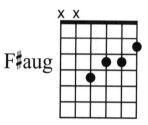

F#dim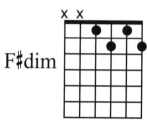

F#M7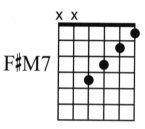

F#m7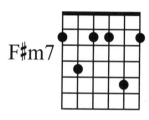

F#7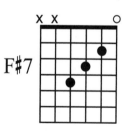

F#m7(♭5)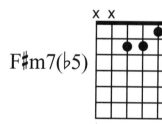

F#dim7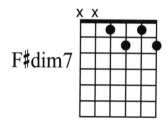

F#miMA7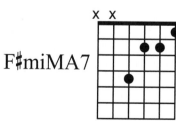

GM

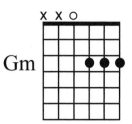

Gm

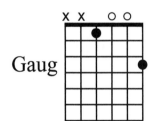

Gaug

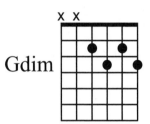

Gdim

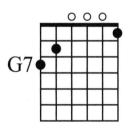

GM7

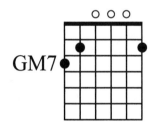

Gm7

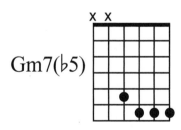

G7

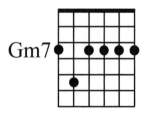

Gm7(♭5)

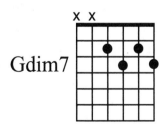

Gdim7

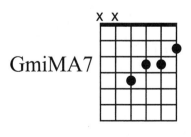

GmiMA7

GbM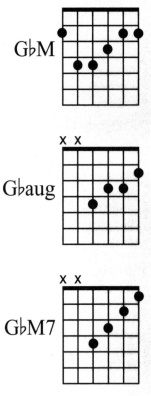

Gbm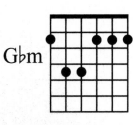

Gbaug

Gbdim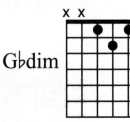

GbM7

Gbm7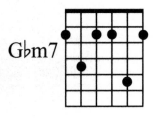

Gb7

Gbm7(b5)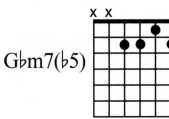

Gbdim7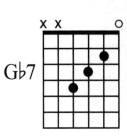

GbmiMA7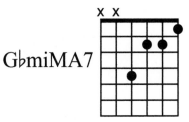

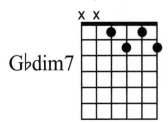

Appendix C

Glossary

accompaniment: The use of additional music to support a lead melodic line.

atonal: Music that is not in a key and not organized diatonically.

augmentation dot: A dot placed after a note or rest that extends its value by one half of the original value. (See **dotted note** and **dotted rest**.)

bar lines: Vertical lines in written music that separate notes into different groups of notes and rests, depending on the time signature used.

bass clef: The lower staff in the grand staff. The bass clef establishes the pitch of the notes on the lines and spaces of the staff below middle C.

beam: A bar used instead of a flag to connect the stems of eighth notes and smaller notes.

beat: A series of repeating, consistent pulsations of time in music. Each pulsation is called a beat.

bridge: The contrasting musical section between two similar sections of music. Also sometime called the B section.

cadence: The ending of a musical phrase, containing points of repose or release of tension.

call and response: When a soloist is answered by another musician or group of musicians.

chord: The simultaneous sounding of at least two pitches or notes.

chord progression: Moving from one chord to another, usually in established patterns.

compound time: A meter whose beat count can be equally divided up into thirds (6/8, 9/4, and so on) with the exception of any time signature that has a 3 as the top number of its time signature (as in 3/4 or 3/8 time).

cut time: Another name for 2/2 time.

diatonic: Conforming to the notes found in a given key. In a piece written in C major, for example, the C, D, E, F, G, A, and B are all diatonic pitches, and any other notes used in the piece are non-diatonic or chromatic.

dotted note: A note followed by an augmentation dot means the note is worth one and a half times its normal value.

dotted rest: A rest followed by an augmentation dot means the rest is worth one and a half times its normal value.

downbeat: The accented beats in a measure.

duplet: Used in compound time to divide a beat that should contain three equal parts into two equal parts.

flag: A curved line added to the stem of a note to indicate a reduced rhythmic value. Flags are equivalent to beams.

form: The overall shape, organization, or structure of a musical composition.

genre: A style or manner of music.

grand staff: The combination of the bass clef staff and the treble clef staff.

half step: The smallest interval in Western music, represented on the piano by moving one key to the left or right from a starting point, or on the guitar as one fret up or down from a starting point.

harmony: Pitches heard simultaneously in ways that produce chords and chord progressions.

homophony: Layers of musical activity that move at the same rhythm, such as melody and accompaniment.

improvisation: Spontaneous musical creation.

key: Normally defined by the beginning and ending chord of a song and by the order of whole steps and half steps between tonic scale degrees (in the key of C, for example, this would be represented by the first C of the scale and the C an octave above the first.

lead sheet: A scaled-down, notated melody with chord symbols, usually for rock or jazz music, on which a musical performance is based.

measure: Also called a bar. A segment of written music, contained within two vertical bars, that contain as many beats as the top number of the key signature indicates.

melody: A succession of musical tones, usually of varying pitch and rhythm, that together have an identifiable shape and meaning.

meter: The organization of rhythmic patterns in a composition in such a way that a regular, repeating pulse of beats continues throughout the composition.

middle C: The C note located right between the two musical staffs in the grand staff, and near the middle of the modern piano.

notation: The use of written or printed symbols to represent musical sounds.

note: A symbol used to represent the duration of a sound and, when placed on a music staff, the pitch of the sound.

octave: Two tones that span eight different diatonic pitches that have the same pitch quality and the same pitch names in Western music.

pick-up notes: Introductory notes placed before the first measure in a piece of music.

pitch: The highness or lowness of a tone produced by a single frequency.

polyphony: Layers of different melodic and rhythmic activity within a single piece of music.

rest: Symbol used to notate a period of silence.

rhythm: A pattern of regular or irregular pulses in music.

scale: A series of notes in ascending or descending order that presents the pitches of a key, beginning and ending on the tonic of that key.

score: A printed version of a piece of music.

simple time: A time signature in which the accented beats of each measure are divisible by two, as in 4/4 time.

staff: Five horizontal, parallel lines, containing four spaces between them, on which notes and rests are written.

syncopation: A deliberate disruption of the two- or three-beat stress pattern, most often by stressing an off-beat, or a note that is not on the beat.

tempo: The rate or speed of the beat in a piece of music.

timbre: The unique quality of sound made by an instrument.

time signature: A notation made at the beginning of a piece of music, in the form of two numbers such as 3/4, that indicates the number of beats in each measure or bar and which note value constitutes one beat. The top (or first) number tells how many beats are in a measure, and the bottom (or second) number tells which kind of note receives the count of one beat.

tonal: A song or section of music which is organized by key or scale.

treble clef: Symbol written at the beginning of the upper musical staff in the grand staff. The treble clef establishes the pitch of the notes on the lines and spaces of the staff existing above middle C.

trill: When a player rapidly alternates between two notes next to one another.

triplet: Used in simple time to divide a beat that should contain two equal parts into three equal parts.

turnaround: A chord progression leading back to the beginning of the song.

whole step: An interval consisting of two half steps, represented on the piano by moving two adjacent keys, black or white, to the left or right from a starting point, or on the guitar as two frets up or down the neck from a starting point.

Index

• E •

E augmented, 184
E diminished, 184
E diminished seventh, 184
E flat
    augmented, 185
    diminished, 185
    diminished seventh, 185
    dominant seventh, 185
    major, 145, 185
    major seventh, 185
    minor, 143, 185
    minor 7 flat 5, 185
    minor seventh, 185
    minor-major seventh, 185
E major
    key signatures, 141, 142
    seventh, 184
E minor
    key signatures, 139–140
    minor-major seventh, 184
    7 flat 5, 184
    seventh, 184
E sharp, 100, 101
eardrum, 97
Eastern music, 100
Egypt, 11
8-bar blues, 243
eighth note
    beat, 24
    common time value, 17
    components, 18
    syncopation examples, 59–60
eighth rest, 35
Ellington, Duke (musician), 246–247
ending, song, 207, 213
enharmonic equivalent
    diminished seconds, 124
    diminished triads, 170
    key signatures, 143, 144
etude, 239
exposition, 230–232

• F •

F augmented, 185
F clef
    definition, 315
    history, 13
    illustrated, 41
    mnemonics, 91, 254
    notation, 81
    overview, 42, 81
F diminished triad, 170, 185
F dominant seventh, 185
F major
    key signature, 146
    major triads, 164–165
    seventh, 185
F minor
    key signatures, 144–145
    minor-major seventh, 185
    7 flat 5, 185
    seventh, 185
F sharp
    augmented, 186
    diminished, 186
    diminished seventh, 186
    dominant seventh, 186
    half steps, 104
    key signatures, 141, 143
    major, 186
    major seventh, 186
    minor, 186
    minor 7 flat 5, 186
    minor-major seventh, 186
fake book, 200
fantasia, 239
Fender, Freddy (musician), 244
Fender, Leo (inventor), 245
fifth
    examples, 116–117
    interval building, 118, 119–120
    overview, 116
    triads, 163–165, 166
first inversion, 189

• *U* •

• *V* •

Notes

Notes

BUSINESS, CAREERS & PERSONAL FINANCE

0-7645-9847-3

0-7645-2431-3

Also available:
- Business Plans Kit For Dummies
  0-7645-9794-9
- Economics For Dummies
  0-7645-5726-2
- Grant Writing For Dummies
  0-7645-8416-2
- Home Buying For Dummies
  0-7645-5331-3
- Managing For Dummies
  0-7645-1771-6
- Marketing For Dummies
  0-7645-5600-2

- Personal Finance For Dummies
  0-7645-2590-5*
- Resumes For Dummies
  0-7645-5471-9
- Selling For Dummies
  0-7645-5363-1
- Six Sigma For Dummies
  0-7645-6798-5
- Small Business Kit For Dummies
  0-7645-5984-2
- Starting an eBay Business For Dummies
  0-7645-6924-4
- Your Dream Career For Dummies
  0-7645-9795-7

HOME & BUSINESS COMPUTER BASICS

0-470-05432-8

0-471-75421-8

Also available:
- Cleaning Windows Vista For Dummies
  0-471-78293-9
- Excel 2007 For Dummies
  0-470-03737-7
- Mac OS X Tiger For Dummies
  0-7645-7675-5
- MacBook For Dummies
  0-470-04859-X
- Macs For Dummies
  0-470-04849-2
- Office 2007 For Dummies
  0-470-00923-3

- Outlook 2007 For Dummies
  0-470-03830-6
- PCs For Dummies
  0-7645-8958-X
- Salesforce.com For Dummies
  0-470-04893-X
- Upgrading & Fixing Laptops For Dummies
  0-7645-8959-8
- Word 2007 For Dummies
  0-470-03658-3
- Quicken 2007 For Dummies
  0-470-04600-7

FOOD, HOME, GARDEN, HOBBIES, MUSIC & PETS

0-7645-8404-9

0-7645-9904-6

Also available:
- Candy Making For Dummies
  0-7645-9734-5
- Card Games For Dummies
  0-7645-9910-0
- Crocheting For Dummies
  0-7645-4151-X
- Dog Training For Dummies
  0-7645-8418-9
- Healthy Carb Cookbook For Dummies
  0-7645-8476-6
- Home Maintenance For Dummies
  0-7645-5215-5

- Horses For Dummies
  0-7645-9797-3
- Jewelry Making & Beading For Dummies
  0-7645-2571-9
- Orchids For Dummies
  0-7645-6759-4
- Puppies For Dummies
  0-7645-5255-4
- Rock Guitar For Dummies
  0-7645-5356-9
- Sewing For Dummies
  0-7645-6847-7
- Singing For Dummies
  0-7645-2475-5

INTERNET & DIGITAL MEDIA

0-470-04529-9

0-470-04894-8

Also available:
- Blogging For Dummies
  0-471-77084-1
- Digital Photography For Dummies
  0-7645-9802-3
- Digital Photography All-in-One Desk Reference For Dummies
  0-470-03743-1
- Digital SLR Cameras and Photography For Dummies
  0-7645-9803-X
- eBay Business All-in-One Desk Reference For Dummies
  0-7645-8438-3
- HDTV For Dummies
  0-470-09673-X

- Home Entertainment PCs For Dummies
  0-470-05523-5
- MySpace For Dummies
  0-470-09529-6
- Search Engine Optimization For Dummies
  0-471-97998-8
- Skype For Dummies
  0-470-04891-3
- The Internet For Dummies
  0-7645-8996-2
- Wiring Your Digital Home For Dummies
  0-471-91830-X

* Separate Canadian edition also available
† Separate U.K. edition also available

Available wherever books are sold. For more information or to order direct: U.S. customers visit www.dummies.com or call 1-877-762-2974.
U.K. customers visit www.wileyeurope.com or call 0800 243407. Canadian customers visit www.wiley.ca or call 1-800-567-4797.

SPORTS, FITNESS, PARENTING, RELIGION & SPIRITUALITY

0-471-76871-5   0-7645-7841-3

Also available:
- Catholicism For Dummies
  0-7645-5391-7
- Exercise Balls For Dummies
  0-7645-5623-1
- Fitness For Dummies
  0-7645-7851-0
- Football For Dummies
  0-7645-3936-1
- Judaism For Dummies
  0-7645-5299-6
- Potty Training For Dummies
  0-7645-5417-4
- Buddhism For Dummies
  0-7645-5359-3

- Pregnancy For Dummies
  0-7645-4483-7 †
- Ten Minute Tone-Ups For Dummies
  0-7645-7207-5
- NASCAR For Dummies
  0-7645-7681-X
- Religion For Dummies
  0-7645-5264-3
- Soccer For Dummies
  0-7645-5229-5
- Women in the Bible For Dummies
  0-7645-8475-8

TRAVEL

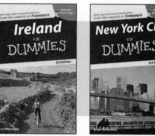

0-7645-7749-2   0-7645-6945-7

Also available:
- Alaska For Dummies
  0-7645-7746-8
- Cruise Vacations For Dummies
  0-7645-6941-4
- England For Dummies
  0-7645-4276-1
- Europe For Dummies
  0-7645-7529-5
- Germany For Dummies
  0-7645-7823-5
- Hawaii For Dummies
  0-7645-7402-7

- Italy For Dummies
  0-7645-7386-1
- Las Vegas For Dummies
  0-7645-7382-9
- London For Dummies
  0-7645-4277-X
- Paris For Dummies
  0-7645-7630-5
- RV Vacations For Dummies
  0-7645-4442-X
- Walt Disney World & Orlando
  For Dummies
  0-7645-9660-8

GRAPHICS, DESIGN & WEB DEVELOPMENT

0-7645-8815-X   0-7645-9571-7

Also available:
- 3D Game Animation For Dummies
  0-7645-8789-7
- AutoCAD 2006 For Dummies
  0-7645-8925-3
- Building a Web Site For Dummies
  0-7645-7144-3
- Creating Web Pages For Dummies
  0-470-08030-2
- Creating Web Pages All-in-One Desk
  Reference For Dummies
  0-7645-4345-8
- Dreamweaver 8 For Dummies
  0-7645-9649-7

- InDesign CS2 For Dummies
  0-7645-9572-5
- Macromedia Flash 8 For Dummies
  0-7645-9691-8
- Photoshop CS2 and Digital
  Photography For Dummies
  0-7645-9580-6
- Photoshop Elements 4 For Dummies
  0-471-77483-9
- Syndicating Web Sites with RSS Feeds
  For Dummies
  0-7645-8848-6
- Yahoo! SiteBuilder For Dummies
  0-7645-9800-7

NETWORKING, SECURITY, PROGRAMMING & DATABASES

0-7645-7728-X   0-471-74940-0

Also available:
- Access 2007 For Dummies
  0-470-04612-0
- ASP.NET 2 For Dummies
  0-7645-7907-X
- C# 2005 For Dummies
  0-7645-9704-3
- Hacking For Dummies
  0-470-05235-X
- Hacking Wireless Networks
  For Dummies
  0-7645-9730-2
- Java For Dummies
  0-470-08716-1

- Microsoft SQL Server 2005 For Dummies
  0-7645-7755-7
- Networking All-in-One Desk Reference
  For Dummies
  0-7645-9939-9
- Preventing Identity Theft For Dummies
  0-7645-7336-5
- Telecom For Dummies
  0-471-77085-X
- Visual Studio 2005 All-in-One Desk
  Reference For Dummies
  0-7645-9775-2
- XML For Dummies
  0-7645-8845-1

HEALTH & SELF-HELP

0-7645-8450-2

0-7645-4149-8

Also available:

- Bipolar Disorder For Dummies
  0-7645-8451-0
- Chemotherapy and Radiation
  For Dummies
  0-7645-7832-4
- Controlling Cholesterol For Dummies
  0-7645-5440-9
- Diabetes For Dummies
  0-7645-6820-5* †
- Divorce For Dummies
  0-7645-8417-0 †

- Fibromyalgia For Dummies
  0-7645-5441-7
- Low-Calorie Dieting For Dummies
  0-7645-9905-4
- Meditation For Dummies
  0-471-77774-9
- Osteoporosis For Dummies
  0-7645-7621-6
- Overcoming Anxiety For Dummies
  0-7645-5447-6
- Reiki For Dummies
  0-7645-9907-0
- Stress Management For Dummies
  0-7645-5144-2

EDUCATION, HISTORY, REFERENCE & TEST PREPARATION

0-7645-8381-6

0-7645-9554-7

Also available:

- The ACT For Dummies
  0-7645-9652-7
- Algebra For Dummies
  0-7645-5325-9
- Algebra Workbook For Dummies
  0-7645-8467-7
- Astronomy For Dummies
  0-7645-8465-0
- Calculus For Dummies
  0-7645-2498-4
- Chemistry For Dummies
  0-7645-5430-1
- Forensics For Dummies
  0-7645-5580-4

- Freemasons For Dummies
  0-7645-9796-5
- French For Dummies
  0-7645-5193-0
- Geometry For Dummies
  0-7645-5324-0
- Organic Chemistry I For Dummies
  0-7645-6902-3
- The SAT I For Dummies
  0-7645-7193-1
- Spanish For Dummies
  0-7645-5194-9
- Statistics For Dummies
  0-7645-5423-9

Get smart @ dummies.com®

- **Find a full list of Dummies titles**
- **Look into loads of FREE on-site articles**
- **Sign up for FREE eTips e-mailed to you weekly**
- **See what other products carry the Dummies name**
- **Shop directly from the Dummies bookstore**
- **Enter to win new prizes every month!**

* Separate Canadian edition also available

† Separate U.K. edition also available

Available wherever books are sold. For more information or to order direct: U.S. customers visit www.dummies.com or call 1-877-762-2974.
U.K. customers visit www.wileyeurope.com or call 0800 243407. Canadian customers visit www.wiley.ca or call 1-800-567-4797.